Allan Maclean

Jacobite General

The Life of an Eighteenth Century Career Soldier

Mary Beacock Fryer

Dundurn Press
Toronto and Oxford
1987

Allan Maclean
Jacobite General

The Life of an Eighteenth Century Career Soldier

Mary Beacock Fryer

Copyright © Mary Beacock Fryer, 1987

All rights reserved. No part of this publication may be reproduced, stored in a retrieval system, or transmitted in any form or by any means, electronic, mechanical, photocopying, recording, or otherwise (except brief passages for purposes of review) without the prior permission of Dundurn Press Limited.

Design and Production: Andy Tong
Printing and Binding: Gagne Printing Ltd., Louiseville, Quebec, Canada

The writing of this manuscript and the publication of this book were made possible by support from several sources. The author is grateful to **The Ontario Arts Council** for a Writer's Grant award, and the publisher wishes to acknowledge the generous assistance and ongoing support of **The Canada Council and The Ontario Arts Council.**

Care has been taken to trace the ownership of copyright material used in the text (including the illustrations). The author and publisher welcome any information enabling them to rectify any reference or credit in subsequent editions.

J. Kirk Howard, Publisher

Cataloguing in Publication Data

Fryer, Mary Beacock, 1929-
    Allan Maclean, Jacobite General: The life of an eighteenth century career soldier

(Dundurn Lives)
Bibliography: p.
Includes index
ISBN 1-55002-009-9 (bound)   ISBN 1-55002-011-0 (pbk.)

1. Maclean, Allan, 1725-1797. 2. Great Britain. Army - Biography. 3. Canada - History Seven Years' War, 1755-1763 - Biography*. 4. Canada - History - 1775-1783 - Biography. 5. Soldiers - Canada - Biography. I Title. II. Series.

FC411.M24F79 1987   971.02'4'0924   C86-094760-2
F1032.M24F79 1987

Dundurn Press Limited   **Dundurn Distribution Limited**
1558 Queen Street East   Athol Brose, Wargrave
Toronto, Canada   Reading, England
M4L 1E8   RG10 8DY

CONTENTS

Acknowledgements

I owe a debt of gratitude, first and foremost, to Alwyne Compton Farquharson of Torloisk, Isle of Mull, for sharing so generously the information kept at Torloisk House. The other person to whom I am most indebted is the late Dr. James Maclean of Glensanda, for writing his fascinating book, *Reward is Secondary*. I thank the Honourable George F.G. Stanley, the Lieutenant Governor of New Brunswick, for introducing me to the work of Dr. Maclean.

While many people have helped me in the preparation of this book, I want to thank the following in particular. Gavin K. Watt, of the Museum of Applied Military History, was always happy to discuss obscure points that puzzled me. Bruce Wilson, of the Public Archives of Canada, obtained documentation for me from the Public Record Office in London. Miss E. Talbot Rice, of the National Army Museum, sent material on Allan Maclean's military record. The Right Honourable Lord Maclean of Duart and Morvern, K.T., G.C.V.O., K.B.E., allowed my publisher to use a reproduction of the minature of Allan Maclean that is in the collection at Duart Castle. Kenneth McNaught, well-known Canadian historian and an amateur artist, very kindly allowed us to reproduce his painting of the castle.

I thank the Ontario Arts Council for grants that helped finance my research. Without the assistance of the Council many books that shed new light on Ontario's past would never be feasible. I also want to express my appreciation to my publisher, Dundurn Press.

M.B.F
16 April 1987

Some Characters Named Maclean

* Not all the Macleans mentioned in the narrative are on this list — only those with the same given names that cause confusion.

Allan Maclean of Torloisk, the central character, lieutenant-colonel, 84th Regiment
Sir Allan Maclean of Maclean, the 22nd chief.

Archibald Maclean of Torloisk, youngest brother of Allan Maclean.
Archibald Maclean, lieutenant in the first battalion, 84th Regiment.

Donald Maclean, 5th laird of Torloisk, the father of Allan Maclean.
Donald Maclean of Brolass, father of Janet Maclean, the wife of Allan Maclean, and father of Hector the 23rd chief.
Donald Maclean, Cadet of Torloisk, husband of Anna, Allan Maclean's sister.

Hector Maclean, 6th laird of Torloisk, eldest brother of Allan Maclean.
Sir Hector Maclean, the 21st chief.
Sir Hector Maclean, the 23rd chief, brother of Janet, wife of Allan Maclean, ensign in the second battalion, 84th Regiment.
Hector Maclean, ensign in the first battalion, 84th Regiment.

John Maclean, lieutenant in the first battalion, 84th Regiment.
John Macleane, son of Dr. Lauchlin Macleane, Allan Maclean's benefactor.

Lachlan Maclean, 7th laird of Torloisk, elder brother of Allan Maclean.
Lachlan Maclean of Drimnin, killed at Culloden.
Lachlan Maclean of Garmony, husband of Elizabeth, sister of Allan Maclean.
Lauchlin Maclean, son of Lachlan of Garmony and Elizabeth

Maclean and nephew of Allan Maclean, merchant in
Baltimore, captain in the first battalion, 84th Regiment.
Lauchlin Macleane M.D., from Dublin, Allan Maclean's
benefactor.

Mary Maclean of Torloisk, sister of Allan Maclean.
Mary (Campbell) Maclean, wife of Donald 5th laird of
Torloisk, mother of Allan Maclean.
Mary (Dickson) Maclean, wife of Donald of Brolass, mother
of Janet, wife of Allan Maclean, mother of Hector Maclean
the 23rd chief.

Allan Maclean of Torloisk, lieutenant-colonel of the 84th Regiment
Royal Highland Emigrants. This miniature is from the collection at
Duart Castle, Isle of Mull, and it was loaned to the Canadian War
Museum to be photographed by The Right Honourable Lord Maclean.

Prologue: Quebec City
30 December 1775

A tall dark man emerged from the Recollect Monastery into the sombre twilight. His hair was powdered and tied in a military queue, and he was attired in the regimentals of an officer in one of King George III's Highland corps. His coat of scarlet was faced dark blue and laced with gold, the sword hilt and the gorget on his chest also of gold. The band of his blue feathered bonnet was diced red-white. The hose were an argyle pattern of red and white. The kilt and short plaid were of "old Government tartan", the dark blue and green first used by the Black Watch, troops raised in the Highlands of Scotland to keep order after the first Jacobite rising of 1715. At that time, Highland clans loyal to the exiled House of Stuart had sought to depose the German usurper, King George I of the House of Hanover.

Perhaps two hours had passed since Lieutenant-Colonel Allan Maclean had risen from Governor Guy Carleton's table. Allan still felt drowsy from the wines he had consumed, and he sought the cold air to clear his head. An alert mind was a necessity. The garrison had been poised for an attack ever since 14 November when a rebel army under Benedict Arnold had appeared on the Plains of Abraham, where Wolfe's army had defeated Montcalm's sixteen years ago. Now, intelligence sources had informed Allan, Arnold had been joined by Richard Montgomery and some 600 reinforcements from rebel-held Montreal.

Since the British garrison had learned of Montgomery's arrival, the governor and Allan, his second-in-command, had slept fully clothed in the Recollect Monastery, ready to spring into action at the first sign of an enemy approach. Tension mounted as one starlit night followed another. Some officers wondered why the rebels were delaying, but Allan thought he knew the reason. As long as the nights were bright the rebels would forbear. Tonight, cloudy with a threat of a snowstorm, might suit their purposes — poor visibility to conceal their intent.

Allan might soon have his chance, for Carleton had promised him the command of the army in the field. [1] The strategy would also be his. Experienced soldier though he was, Allan had never taken command of a battle, but he knew he would win this one. Thus far, the rebel posturing around the fortress city above the St. Lawrence had seemed to Allan a comic opera. The wonder was not that he could defeat Arnold and Montgomery, but that with a very small army and only a few pieces of artillery, the two rebel leaders should dare to attack the rock at all.

Allan was ready. At age fifty, he reckoned he had been thirty-two years a soldier. For the past twenty-nine years, as a means of survival, he had been a mercenary in the service of foreign monarchs, first the House of Orange, and now the House of Hanover. His true allegiance he saved for his own sovereign, the exiled Stuart o'er the water, the man he regarded as King James III (and VIII of Scotland), who was known by the Whigs as the Old Pretender. The name used by his followers derived from Jacobus, the Latin for James II, the last Stuart king who reigned. A Jacobite Allan had been born, a Jacobite he would die!

The wind was stronger now, the night very black, sleet beginning to sting his face. If this storm developed, the rebels might think they had the conditions they sought. Allan's dark eyes glinted in anticipation. The new year, more sacred to a Highlander than Christmas, was upon him.

"New Years' Eve — our hogmanay — could be a very noisy celebration this year", he said aloud.

Drawing his plaid more tightly around him, he turned back towards Recollect Monastery, praying his premonition was sound. Braced against the wind, his mind flew back to that April day of 1746. Then, as now, sleet had stung his face, as he met his baptism of fire on Drumossie Moor near Culloden House, the day his boyhood dreams were shattered.

Duart Castle, Isle of Mull. Watercolour by Kenneth McNaught

Chapter One

The Fiery Cross 1746

That Allan Maclean would participate in the last attempt to restore the House of Stuart and depose that of Hanover was fore-ordained by his heritage and his upbringing. He was born, in 1725, into a family obsessed by loyalty to the exiled Stuarts, love and pride in clan Maclean, and hatred of clan Campbell.

Allan's father was Donald Maclean, the 5th laird (proprietor) of Torloisk, an estate on the northwest coast of the Isle of Mull, one of the inner Hebridean islands off Scotland's west coast. Some lairds owned their land outright, but others leased their estates. Whether owner or lessee, a laird owed allegiance to his chief, and was responsible for providing clansmen when the chief wanted to go to war. The clansmen who marched with their chief were known as his fighting tail.

Mary, Allan's mother, was a daugnter of Archibald Campbell of Sunderland, but like her husband she had no love for the Duke of Argyll, the chief of her clan, nor for most of his adherents.[1] When she married she became a Maclean and gave her allegiance to her husband's family, a family that had suffered at the hands of the Dukes of Argyll, who owned the estate.

At one time all the land on Mull had been the property of clan Maclean, except for the north end which belonged to clan MacKinnon. Since 1691, the year when clan Campbell, led by the 10th Earl (and 1st Duke) of Argyll, had defeated the Macleans of Mull, successive Dukes of Argyll had exacted rent from the lairds of Torloisk.[2] Donald Maclean bitterly resented parting with money that might have gone to support the present chief, Sir Hector Maclean, the 21st of his clan. Sir Hector had been born in France, and had spent most of his life there or in Italy, because his father, Sir John the 20th chief, had led the battalion of Macleans during the rising of 1715 against the Hanoverian imposter, George I. Allan's father had been a major under Sir John, and had fought at the Battle of Sheriffmuir. Fortunately the laird of

Torloisk had not been recognized and had not gone into exile on the Continent with his chief.

The 21st chief was known as Sir Hector Maclean of Maclean, because he had no land. His ancestral home was Duart Castle, on the east coast of Mull, for which earlier chiefs had been called Macleans of Duart. Since 1691, following the defeat of the Macleans, the Duke of Argyll had kept a garrison of Campbells in the castle. Not long after that defeat the Campbells also demolished the stone house of Torloisk and loaded the furnishings, the door and window sills, joists and slates, aboard a galley and carried away their loot. The stones from the walls they scattered over the moor. When Allan's father became the laird, all he could afford to build was a two-roomed cottage with a dirt floor and roof of turf, and two small windows facing the sea that did not let in much light. Donald had used the scattered stones from the once proud ancestral home.[3] In the main room were Allan's parents' bed and a few sticks of furniture. The second room was divided by a curtain. On one side of it was the bed Allan shared with his younger brother Archibald; on the other side was that used by their two unmarried sisters, Mary and Betty.

The estate of Torloisk consisted of many crofting townships — settlements of tenants who grew oats and barley on the unproductive land. On the bare hills above the shore grazed stunted black cattle and miniature Highland workhorses, black-faced sheep and goats belonging to the crofters. Their owners existed in stone cottages even smaller than Allan's home, on whose roofs of turf a hole served as a chimney. Each township shared a heavy plough, a fishing boat and nets. The hills, long denuded of trees, yielded no timber, but for fuel Mull had no lack of peat bogs.

The family cottage stood on a rise overlooking Loch Tuath, where white sand gleamed along the shore, backed by a row of sentinel-like boulders below steep cliffs. A home farm surrounding the laird's dwelling was worked by landless cottars who lived in huts dotted about. Nearby was the village of Kilninian, with its stubby church spire and stone cottages. The crofters paid their rents in kind, which the laird sold in Glasgow. At Torloisk hard cash was scarce and used sparingly.

The Isle of Mull

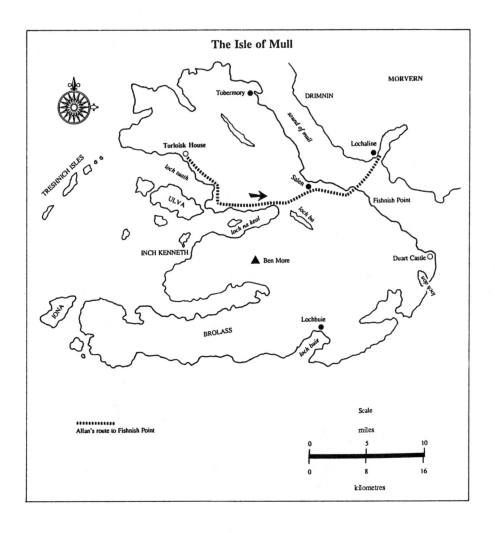

MORVERN

DRIMNIN

Tobermory

Torloisk House

TRESHNISH ISLES

sound of mull

Lochaline

Salen

Fishnish Point

ULVA

loch tuath

loch na keal

loch ba

INCH KENNETH

Duart Castle

loch spelve

Ben More

IONA

BROLASS

Lochbuie

loch buie

••••••••••••
Allan's route to Fishnish Point

Scale

miles

| 0 | 5 | 10 |

| 0 | 8 | 16 |

kilometres

Allan was one of ten children — four sons and six daughters. Hector, the eldest son and the laird's heir, was studying law in Edinburgh, and was a captain in the battalion that was the clan's own army. Lachlan, the second son, was an officer on a merchantman that plied between Port Glasgow and the West Indies, who hoped one day for a ship of his own. Allan, the third son, wanted a military career. On his eighteenth birthday he had been appointed a lieutenant in the battalion under his brother Hector, but the clan had not been in action since 1715, a decade before Allan's birth. Archibald, the youngest son, was a rather dull youth who did not know what he wanted to do with his life.

Mary, the eldest daughter, seemed destined for spinsterhood, but the laird hoped that some man who was not greedy would marry Betty, the youngest. Anna had married Donald Maclean, the head of a lesser branch of the family, and who was known as the Cadet of Torloisk. Their small holding yielded a more meagre living than the lands of the laird. Alicia was the wife of Lachlan Macquarrie, the debt-ridden laird of the Isle of Ulva. Their house, which could be seen from Torloisk on clear days, was also humble, with a dirt floor and so many broken windows that rain poured in on wet days. Christiana had married Alexander Maclean, a cousin and the minister of the Presbyterian church in Kilninian. Elizabeth was the wife of Lachlan Maclean of Garmony, a member of the Lochbuie branch of the clan, and had emigrated with her husband to Jamaica.

Otherwise the laird's family consisted of elderly relatives who had no other means of support. Some of the men had spent time in exile in France and served as tutors to the children. All lived in a second stone cottage erected from the ruins of the old house of Torloisk. With so many people to care for, Allan's father was hard-pressed to provide adequately for his children. None of his daughters had married well for the dowries he could afford were small. Hector would soon be a qualified lawyer and might help Lachlan purchase a ship. Once the Stuarts were restored, Donald hoped to purchase a commission in the British army for Allan, and the cheapest was 400 pounds. Archibald, his family suspected, would be content to pass his days roaming the hills and going to *céilidhean*.

Most of the crofters spoke only Gaelic. The members of the laird's family were fluent in the native tongue, but all the children were taught English. To Donald Maclean education was an end in itself. No Highland gentlefolk should grow up ignorant even though they lived in a hovel. Lessons had embraced history and geography as well as French.

An important part of Allan's education was Presbyterian catechism with its Calvinistic ethics. For a family impoverished by the Campbells and its loyalty to the Stuarts, respectability was the only lifeline to success. A wealthy man might keep mistresses; the sons of Torloisk had only their code of honour and their good name to help them get on in the world. All four brothers were warned to be wary of indiscretions that might prevent them marrying well-born ladies of their own class — preferably wealthy ones who could restore the fortunes of Torloisk.[4]

After the rising of 1715, English soldiers had destroyed the country and driven off the livestock, and Torloisk was left in worse state than ever. Because of his father's teachings, Allan was convinced that prosperity would never return until his chief was back in Duart Castle taking care of the clan. To be sure, the Mackinnons, whose occupation of the north part of Mull the Macleans resented, had been a source of conflict, but that had never interfered with Allan's family's well-being. Only the troops of the German imposter monarch and clan Campbell had accomplished that. During Allen's youth the Campbells, the most powerful clan, were the instrument of royal power in the Highlands. Through a system of indirect rule, the crown controlled the lesser clans by allowing the Campbells a free hand.

Although Allan's family and most other Macleans were Presbyterians, none saw any conflict in supporting the Roman Catholic Stuarts. As far as Donald Maclean was concerned, the Stuarts had been wrongly deprived of the throne. Because of his position as head of a senior cadet branch of the clan, Donald regarded himself as belonging to the Highland nobility whose duty it was to aid the royal family which had the higher claim to the throne. Part of that duty was instilling into his children respect and love of the history of the clan. One of Donald's tales of derring do told of a Spanish galleon from the great Armada that had strayed into Tobermory harbour on the Sound of Mull. Some

Macleans blew up the galleon and sank it. Aboard, supposedly, were thousands of gold coins, for this was the Armada's treasure ship.

Another saga concerned a Maclean of Duart, a chief in the misty past, who drove the chief of the clan Mackinnon from Mull and forced him to take shelter on the mainland. One evening Duart and his men lay in Mckinnon's house, drunk on the contents of their banished host's wine cellar. Mackinnon made a clandestine visit to the house and cut a piece from Duart's plaid. This he tied to a staff which he stuck in the ground outside, encircling it with rods topped with scraps of Mckinnon tartan. When Maclean awoke, the sight of those rods cleared his head with a vengeance. He knew that he might have slumbered into eternity, throat slit from ear to ear. In return for sparing his life, Duart restored Mckinnon's lost property.[5]

Allan was fiercely proud of his given name, a special one in his family. Torloisk had been founded by *Alean-nan-Sop* — Allan-of-the-Straws — whose mother was disowned by her parents when they discovered that she was carrying the child of a Duart chief, without the benefit of wedlock. Her parents put her to work as a kitchen maid. An aged crone in the service of Duart cast a spell that caused the pregnancy to last many months too long. When labour finally began the birth was so rapid that the midwife had only time to lay the mother on some straw. The newborn grasped a few strands in his tiny fists and acquired his nickname.

When he grew to manhood Allan-of-the-Straws built a fortress at Torloisk, then uninhabited and remote, and made a fortune as a pirate. The first laird of Torloisk was Lachlan Mor, the second son of an earlier chief. Lachlan Mor unseated Allan-of-the-Straws' son, so that while Allan was not a direct descendent of the famed pirate, he felt a sense of kinship. He, too, carried the blood of a chief in his veins.[6]

Seeing no prospect of gaining military experience at home, Allan often begged his father to let him go to the Continent to seek a commission with the French or Dutch. Donald Maclean refused to give his consent, for the laird had other priorities. He wanted Allan to assist the Stuarts if the opportunity arose and to be ready to help drive the Campbells from Mull. When Allan pointed out that he had to learn how to be an officer, his father's reply was always the same.

"A Highland gentleman does not need training. Fighting is in our blood and in the blood of our clansmen. When the time comes, we will remove the weapons from between the layers of turf where I hid them after the '15. Be patient my son."

Allan obeyed his father, as was his duty, but he envied other Highlanders who had left to serve abroad. Some had enlisted in regiments established by foreign monarchs especially for Highlanders. France had the French Royal Scots; the Netherlands had a Scots Brigade. On duty at The Hague was another Allan Maclean, the man destined to become the 22nd chief of the clan. Sir Hector Maclean was a bachelor. The other Allan Maclean, his heir and a distant cousin, like the chief was known as Maclean of Maclean, although his father had once been laird of Brolass, in the south of Mull. Like Torloisk, Brolass now belonged to the Duke of Argyll.

A close relative of the Macleans of Torloisk who had served in the Scots brigade in the Netherlands was Captain William Maclean of Blaich, an estate on the mainland near Fort William. The captain had retired but his son Francis was a subaltern in the Brigade, and Allan had long wanted to join him.[7]

By 1745, the year Allan turned twenty, rumours circulating suggested that another attempt to restore the Stuarts would soon be made. In Paris, Sir Hector Maclean heard that Prince Charles Edward Stuart, the rightful king's elder son, would lead an army to Scotland. Sir Hector left France for Edinburgh, where on 5 June he was arrested and later taken to London. Because he had been born in France, he was regarded as a foreigner and allowed the status of a prisoner of war. Then Prince Charles landed on the west coast, raised his standard at Glenfinnan, and called on the loyal Jacobite clans to join him. To the disappointment of many friends, the Prince had come in one ship, and with only a handful of soldiers, most of them French Royal Scots, not the army which King Louis of France had once promised him.

The Macleans of Mull were eager to fight for the Prince, but for the moment they were frustrated. The garrison of Campbells still in residence at Duart Castle stood in the way. A sorrowing Allan had to sit on the sidelines at Torloisk as the Prince led his army into England, along the way handing out some severe drubbings to the troops of George II before giving up the attempt to reach London. Nevertheless the situation still looked promising. On returning to Scotland the Jacobite army roundly defeated the King's soldiers at Falkirk in January 1746. The Prince was calling for fresh volunteers, and the Campbells left Mull to join the army that opposed him. Since Sir Hector, the chief, was still a prisoner in London, the man who would lead the battalion was Charles Maclean of Drimnin, the laird of an estate on the Morvern peninsula, across the Sound of Mull on the mainland. A robust man in his middle-forties, Maclean of Drimnin had served in foreign armies and was thus an experienced soldier.[8]

Towards the end of February 1746, Hector Maclean, Allan's elder brother, arrived from Edinburgh, and Drimnin sent the fiery cross around Mull, the signal for the clan to rise. The cross consisted of two crossed sticks, each somewhat charred, to which was attached a bit of cloth that had been dipped in blood. A runner carried the cross from croft to croft, informing the clansmen. Hector would soon take his place in the battalion, the men of Torloisk as his fighting tail and Allan as his second-in-command. The men of Mull were to gather at Fishnish Point, ready to cross the Sound of Mull in small boats to join the members of the clan who lived on the mainland.

From within the turf roof of the cottage Donald Maclean drew out weapons that had been secreted there since 1715. Opening oilcloth-wrapped packets the laird exposed muskets, pistols known as Highland dags, basket-hilted broadswords, sheathed dirks, and bullskin shields called targets, which he distributed to his warrior sons. Then Hector took Allan's bonnet and pressed into the band a white linen cockade — a rosette, symbol of the white rose of the Stuarts. On it was embroidered "With Charles our brave and merciful P.R., we'll greatly fall or nobly save our country." To this Allan added a sprig of crowberry, the symbol of the Macleans of Mull.

When they left the small house, Allan carried on his shoulders a sack of oat meal to sustain them. In his sporran was a small leather bag of coins which the laird pressed on him, money Allan accepted with reluctance, suppressing mounting indignation at the implication that the Prince might not triumph and he would need funds to escape the country. Mary Maclean knew the risk they were taking, but she accepted that they must do their duty.

The brothers went first to the cottage of their father's piper, Rankin, and told him to take post at Kilninian church. Then they went from croft to croft. Most of the men and boys came willingly, but some responded only to threats to burn their roofs to remind them of the allegiance they owed to their absent chief.

In a few hours the warriors of Torloisk were milling about the church, where Hector formed them into a column. Their march took them along the shore of Loch Tuath to the strains of *Spaidsearachd Chlann Ghilleathain* — Maclean's March — played by Piper Rankin, which almost smothered the occasional war cry of *Bas na Beatha* — Death or Life — and *Fear eile airson Eachinn* — Another for Hector. One who stayed behind was Donald the Cadet of Torloisk, to administer the estate for the aging laird in the absence of so many men.

Allan marched behind Hector, proud of their fighting tail as they followed the shore of Loch na Keal. At Salen, on the Sound of Mull, the column halted for some sleep. There they were joined by men from that coast making for Fishnish Point. When the enlarged host reached its destination, Hector and Allan went in search of Maclean of Drimnin. They found the chieftain standing with his sons, Alan, Lachlan and Donald, all in the tartan of Drimnin. Hector and Allan doffed their bonnets in respect, and Drimnin welcomed them gravely.

The commander shouted for order and addressed the men in Gaelic. Officers were to see to the loading of their men on the boats that were drawn up on shore ready for the crossing to Lochaline. The Prince's army was marching for Inverness, where the battalion would join him. A rumble of dismay surged through the crowd and Allan's heart sank. If the Prince had withdrawn so deeply into the Highlands, he would face a long and difficult march before he could make a second attempt on London.

Drimnin strove to reassure the clansmen. The Jacobite host was rallying at Inverness because the Duke of Cumberland's army was marching for Aberdeen. The duke, King George II's younger son, had been brought home from the Continent especially to take command of the army for his father. His Royal Highness Prince Charles' advisers, the Duke of Perth, Lord George Murray and Lord John Drummond, had recommended Inverness as the best place to gather the Jacobite force. There, the Jacobites would defeat the flower of England's army, the Lowlanders and the perfidious Campbells and other Highland Whigs, and few soldiers would then stand between the Prince and London. At Inverness, Drimnin proclaimed, the Jacobites would extirpate the Duke of Cumberland's army, much as the Picts of old had butchered the legions of Rome!

A cheer rose from the assembled gathering, none louder than the chorus from the men of Torloisk. Even the reluctant ones were caught up in the adventure. As a wintry night was falling, some nine score Macleans were mustered at Lochlaine, crouched around peat fires, refreshing themselves on oat meal and roast venison, talking of the coming campaign with enthusiasm.

They slept close to the fires rolled in their plaids, arms at hand, and before first light the camp was stirring. Drimnin formed the men of Mull into a company with Hector as the captain and Allan as his subordinate in charge of a platoon. To the skirl of the pipes the straggly column wound its way into Glen Gael, thence towards Loch Linnhe. At intervals the men stopped to drink from a burn, which caused the dry meal they had consumed to swell and kept hunger at bay for hours. The days were short, and Drimnin had the column on the move before dawn, not calling a halt until after dark.

As they neared Ardgour, some scouts joined them. They had come from two Jacobite leaders — young Donald Cameron, son and heir to old Donald Cameron of Lochiel, and Macdonald of Keppoch. The Camerons and Macdonalds were trying to dislodge a British garrison from Fort William, thus far to no avail. All they had achieved was to bottle up the garrison and its vicious commander, Captain Caroline Scott, a hated Lowland Whig, so that they could not harm any local Jacobites. Drimnin agreed to cross the loch and help them, for he disliked leaving an enemy garrison at his rear.

In Glen Nevis, beneath the shadow of Ben Nevis, the tallest mountain in Scotland, they were guided to a moated hillock called Dun Dige. On top stood the house of

Alexander Cameron of Glen Nevis. Alexander, who was not a Jacobite, had absented himself; young Donald Cameron of Lochiel, who was an ardent Jacobite, had taken over his kinsman's house for a headquarters. Young Donald was in command of the Camerons because Old Lochiel, the chief of the clan, was unfit for the task. The Macleans would serve for a time under Young Lochiel, guarding the approaches to Fort William to prevent supplies reaching the garrison.

Chapter Two

Blood on the Moor
16 April 1746

The siege of Fort William proved fruitless, as the Highlanders had no artillery to use against the walls. The fort stood close to Loch Linnhe, astride the military road that stretched from the narrows of the loch northwards all the way to Inverness. Both the fort and the road had been built after the rising of 1715 to control the Highlands. As the men probed the defences Allan had his first taste of grape shot, which may have shaken his confidence in the Jacobites' ability to defeat a regular army. On one foray, cannon boomed from the walls of the fort, and puffs of blue smoke floated up from the batteries. Throwing himself face down, he heard what sounded like hailstones falling on the moor ahead of him. Grape shot, he learned, was little bags of canvas filled with bits of metal, even stones. While a musket ball, even a cannon ball, might kill one man, grape could claim many when a cannon found the right range.

One service Hector and Allan almost certainly performed was obtaining supplies for the Highlanders stationed in Glen Nevis. Their kinsman Captain William Maclean of Blaich lived scarcely two hours by boat along Loch Eil. Later events suggest that Allan received sound advice on the most expeditious way of leaving the country from Maclean of Blaich, the veteran of the Scots Brigade in the Dutch service in which his son Francis was still serving.

For what remained of February the garrison stayed bottled up, the clansmen unable to force an entry. The men from Mull grew restive, asking to be allowed to return to their crofts. With the coming of March and no change in their situation Allan found that he and Hector had to keep a constant watch to prevent desertions. The brothers were successful, for not a man succeeded in slipping away. Allan was having his first taste of command and enjoying himself.

On 9 March a scout returned with news that put fresh hope into the hearts of the besiegers of Fort William. Fort

Augustus, at the foot of Loch Ness, had fallen to the Jacobites on the 5th, while Fort George, at Inverness, had been in the hands of the Prince's army since 20 February. Everywhere the German King's garrisons were on the run, and surely Fort William could not hold out much longer. Young Lochiel sent a runner to Fort Augustus asking that cannon and ammunition be moved from there to Fort William. In due course Brigadier-General Walter Stapleton, an Irish Jacobite, arrived at the head of a train of artillery, and these guns were soon answering those of Fort William's defenders. Allan was soon disappointed. Captain Caroline Scott and his redcoats showed no sign of surrendering, and the walls of the fort remained intact.[1]

Towards the end of the month Brigadier Stapleton was joined by a French engineer, Monsieur Mirabelle. This gentlemen, too, proved ineffective. Now Allan was wondering where the Duke of Cumberland might be. If the besiegers lingered much longer they might miss the encounter between the Prince and the German imposter's son entirely.

On 6 April Allan's question was answered. A courier came galloping from Fort Augustus with word that Cumberland was just a week's march from Inverness. The Prince wanted the Jacobites to abandon the siege of Fort William and come to join him at Inverness. Drimnin agreed to march at once, and Lochiel and Keppoch promised to round up their men from their scattered positions and follow them. By the time the battalion was nearing the northern capital on 11 April, provisions were short but no one was concerned. The Jacobite army was being fed and sheltered by loyal people around Inverness, and French ships must be landing supplies and weapons to use against Cumberland.

Allan was not impressed by Inverness. The town consisted of 500 red sandstone dwellings and 3,000 souls, and the streets were filthy. Hovering above was the castle, which had had a garrison of English soldiers and Scots Whigs under John Campbell, the 4th Earl of Loudoun, until the Prince's army drew near. Now it was his headquarters and there Drimnin marched the battalion. The officers and men waited while he went inside to report their arrival. When he emerged his face was grim.

" There's no room for any of us," he said. " The town is so crowded that we'll have to sleep in a field outside. And there are few provisions. The French have not sent any supply ships. Thank God Cumberland is at hand and we won't have to wait long."

The following morning, accompanied by Hector and a detachment of men who were carrying some scanty provisions from the depot at the castle, Allan caught his first glimpse of Prince Charles. His Royal Highness often rode through the streets and encampments, stopping to speak with his followers. The exiled King's son, dressed in a tartan coat, waistcoat and trews, blue bonnet with its white cockade, was a slender man of medium height, with red-gold hair worn in neat side curls and long military queue. No wonder he was called Bonnie, Allan reflected, thinking somewhat ruefully of his own appearance.

His eyes were brown beneath thick, dark brows, his countenance craggy as the cliffs of Mull, rather than handsome. While he was considerably taller than the Prince, and sturdier, his shoulders tended to slope. He disliked his long, aquiline nose, the lips thick enough to suggest a sensuous nature.

On 12 April a rider brought news that sent cold iron up Allan's spine, and that of every Maclean in the Jacobite army. A large band of Campbells who had not yet joined the Duke of Cumberland had gone marauding through the clan's lands on Morvern and Mull, stealing from and abusing the women, children and the elderly. As tales of rape and lootings surged through their encampment, every man resolved to avenge this dastardly deed committed in his absence. Allan tried to blot out pictures of a devastated Torloisk, all food and livestock stolen, his sisters carrying Campbell bastards in violated wombs. Enraged, he told Hector that the battalion would be better employed intercepting Campbells, which would also help the Prince, instead of waiting to fight the Duke of Cumberland.

" We can't desert the Prince," Hector said bluntly.

" We wouldn't be, not if we were after damn Whigs," Allan maintained.

" No, we must stay here," Hector said firmly. " The stories could be exaggerated, to make us do just that, desert from Inverness. We'll have our chance when we face Cumberland."

On the evening of 14 April, a Monday, Drimnin called his officers together and told them that the Jacobite army would await the arrival of Cumberland's on Drumossie Moor, hard by the estate of Culloden. The laird, Duncan Forbes, the Lord President of the Court of Sessions in Scotland, and a Whig, had fled when the Prince's army approached.

"Cumberland reached Nairn today," Drimnin told them. " Twenty-five miles from here, and twenty from Culloden House."

The Jacobite army was to draw up in three divisions, each two lines deep. Lord George Murray would lead the right division, Lord John Drummond the centre, and the Duke of Perth the left. The Macleans would be combined with nine score MacLachlans to form one large battalion under Drimnin, and placed in the front line of Lord Drummond's central division. On the right side of this division the Frasers and clan Chattan (Macintosh) would stand. Next to them Lord Drummond would place four cannon and artillerymen. On the left of these guns he would position the Farquharsons, a few Macleods who defied their Whig chief, the Grants, the Macleans and Maclachlans, the 1st Edinburgh Regiment, and some Chisolms.

The second line in all three divisions would be of Jacobites from the Lowlands, some Irish volunteers, part of clan Gordon, and the few French regulars who had come with the Prince the year before. Each division would be supported by a field battery. The battalion would march to Drumossie Moor at dawn.

Allan scarcely closed his eyes that night, and as the first pale streaks crossed the sky he was stirring and began rousing his platoon. With the prospect of imminent action he hardly noticed the lack of breakfast. Not even the awareness that Drimnin had no food to send with the men could dampen his ardour, nor were the men complaining. All felt able to wait until after the battle, hunger rendering them the more fierce.

Outside the estate of Culloden, Drimnin positioned the Macleans and Maclachlans near the left of the centre division. All that Tuesday the men stayed on the greening heather, while Hector and Allan moved among them to bolster their morale. Still there was no sign of Cumberland's army. At length, in the late afternoon they saw Drimnin coming towards them.

" What's happening, sir?" Hector enquired.

" Someone has remembered it's Cumberland's birthday, and his army will be celebrating," Drimnin replied. " The Prince wants a formal battle, but our commanders have persuaded him that this field will give Cumberland the advantage. Instead we are to make a night march and surprise his camp before dawn tomorrow, when his soldiers will be drugged with rum."

The divisions swung into marching columns and moved off over the moor towards the northeast. The march became a nightmare as the clansmen stumbled through swamps. Picking himself up for the hundredth time, Allan felt light-headed as he drove himself forward, begging his platoon not to fall behind. The sky was lightening and he feared they still had far to go. An hour later he heard a distant roll of drums. The column slowed and stopped. Drimnin came striding back to the company where he spoke briefly to Hector and passed on to the next company.

" What did Drimnin say?" Allan asked as his brother approached.

" Cumberland's drummers have sounded reveille. We're too late to surprise him, and we're to march back to Drumossie Moor" , Hector said.

Allan groaned. " Back through those swamps?"

Hector's shoulders slumped from exhaustion. " No, thank God. We're to take the road."

When the weary Jacobite army had struggled back onto the moor, Drimnin allowed the officers to take their men to Culloden House, outside which there were supposed to be provisions, and then they could snatch two hours' sleep. Allan managed to scrounge a biscuit per man and a few handfuls of oat meal, which did little to allay their hunger. Then he wrapped himself in his plaid and lay down beside Hector on the damp ground, shivering from cold and starvation. By nine o'clock that morning of Wednesday 16 April, Allan and Hector had their men back in position on Drumossie Moor. The Prince was to have his way after all over where the Jacobites would make their stand.

Bonnie Charlie, still in his tartans and bonnet with its white cockade, rode along the front line, exhorting the men to make this another battle like Prestonpans, which the Jacobites had won before they marched into England, or Falkirk, their victory after his return to Scotland. Hector and Allan doffed their bonnets as the Prince passed by. As the young man rode on, Allan stood grim-faced, the spectre of suffering at Torloisk haunting him, hunger far from his consciousness. Towards noon a breeze carried the sound of fifes and drums, and straining his eyes he thought he could discern the banners of Cumberland's vanguard, fluttering behind the advancing scouts.

The Jacobite pipes and drums struck up a rant, and Allan, a chill wind whipping his face, watched as Cumberland's line halted, out of range of the Prince's cannon, he thought. A cheer rose from the Jacobite line as the Prince rode towards the centre where Lord Drummond stood. Still no one moved. The weather was deteriorating, the wind now biting. Just before one o'clock hail fell which turned to sleet, lashing the faces of the Jacobite army. Lord Drummond rode by, exhorting his division to stand firm until the enemy was at close range. Let Cumberland advance if he wanted to do battle.

Tension mounted as Cumberland's men swung from marching columns into battle line perhaps 500 yards off, Allan reckoned. Suddenly his men were pushing him forward; cursing he ordered them back into formation. Cumberland's artillery suddenly spoke, but the shots fell short. When the noise died down, Drimnin yelled hoarsely for the battalion to stand fast, but his words were almost lost by a skirl of pipes. Without waiting for the drummers to beat the advance, the Macintoshes, ignoring the shouts of Lord Murray, surged forward before the Jacobite artillery had fired. At the sight of clan Chatten all discipline among the Macleans and the other clans vanished, and resorting to their traditional form of warfare they charged, shrieking their war cries.

Allan was swept along with the rest. He fired his musket, dropped it and ran towards Cumberland's line brandishing his broadsword in his right hand. His target was over his left arm, dirk clasped in that hand, loaded dag tucked into his belt ready for the next opportunity to fire. A hail of grape shot shattered the Highlanders' charge but did not break it. On the front line rushed, scattering Cumberland's line in confusion.

Dimly Allan suspected he was in the midst of Cumberland's second line, and the tide was turning against the Jacobites. All around him men were dropping, their cries echoing above the boom of the cannon and the pop of the muskets. The moor was blanketed in blue smoke through which Allan, hoping in particular to attack men in Campbell tartan, could see little. He was forced back, stumbling over dead and maimed men, aware that drums were sounding a retreat. Calling to his men to fall back, Allan prayed that some were with him but he recognized no one as bodies hurtled towards the Prince's second line.

Soon this line, and the survivors of the first, were falling back, tripping over more dead and wounded. Allan saw that all were lost. He looked in vain for Hector, or any of the other men from Mull, but could not spot one of them nor Piper Rankin. Heart pounding as though it would burst, Allan felt hot, angry tears dampening his cheeks. He ran westwards, up into the high moor, wondering how long he could keep up the pace. Just when he thought a redcoat's bayonet would be a welcome end to his agony he beheld a miracle.

Grazing was an empty horse, reins dangling as it munched. Allan crept forward quietly so as not to startle it, seized the reins and mounted. He would ride southwards to the Streen River, which joined the Findhorn River in the vicinity of Darnaway, and could serve to guide him to a part of the coast which Cumberland's men would not get round to searching for some time. Now his most urgent need was food. He dismounted and drank from a burn, watered the horse and continued up into the high moor. At length he came upon a hut of turf. The tenant, a shepherd, gave him some oat meal and begged him to be gone.

" You know what the soldiers will do to me if they suspect I have given succour to a Jacobite."

" I know," Allan said wearily. " God keep you safe, good man."

He continued towards the Streen River until twilight, when he tethered the horse to a bush, loosened the saddle girth, and lay down to rest. He slept out of sheer exhaustion despite the danger, and awoke when the sun was high, relieved to find the horse standing where he had left it, head hanging.

Reality faded, and he was back among the maimed and dying on the blood-soaked moor near Culloden House, searching for the men of Torloisk who had vanished in the chaos. Where was Hector? Allan felt honour-bound to retrace his flight and see if he could find any of the men for whom he was responsible. Then he shook himself. That was impracticable. Cumberland's soldiers would be guarding the field, and every able-bodied man would have fled long since; the wounded would be prisoners or worse. He cinched the girth, mounted, and finding how chafed his bare legs and bottom were, rose in the stirrups and tucked his kilt under him before riding on, keeping the high moor above the Streen River.

Two days later, after skulking in the heather away from habitations, Allan reached the fork in the river and knew that the northwards flowing stream was the Findhorn. Here he abandoned the horse, too conspicuous when he was moving through more inhabited country. He removed the saddle and bridle and hid them in some gorse, slapped the horse's rear which sent it trotting over the moor, and strode towards the river bank. Four days after the battle he crossed a bridge over the Findhorn and made his way to a tiny fishing village, arriving days before Cumberland's soldiers had had time to widen their net.

For a sum, a fisherman was willing to transport Allan and a handful of other refugees from the Prince's army, now hiding in the village, to the Continent. Did the young gentleman prefer France or the Netherlands? Allan hesitated. He thought first of France, for he spoke the language although not very well, but he changed his mind. The French had let down the Prince and caused the debacle on Drumossie Moor. He preferred The Hague, the Scots Brigade with Francis Maclean of Blaich, but the decision must be Hector's if he had survived. Allan asked the fisherman to wait as long as he dared, in the hope that his elder brother would arrive to join him.[2]

Chapter Three

Exile 1746-1750

Hector did not come. As May approached, the fisherman was afraid to wait any longer, and a sorrowing Allan acquiesced. Hector must be dead now, or lying in some filthy gaol where he would not live long. The heir to Torloisk had never been as strong as his younger brothers.

Allan announced his intention of joining the Scots Brigade, and the other fugitives agreed to be left on the Dutch coast, too. One place was as good as any other as long as they were beyond the reach of Cumberland's vengeance. On a grey morning in late April the fisherman guided the Jacobites to his ship's boat and they rowed out to his vessel. The crew hoisted sail and the ship moved out of the harbour towards the open sea.

Allan studied the retreating shore, his thoughts leaping across the Highlands to his native isle, to the loved ones who must by now know of the rout at Culloden. He shuddered at the thought of the brutal pacification the Highlands would suffer, and prayed that the soldiers would not ravage Torloisk. Visions of his mother's grieving countenance flashed before his eyes. He would have to find a way to let his parents know he was safe.

A fair wind carried the ship southeastwards across the sea towards the Dutch coastline. Seven days out, the flat shore was in sight. The fisherman landed the fugitives a short piece north of The Hague, and told them to walk inland until they came to a road, where they should turn right and walk until they saw the city. In a mid-morning drizzle that did little for their flagging spirits the little party of Highlanders climbed up over the dunes that protected the cultivated fields from the sea, found the road, and in a few minutes were entering the outskirts of the city. As they marched, the others, who had only the Gaelic, asked Allan to be their spokesman. He wondered what use English or French would be in this foreign-looking land, without a hill in sight, let alone a mountain, where every scrap of land was so neatly manicured. He soon found that the men's confidence was not misplaced. English was important for commerce, and the Dutch were a nation of merchants. He received clear instructions for finding the headquarters of the Scots Brigade.

Allan marvelled at the cleanliness of The Hague. The only cities he had seen were Glasgow and Edinburgh, where garbage and slops were thrown into the streets from the upper windows. The Hague was criss-crossed by a labyrinth of canals into which the Dutch threw their wastes, canals that carried as much traffic as the streets.

The Scots Brigade was quartered in barracks that served the Dutch Army, as well as a contingent of Swiss soldiers. Inside the barracks Allan found a small office where a clerk in uniform was writing. At the sight of Allan, flanked by the other unkempt Highlanders, the clerk rose and fetched the officer of the day. Allan asked the way to the lodgings of Lieutenant Francis Maclean. Instinct warned him to be introduced to the Brigade by an officer, and not to appear a potential recruit for the ranks. Before committing himself he wanted to investigate the prospects for a commission.

The officer of the day kept the other Highlanders, and he arranged for a Dutch soldier to escort Allan to the tall, narrow house on a side street overlooking a narrow canal. Of the stout, fair-haired, pleasant-looking woman who opened, he asked for Lieutenant Maclean.

"Lieutenant Maclean not here," she said in halting English. "You wait. He come soon, before dinner."

She showed Allan into a spotless parlour and left him to his thoughts. He was amazed at such hospitality, remembering how filthy he was, not having bathed for weeks, the checks of his plaid and kilt almost invisible under a layer of mud and grime. How he must stink! His odour must be filling the parlour. At what he guessed was noon, he heard the front door open and the woman speaking quickly in Dutch, and the deeper tones of a man responding. The door of the parlour opened, and Allan beheld a man in military dress, tricorne hat, red silk sash round his waist, a silver gorget on his chest, who looked at him curiously, wrinkling his nose.

"I am Allan Maclean of Torloisk," he said quickly. "I escaped from the battle near Inverness, and want to join the Scots brigade."

"Let's go to my room," Francis said, leading the way. "My father wrote that you were near Fort William. Did the Prince fail?"

"Aye." Allan's voice sounded weary as he followed his cousin up the staircase. "I shudder to think how many good men died that day."

Francis' room was small but comfortably furnished, and he brought out a razor, some towels, and called downstairs in Dutch. Soon servants appeared with large jugs of steaming water and a hip bath. Allan bathed, washed his hair, and removed the tattered growth of beard. Francis rummaged in a large chest and drew out a pair of breeches, a shirt and stockings, and eyed a worsted coat critically.

"You're only a bit taller than me," he said. "These may do."

As he donned the unfamiliar apparel, Allan told Francis briefly what had occurred at Culloden. The clothes almost fit, the coat tight through the shoulders, the breeches stopping at mid-knee. Francis inspected him, pronounced him presentable, and they set out for the lodgings of Maclean of Maclean, their future chief and a captain in the Scots Brigade.[1]

As they walked, Francis told Allan that his arrival was timely. The Dutch Republic, a union of several provinces, was at war with France, part of a conflict that had broken out in 1740 over the question of the Austrian succession. Upon the death of Charles VI, the Holy Roman Emperor and Archduke of Austria, his daughter, Maria Theresa, succeeded him as ruler of all the Austrian possessions. France, Spain and Prussia were determined to help themselves to parts of Maria Theresa's inheritance. The Dutch and the English were allies of Austria, who opposed the dismembering of the Austrian empire, which led to France's declaration of war in 1745. Louis XV of France had sent an army to conquer the Belgians of the Austrian Netherlands, and the French might well decide to occupy the southern provinces of the republic. The Dutch government was hiring mercenaries and recruiting among its own citizens, but the republic lacked a competent military leader. Some of the provinces had elected governments, while others were ruled by stadholders. Rumours hinted that the government would appoint William IV, the Prince of

Orange, the principal stadholder, as captain-general of the army.

"I hope the rumours are true," Francis finished as they halted before another tall, narrow house. "The Dutch officers think that the Prince would make an excellent commander-in-chief."

Maclean of Maclean, whose given name was also Allan, was in, for he, too, had come home to freshen up before dining in the mess. Francis introduced Allan, and began telling him of the disaster at Culloden, but Maclean of Maclean interrupted him. A letter from Inverness was waiting when he reached his lodgings. The news was indeed tragic. Of the 180 Macleans who went to Culloden, scarcely thirty survived. Allan asked about word of Hector, but Maclean of Maclean shook his head. The letter said nothing about the heir to Torloisk, but Charles Maclean of Drimnin and his son Lachlan were dead. Drimnin might have lived, but when he learned that Lachlan had been killed, he shouted that he would be avenged, rushed at some redcoats and was speedily cut to pieces, a gallant gesture but a waste. Of his other sons, Alan was wounded, but Donald was unscathed. The future chief now asked Allan to describe the battle, and when he got to the artillery barrage that had shattered the front line of the Jacobite army, Maclean of Maclean's eyes glinted angrily.

"Butcher Cumberland brought up his second line and drove you back," he said. "Now, Allan of Torloisk, you must have a commission in the Brigade."

"I want one, but I have no money to purchase," Allan said.

Maclean of Maclean waved a hand airily. "Commissions here are earned," he explained. "As a son of Torloisk you will be a subaltern."

Allan sighed with relief. Here was an opportunity to learn soldiering at no expense to himself. Maclean of Maclean promised to arrange an interview with the commander of his battalion, Lieutenant-Colonel Henry Dundas the Earl of Drumlanrig, and the two officers took Allan to their mess. Allan found the food overwhelming, both in quantity and quality, the wines and port too rich for him after so long on a skimpy diet. Never before had he been confronted by such a bewildering variety of vegetables and fruits.

Maclean of Maclean was as good as his word, and the following day Allan would have his interview with the Earl of Drumlanrig. He shared Francis' room that night and kept his appointment promptly. The commanding officer loaned him a manual of arms in English, and had him take an oath of allegiance to the republic. Allan needed a place to live, and he obtained a list of houses that let rooms from brigade headquarters. He chose an attic room in a small but clean house not far from Francis' lodgings. The new quarters were hardly fit for an officer, but the attic was cheap, and Allan had to stretch the sum his father had given him as long as possible.

Now he must send a message to Torloisk, to let his family know his whereabouts. He consulted Francis, who agreed to write to his father at Blaich. "There's an old Jacobite code which exiles used after the '15," Francis said. "Your father will know it, and mine can send his reply."

Allan felt hot tears welling in his eyes, as, in a choked voice, he told his kinsman of the Campbells' raid on Mull and of his fears for his family. An angry flush darkened Francis' face, and he promised to ask his father to find out what had happened at Torloisk.

Despite tensions wracking him, Allan threw himself eagerly into learning his duties, and he returned the manual arms to the Earl of Drumlanrig. He was assigned a platoon, and one of his most important tasks was inspecting the men's weapons and accoutrements, to ensure that everything was clean and in perfect order. He attended brigade drill, watching intently as the drummers put the rank and file through musket practice and formed their hollow squares, the sergeants shouting at men who were clumsy. He saw the weakness of his father's assumption that a Highlander did not need formal training. These parade ground manoeuvres by disciplined troops could be enacted under battle conditions. Recalling the confusion at Culloden, he wondered what might have happened had the Macintoshes not rushed forward, followed by his own clan, before the Prince's artillery had had time to respond to Cumberland's.

After Allan had been with the Brigade for six weeks the Earl of Drumlanrig sent for him and told him that he had carried out his duties satisfactorily. He could now have a lieutenant's commission, and draw an advance on his pay to purchase his uniform and other accoutrements, and black riding boots. From the advance Allan hired a servant and bought a horse. Part of each day he took fencing lessons, a necessary skill for an officer.

In July, Francis brought him a letter from the laird of Blaich. His coded message had reached Torloisk, and things were going about as well as could be expected. Hector was alive, hiding somewhere until it was safe to return to his law studies in Edinburgh. The Campbells had stolen all the stored food and driven off the livestock, but Allan's brother Lachlan had arrived in Glasgow from Jamaica in time to send food to keep the family and crofters until the next harvest. Now Allan could carry on with a light heart and begin to enjoy his new life, and he might soon see action. The French army was moving ever closer to Dutch territory.

The Dutch people were very kind to the foreigners in their army, both the exiled Highlanders and the Swiss. Allan found a schoolmaster who coached him in Dutch, so that he would not be isolated in the society of his fellow officers. As summer passed into autumn he found that when visiting Dutch homes he could understand much of what was said. With marriageable women he cultivated a reputation as a pleasant companion but a confirmed bachelor. One day he would marry, but his wife must be one of his own kind — a Highland lass.

In October, Allan heard that Prince Charles had reached France after being in the Highlands more than five months since Culloden, sheltered by people whose lives would have been forfeit had they been caught. The Highlanders acquired a heroine in the person of Flora Macdonald, who brought the Prince, disguised as a seamstress, from the outer Hebrides to the Isle of Skye. Other stories told of arrests, of murders of innocent people, of cattle driven to the Lowlands. Soldiers had burnt the crop at Torloisk, but again Lachlan had come to the rescue.

As the year 1747 opened, the French were threatening the Dutch garrisons stationed along the border. In May the government appointed the Prince of Orange the commander-in-chief, and early in September the Scots Brigade received orders to mobilize. The Brigade's destination was the coastal port of Bergen-op-Zoom, in the south, where the garrison of English and Dutch soldiers, under seige since July, needed a reinforcement. The column that left The Hague was 1,450 strong in three battalions. Allan rode at the head of his platoon, the column followed by a train of baggage wagons. Pipers played nostalgic tunes for the men on foot. At night the rank and file slept in small canvas tents; the officers were quartered in inns.

Allan swelled with pride as he contemplated the fine fighting force. The men of the Brigade were amenable to discipline. While most were exiles they were also volunteers who had not been pressed into the service. Physical punishments were rare. The men made a great spectacle, uniforms tidy, the white portions gleaming from fresh laundering or pipe clay, accoutrements shining, hair well powdered and neatly tied in long queues, snakelike in their black ribbon bindings. Allan hated having his hair powdered each morning by his servant, and the powder shaken out when the queue was undone each evening. Yet had Prince Charles unseated German Geordie, he would be in the British army, enduring this same procedure.

At the walled town of Bergen-op-Zoom, a French fleet lay offshore, while troops of the line were drawing near. The French ships began firing and the Brigade stood to arms, but for a time the only action was the answering guns of the Dutch shore batteries. Then on September 16 scouts reported the approach of a French column, and the Brigade was ordered to accompany a Dutch regiment to meet it.

For the second time in his life, Allan found himself in the front line, watching while an army with banners fluttering moved from marching column into line of battle to the martial tunes of the fifes, the signal drums beating, tension mounting in his breast. The French artillery boomed, the Dutch replied, and after the first musket volley many men fell near him, some shouting in agony. A wave of nausea, followed by fury, swept over Allan. Never, throughout his life, would he come to accept the carnage of war, no matter how often he saw dying and maimed men.

The drums sounded a flanking movement, and the Brigade swung to the left, soldiers jogging, Allan trotting his horse beside his platoon. Casualties seemed appallingly heavy, but the French were falling back. Drums signalled a retreat; in the fray survivors had to abandon the dead, making every effort to carry off the wounded unfit to walk. Many more died before they gained the security of the town walls. To Allan's horror, of 1,450 men, 1,120 were dead or wounded, the Brigade decimated. Yet French losses during the seige were some 22,000 men, while the garrison had lost some 4,000.[2]

The following day the town surrendered and the French marched in. Still in shock, Allan suffered the humiliation of handing his sword to a French officer and having it returned. When he recovered from the disgrace of surrender, he found that the Scots were being well treated. They were the darlings of the French, who regarded them as unfortunate souls, in the Dutch service in order to survive after the sad affair at Culloden. One officer told Allan and Francis that had the Brigade not withdrawn, the French would have been forced to abandon the seige.[3] Clearly, he had no notion of how badly the Brigade had suffered.

A few days later the officers were exchanged. The surviving rank and file were allowed to march to The Hague on parole, and would return to duty when a like number of French soldiers had been exchanged. A subdued Allan rode at the head of what remained of his platoon, the many wounded riding in wagons with the baggage train. The war soon ended, with the signing of the Treaty of Aix-la-Chapelle. Under its terms the French withdrew from the Austrian Netherlands, although Maria Theresa lost other territories to France's allies.

A few more Jacobites arrived, bringing word that conditions were very bad in the Highlands. Many chiefs and lairds had lost their lands, and the wearing of Highland dress was proscribed. Then Francis brought Allan a letter he had received from Blaich. On 20 August 1748 Allan's father had died at Torloisk.[4] His eldest brother, Hector, out of hiding and now a qualified lawyer in Edinburgh, was the 6th laird. Allan involved himself into his duties to take his mind off his grief, but he longed to be free to return home and comfort his mother, aware of how much his presence would mean to her,

Despite some recruitment, the Dutch government reduced the Scots Brigade for reasons of economy. Many officers resigned, and the rank and file that had not been at Culloden

Frederick Haldimand. This Swiss professional soldier rose to the rank of major-general in the British army. After his service in Canada during the revolution he was made a knight of the Bath by George III. Haldimand first met Allan Maclean in the 1740s.

were drifting home. One who left was Maclean of Maclean, who promised to visit Torloisk and give Allan's mother a first-hand account of him.

Allan became reconciled to the loss of his father, and life at The Hague became pleasant once more. His circle of friends was growing, and included a Lowlander named John Small, and two Mackay brothers, Samuel and Francis. He had become acquainted with several Swiss officers, and was impressed by two in particular — Henry Bouquet and Frederick Haldimand.[5] Both spoke French, and from their junior officers Allan picked up a working knowledge of German, which he found similar to Dutch. He would serve with all these officers later on.

He invested his savings in a mercantile house, but they remained discouragingly small. Officers had to keep up appearances, and very little was left of his pay after each muster. Time passed, until the year 1750 arrived. Allan had now spent almost four years in the Scots Brigade, a life that suited him well. One June day after he came off duty, he found a letter waiting for him at his lodgings. It was from his brother Hector in Edinburgh.

Hector informed him that King George II had agreed to an amnesty under certain conditions. He ordered Allan to resign his commission and return to Scotland as soon as possible. Puzzling over what Hector meant by certain conditions, Allan prepared to obey his laird.

Chapter Four

Edinburgh Years
1750-1756

Allan had no difficulty resigning his commission. Many young men were anxious to replace him, and he arranged passage on a packet to Leith, the port for Edinburgh. There he hired a horse and early on a summer morning rode up Leith Walk and over the bridge spanning the North Loch and gained the High Street. Hector lived in a flat in one of the narrow closes that opened off this principal street in the densely populated city, where everyone existed in six-storey tenements. Uphill the Castle loomed on its great rock, while downhill the High Street became the Cannongate that ended at the Palace of Holyrood. He left the horse at a livery stable and walked to the close, climbed to the fourth storey by a narrow dark stone stairway and rapped, still apprehensive over what conditions were required for an amnesty. Yet Hector was head of the family and Allan would never have thought of disobeying his order to come here.

A servant opened, and Hector leapt up from a desk in what was clearly his bedroom. Like every home in Edinburgh, and in most of Scotland, every room had a bed in it. Hector met his clients in a nearby tavern. "At last!" Hector exclaimed, flinging his arms around his younger brother.

Allan's eyes felt damp, as the loss of his father was brought home again forcibly. Hector, however, was all business and did not notice as he came right to the point. Allan would be granted an amnesty as soon as he took an oath of allegiance to the King.

Allan's voice rose in anger. "My loyalty will always be to the Stuarts!" he exclaimed in turn.

"Of course, and mine, too,"Hector said soothingly. "Yet you took an oath of allegiance to the Prince of Orange."

"I did," Allan admitted.

"As soon as I can arrange it, I want you to have a commission in the British army. Then your loyalty to King George can be to him as head of the service, the same loyalty you gave the Prince of Orange. Will that satisfy your conscience?"

"It will," Allan said, reconciled. "But how am I to get a commission? I've saved some money but not nearly enough to purchase in an established regiment, and with the country at peace I doubt if new regiments will be raised."

"Take the oath and let me worry about that," Hector replied.

Allan did. With Hector he walked to another close and found the flat of a magistrate. He swore his oath on a Bible,[1] and the magistrate gave him a certificate which he was to carry as long as anyone was likely to point a finger of suspicion at him.

Back at Hector's, the brothers talked over glassfuls of whiskey. Hector had recently been appointed a Writer to the Signet, the Scots term for solicitor, and he was acquiring some clients, most of them Macleans. Their brother Lachlan now had his own ship, the *Mary*, named for their mother, for which Hector had raised a loan. Their youngest brother Archibald was at Torloisk, as were their sisters Mary and Betty, and all were still unmarried. When both men were feeling mellow, the servant called them to dinner, and Hector led Allan into an adjoining room with the inevitable bed in it, where a table was spread. Dishes were filled with slices of beef, potatoes in a cream sauce, cucumbers in ginger pickled in vinegar, Madiera wine, a currant pudding and steaming bowls of broth — barley with chunks of mutton and vegetables floating it it. Allan was delighted with the familiar fare. At Hector's at least, a man could eat well.

He stayed with Hector a few days, then he set out on the hired horse for Torloisk. Once out of the malodorous city, he took deep breaths of sweet air as he found the road to Stirling. Each night he slept with his head on his saddle. He longed for the old plaid, but he had left his in The Hague since that garment was proscribed. Before he settled down, he hobbled the horse and buried his supply of coins, for robberies, though uncommon, did occur occasionally.

His way lay across the Bridge of Allan, to Lochernhead and into Glen Dochart. At Tyndrum he turned west into Glen Lochy to Dalmally, through the pass of Brander, along the shores of Loch Etive and Loch Linnhe, with its memories of 1746, to Oban. There he caught the ferry to Mull. The boat was a row galley, where a wide plank had been laid up to the gunwale, another down to the floor boards that were piled with straw. Urging the horse gently, Allan led it along the planks and stood by its head as the boatmen pushed off and rowed round the end of Kerrera Island. Mist lifted and Allan caught a glimpse of Mull, two leagues off.

Ashore, he rode into Glen More, with Ben More, the highest mountain on the island to his left. He followed the foot path to Loch Ba, and by the time he was descending to the shore of Loch na Keal his heart seemed to be thumping in his chest. There lay the Isle of Ulva, outlined in the distance. He was eight hours' ride from Torloisk, and was grateful that in summer the sky never grew fully dark.

At what he guessed was midnight he stopped to let the horse rest and graze. As he followed the shore of Loch na Keal, crofters were emerging, all in drab clothes, dyed black or grey in obedience to the proscription. To his joy he recognized some who had followed him at Culloden. Not all had perished on the bloody field. The little house looked even meaner than his recollection of it, but at least Cumberland's soldiers had not demolished it. At last he was home, walking arm in arm with his mother into the house where she placed a bowl of steaming broth before him, some oat cakes and a glass of whiskey. In his own bed, in womblike surroundings, Allan was transported over the years, as though he had never been away.

When late September set the bracken aflame on the hills, Allan received a letter from Hector. He had enquired about purchasing a commission, but none were available. Too many officers on the half-pay list wanted to return to duty, just as Allan suspected. Hector invited him to spend as much time as he liked in Edinburgh, until a commission could be secured. Some officers among his friends thought Allan might not have to wait long. Rumblings from America — tension between the English and French colonists — implied that troops might soon be needed.

For the moment Allan was happy at Torloisk. While he was capable of bursts of activity, he was accustomed to long months occupied with very little. Apart from the siege of Bergen-op-Zoom, life in the Scots Brigade had placed few demands on his energy. Like all Highlanders he spent hours at *céilidhean*, socializing and conversing. The pipes were banned — since they had been declared instruments of war after Culloden — but no one could silence the *clarsach* and the *port a beul* —the Gaelic harp and the rhythmic mouth music.

Just before Christmas, letters arrived from Lachlan and Hector. Lachlan was about to sail for Jamaica with a cargo. Hector informed the family that Sir Hector Maclean, the chief, had died that October in Rome. Maclean of Maclean, now Sir Allan, had become the 22nd chief.[1]Since his retirement from the Scots Brigade, Sir Allan had lived on the Isle of Coll. His wife Una was a daughter of Hector Maclean, the laird of Coll. Allan wondered what the new chief would do about the battalion, but neighbouring lairds such as Maclean of Lochbuie and Macquarrie of Ulva felt the time of a chief having a fighting tail had ended with the defeat at Culloden.

The wild days when a clan survived as much by stealing from its neighbours as from its own industry had already passed. Land once held in common by the clan had become the property of the chief once he realized the legal implications of securing a deed. Over the years, Parliament had come to exercise more control over events north of the Highland Line. Culloden had been the *coup de grace*. The clan system was dead, and thus far the military rule that had replaced it had done little to improve the lot of the inhabitants, laird and tenant alike. Roaming the hills, Allan saw around him the drabness, the poverty he had been too happy to notice when he first set foot on Mull after four years away.

With the spring he returned to Edinburgh, hoping to be on the spot to advance himself and procure a commission. At Hector's home he found his cousin Francis in residence. Francis had resigned from the Brigade and was also hoping for a commission, either by purchase or in a new regiment. After so many years in the Netherlands Francis' savings were greater than Allan's, who admitted that his only hope lay in joining a new regiment where purchase was not required. Hector could not raise a loan, for no mercantile house would extend him credit. He had borrowed heavily to help Lachlan finance his ship, and Lachlan did not expect to be able to repay Hector for a year or two yet.

In the meantime, Allan lived with Hector, making visits to Torloisk, while he waited until Britain should need an enlarged army. He fitted comfortably into Hector's circle of friends, sharing a room with Francis. Hector's was an all-male society, which suited Allan, who could not afford to entertain ladies or think of marrying until he had a regular source of income. Hector's cronies were a blend of lawyers, officers of the garrison, young doctors and medical students. They had two things in common, literary interests and firm Jacobite convictions. Allan was bored by their intellectual pursuits, but the nightly sessions in Hector's bedroom invariably turned to the Stuart cause.[2]

One evening in 1752, two new faces appeared, men Hector introduced as medical students. One was John Stuart, nineteen years old and English by birth, but claiming kinship to the Royal Stuarts. The other was an Irishman who spoke with a brogue and a stammer. He was Lauchlin Macleane, four years older than John Stuart, with prior medical training in Dublin. Despite the spelling of his name, Lauchlin was descended from the Macleans of Coll. Stuart was tall, slender and handsome; Macleane although equally tall, was ugly yet arresting.

As soon as the whiskey was poured, Lauchlin dropped to his knees, raised his glass for the Jacobite toast, and in halting tones proclaimed, "To the King o'er the water!"

From then on, Lauchlin dominated the conversation, although John Stuart held his own better than the others. Allan was fascinated by both men, especially Lauchlin. Yet he wondered whether a Sassenach and an Irishman could be trusted, even though they had Scottish forbears. They were romanticizing Culloden, and would have been astonished had they known how defeated the new chief of clan Maclean now appeared. Since Hector and Allan had both been "out with the Prince" they were lionized. While he would never forget the nightmare that was the reality of Culloden, Allan relished his place of honour among the Jacobites of Edinburgh a mere six years after the defeat.

Both Stuart and Macleane were fond of introducing Allan as one who had been "out with the Prince. " For one who had lived in poverty, and on a tight budget while in the Netherlands, this was heady praise. Although still poor, Allan never forgot that he was of noble blood, a son of a senior cadet branch of the clan and related to the chiefs. He accepted reverent flattery as no more than his due.

By the spring of 1753 Allan had high hopes for a commission. The Edinburgh garrison had been increased and rumours were rife that tension was mounting in the colonies. Troops would soon be needed beyond the Atlantic. More officers joined Hector's gatherings, and all were Jacobites, loyal to the service while longing for the restoration of the Stuarts. On one of these evenings, Lauchlin Macleane appeared with Dr. Richard Huck, a surgeon in the 33rd Regiment stationed in the city. Lauchlin was certain that Allan would soon find a new regiment and Huck agreed with him, but still Allan had no luck.

On 30 March 1755, Allan attended the wedding of Lauchlin Macleane and Elizabeth Hewitt, whose late father had been a surgeon to Czar Peter II of Russia. To Allan the bridal pair seemed ill-matched, Lauchlin large and ugly, Elizabeth short and plain. Following the ceremony Allan asked Hector why Lauchlin had chosen her.

"For her inheritance," Hector said with a laugh.

That summer Lauchlin finished his studies, but showed no inclination to set up a medical practice. Francis purchased a commission in the 42nd Regiment, the Black Watch, and Allan could not help feeling envious. Surely new regiments would soon be needed. The news from America was encouraging for a soldier anxious for duty. He devoured newspaper reports. The French were inciting their Indian allies to attack frontier settlements, and General Edward Braddock had been sent with an expedition to capture Fort Duquesne, on the Pennsylvania frontier, an important French base. For the security of her American empire, Allan suspected that Britain would have to take over New France, or Canada, as it was sometimes called.

He was right. During the summer Braddock took a drubbing in Pennsylvania, but a force under William Johnson, the Superintendent of Indian Affairs for the Northern District, had routed the French on Lake George. Allan bought a map and studied the reports. Britain's colonies were more populous, but the French, aided by their native allies, appeared by no means the underdogs. Newspapers advertised for recruits to fill the Highland regiments. Sir Allan Maclean received a captaincy in Montgomery's Highlanders, a new regiment that did not require purchase. Allan applied but received no reply.

Finally, at one of Hector's gatherings, everyone was discussing the coming campaign, and many officers expected to be sent to America, among them Dr. Richard Huck. "Have you heard of the Royal American Regiment, the new 62nd?" he asked Allan.

"No," Allan admitted. "Tell me about it."

"It's to be raised in the colonies, making use of provincials to fill the ranks. The officers can be British or foreign, as long as they are Protestants," Huck explained. "The commander is Lord Loudoun, who will be sent to America as the commander-in-chief."

"Loudoun's also a Campbell and a damn Whig," Allan protested, flushing angrily.

"And a fine soldier," Huck said. "He's looking for officers with experience. He dislikes awarding commissions by purchase, and he has no objections to employing men who were out with the Prince. You would be wise to consider the Royal Americans."[3]

When the gathering broke up, Allan asked Hector what he thought of Dr. Huck's idea. To his surprise his brother counselled him to write Lord Loudoun, as Allan had to start somewhere. Then, Allan should go to Torloisk and take leave of their mother in case Loudoun's response was favourable.

When the time came to leave Torloisk, Allan could not help comparing this departure with the time the fiery cross went around Mull in 1746. Now, almost ten years later, he was again setting out, this time not as a rebel but as a soldier of George II, assuming that Loudoun wanted him. As he bid his mother farewell, she smiled at him. "Some day you will be a major like your father."

"No I won't," he replied, teasing. "I'll be a general."

In Edinburgh a letter from Lord Loudoun was waiting for him. The future commander-in-chief of His Majesty's forces in America was indeed offering him a lieutenant's commission in the 62nd Regiment. He wanted Allan to come to London as soon as possible, and he anticipated that the officers would be sailing for the colonies early in the spring. As it was now mid-December, Allan resolved to stay with Hector until after Christmas, then foregoing the joys of

Hogmanay, ride to London to arrive there early in January. Hector had arranged for him to draw bills on one Archibald Maclaine, a merchant in Cheapside. Allan objected, but Hector was adamant.

"You will be needing many things your wages won't cover," he said. "For these you must have credit. I won't have my brother living like a pauper when associating with fine gentlemen officers."

On 26 December Allan clattered over the cobbles on a hired horse, along the road that followed the coast to Berwick-on-Tweed, which joined the Great North Road, the busiest route with many inns. Hector had ordered him not to sleep on the ground, or he would not be in a presentable condition when he reached London. As he rode along, Allan felt elated. At last his life was taking the turn he had longed for since he left the Netherlands. America! The very name hinted at adventure. He knew little about that part of the world beyond the fact that it was covered with dense forests, something he could hardly imagine. He fancied that America must resemble the patches of woodland he was noticing as he rode south through the English countryside, but with painted Indians behind every tree.

On a grey afternoon ten days later, he entered the capital for the first time, found an inn, and set out for Whitehall and the War Office. There he was given directions to Lord Loudoun's house in Southampton Street, where he was shown into an anteroom by a servant. The room was crowded, but Allan recognized the two Mackay brothers, Samuel and Francis, from the Scots Brigade, and two Swiss officers, Henry Bouquet and Frederick Haldimand. From Haldimand, Allan learned that there would be four battalions. Henry Bouquet would be the lieutenant-colonel of the first battalion, Haldimand of the second, the latter to be raised among German-speaking colonists. They were interrupted when a secretary called Haldimand's name and he excused himself.

The shadows were long by the time Lord Loudoun was ready for Allan, who was shown into a parlour. The earl rose and held out a hand that Allan failed to grasp. He stood transfixed at His Lordship's attire for he was dressed as a Highland officer, with belted kilt, waistcoat and plaid of matching tartan, a red coat faced blue with silver lace. On a table where he had been sitting lay a blue bonnet. Of course, Allan thought as he belatedly accepted the earl's hand. Highland dress was permitted for military uniforms. How strange it was to find in London the beloved costume, even though the tartan displayed a hated Campbell check.

John Campbell, 4th Earl of Loudoun, was a small, neat man. Allan liked him instinctively despite his name. The earl perused a letter which Allan recognized as his own, and looked up.

"Colonel Haldimand tells me you speak acceptable German," the earl said."I have therefore assigned you to the fourth battalion under a Swiss officer, Colonel-Commandant James Prevost. The lieutenant-colonel is Sir John St. Clair, the major, Augustine Prevost. Colonel Prevost is in Hanover, and Sir John St. Clair, wounded on Braddock's campaign, is in America. Major Prevost has rooms at the Black Lion in Water Lane, off Fleet Street. Kindly wait on him tomorrow morning at ten o'clock, Lieutenant Maclean."[4]

Allan thanked him and withdrew, sorry that he would not be in Haldimand's battalion, but relieved to have a posting after nearly six years. On time he was at Black Lion, where a servant led him to the second floor and rapped on a door. A man dressed as a private opened. Major Prevost was seated at a table finishing his breakfast. The private brought Allan a cup of coffee and the major motioned to a chair beside him.

With an accent that implied Swiss origins, the major briefed Allan. He would be in the major's own company, and the other lieutenant was Peter Van Ingen, already in America. As yet no ensign had been appointed. Each company would have 100 rank and file, and each battalion ten companies. The officers hoped to sail early in March. Allan's pay would be seven shillings and sixpence a day, commencing 8 January, the date of his commission. He was to hire a servant who would receive sixpence a day from Allan's funds, with deductions for food and medical expenses.

"Have you any questions, Lieutenant Maclean?" the major asked.

"One, Major, if I'm not being impertinent."

"Yes?" the other enquired, a dark eyebrow raised.

"Are you related to Colonel Prevost, sir?"

"We are cousins," the major said, without enthusiasm, Allan thought. "The regiment is being raised in the colonies, but Colonel Prevost has permission from the Duke of Cumberland to bring some recruits from Germany. He will be joining us later in America."

As he dismissed him, the major told Allan to visit a tailor in Oxford Street to order his regimentals, the red coat faced blue, the silver lace specified for the officers. Allan obeyed and afterwards arranged for credit from Archibald Maclaine in Cheapside before returning to the inn. Then he found a cheap lodging house to save money.

He passed the following weeks becoming acquainted with his brother officers in the fourth battalion, two of whom were Samuel and Francis Mackay, who had ensigns' commissions. The officers speculated on the quality of the recruits they would be training — colonials who might not be amenable to military discipline. They wondered, too, about their superior officers. Sir John St. Clair had field experience in America. Major Prevost they respected, but all had perceived his coldness when his cousin was mentioned, and a junior officer who was Swiss warned them that Colonel James Prevost had been refused a commission in the Dutch service. The Duke of Cumberland, the King's commander-in-chief, however, favoured him, which was cold comfort to Allan. His absent colonel-commandant was a protegé of the butcher of Culloden.

On 22 March, with Major-General Daniel Webb, Loudoun's third-in-command, the officers and their servants left in stage-coaches for Portsmouth to meet the convoy of transports bound for New York. The non-commissioned officers would sail on a later convoy. As he sailed away on the *Nottingham*, Allan was content, except for nagging doubts about Colonel James Prevost.

Chapter Five

The Royal Americans
1756-1758

Early in June the convoy lay off Sandy Hook. Once the fleet had anchored inside New York's harbour, ship's boats took the officers and their servants ashore. Allan heard someone calling for Lieutenant Maclean, and he beheld a sturdy young man of fair complexion who introduced himself as Lieutenant Peter Van Ingen, a colonial of Dutch descent. With Van Ingen's help, Allan and the two Mackay brothers found lodgings and set out to explore New York, very much a Dutch town except that where there were canals in the Netherlands, here the tall, narrow houses overlooked broad, grassy streets along which cattle grazed, pigs rooted and children frolicked.

Each morning the officers went to brigade headquarters, in Fort George at the foot of Broadway, to read the regimental orders posted there. Officers of the 62nd Regiment were to be sent to widely separated points to recruit. Lieutenant-Colonel Bouquet and the officers of the first battalion would sail for Philadelphia. Lieutenant-Colonel Haldimand was to take his officers north to Albany. Lieutenant-Colonel Russell Chapman of the third battalion was bound for Halifax. Major Prevost and his officers would remain at New York City, for they were to recruit in that neighbourhood.

Two weeks later the non-commissioned officers arrived, and Allan received his beating order from Major Prevost. He was to proceed with a sergeant and a drummer up the Hudson Valley. Beforehand, Prevost briefed the recruiting parties. Strict rules had to be followed to avoid annoying local people. Each officer must present his beating order to the magistrate of the main town in a district before his sergeant and drummer could go into the streets. An enlistment was valid only if, within not less than twenty-four hours or more than four days, the recruit appeared before a magistrate and swore that he was a Protestant, had enlisted as a soldier, had been read the Second and Sixth Articles of War on mutiny and desertion, and had taken the oath of allegiance. If a recruit refused to take the oath, he must be released provided he returned the guinea bounty money he was to receive when he agreed to enlist, and paid a fine of twenty shillings.

Indentured servants were eligible, but the bounty money must go to the servant's master, as well as the amount owing for his indenture. Prevost warned the officers to accept such servants only if their terms of indenture were nearly over, to save money. Officers could draw fifty pounds at a time to pay expenses and bounties. They were to accept only men who were free of ruptures, convulsions and other infirmities, and at least " five feet five inches tall," or for a growing boy, " five feet four inches."[1]

Allan left on a hired horse, his sergeant and drummer marching behind. At the first town he chose, no one would divulge where the magistrate lived. By bribing a boy with a shilling, he got his directions, but the magistrate was unwilling to hear the oaths from the recruits. Temper flaring, Allan left the magistrate's house to find a hostile crowd around his sergeant and drummer. Deciding to seek out friendlier territory, he mounted and beckoned to his subordinates.

" Damn them," he said when they were at a safe distance from the mob. " They deserve to be overrun by the French."

At Poughkeepsie they took a ferry across the Hudson River and went inland, to avoid competing with officers of the second battalion working from Albany. The nearer to the frontier they went, the more recruits Allan enlisted. Since their own homes were endangered by Indians, abetted by the French, they were more willing to serve. Allan turned south into New Jersey, and by late August he had enlisted the thirty men he needed to fill his platoon. Most were Scots and Irish from the frontier, but a few were German lads — farm labourers and drifters he found in the villages. As he began marching to New York City he was nearly out of funds.

Major Prevost was pleased with his success, but for the time being the recruits had to be housed in tents. He had been urging the provincial assembly to grant funds for a barracks, but without success. He hoped that Lord Loudoun, who had arrived late in July, accompanied by his second-in-command, Major-General James Abercromby, would have more influence with the assemblymen.

The war news was bad. The French had captured Oswego. While Allan was in New Jersey, the French commander, the Marquis de Montcalm, had attacked the British posts at the east end of Lake Ontario. After the garrison capitulated, the Indians with Montcalm had gone on the rampage, looting, murdering the wounded and many civilians. In the eyes of the British officers, the Frenchman was guilty of a grave breach of the rules of war. Worse, the French controlled Lake Ontario. Thus far, the British had suffered all the setbacks.

In his lodgings Allan struggled to balance his accounts. Bringing recruits from the frontiers had proved costly, and his travelling expenses far overran the amount assigned for them. Somehow the money must be made up by cutting down elsewhere, or he would find himself in debt to the regiment.

With the other junior officers, Allan began training the recruits. The regiment, now renumbered the 60th Foot, would become skilled in tactics suitable for frontier warfare, and would be armed with rifled carbines, more accurate than the Brown Bess musket.[2] After seeing forested country on his travels, Allan approved. Concentrated volleys and parade ground drill would be ineffective among the forests inland where the French and Indians had been so successful.

"We've learned from Braddock's defeat," Lieutenant Van Ingen observed to Allan as they watched the recruits marching in open formation after marksmanship drill. "Lord Loudoun wants us to be as proficient as the ranger companies being formed at Albany."

In October, by which time a new barracks was completed for the battalion, Colonel James Prevost arrived with some sturdy German lads and a few were assigned to each company. Soon Allan heard rumours that his commander-in-chief wanted to dismiss Colonel Prevost, but he did not want to incur the wrath of the Duke of Cumberland. Everyone knew that the two Prevosts were quarrelling, and Allan recalled the major's coolness when he explained that the colonel was his cousin.

Soldiers brought before Colonel Prevost were given brutal beatings without a fair hearing before a court martial.

Matters came to a head when a soldier was beaten to death by two corporals. When this atrocity was reported to Lord Loudoun, he ordered the corporals broken at a court martial. Officers who overheard a confrontation between Loudoun and the Swiss reported that Prevost had denied all knowledge of the murder. When Loudoun told Prevost that soldiers were to have their rights as British troops, the other sneered.[3]

Recruiting had been successful, but now the battalion lost its spirit, and the officers were disgruntled. Even after the beatings ceased, the colonel found other ways of degrading the rank and file. He allowed his quartermaster to knock the heads off barrels and dump the mens's food on dirty blankets, where they were expected to fight over it. At this Allan fumed. How could that strutting martinet expect to build a fighting force when he treated his men worse than farmyard animals?

During the winter of 1756-57, deep gloom pervaded the entire battalion. Equipment was vanishing because Colonel Prevost, who delighted in parading in his fine uniform, was inept at keeping records, and at having the battalion's supplies properly guarded. Pilfering was rife, and while reports were dropped at Lord Loudoun's headquarters, he dared not offend the Duke of Cumberland's favourite.

Allan's mood was bleak, the long days relieved only by the society of his brother officers. The people of New York, although many were Dutch in origin, were not like the friendly people of the Netherlands, and they resented the British troops. Meanwhile, Allan prayed that Lord Loudoun would dismiss Colonel Prevost. On 15 March, without Major Prevost's knowledge, the officers of the fourth battalion compiled a report for Lord Loudoun on their colonel's abuses, and requested that Sir John St. Clair, their lieutenant-colonel, be assigned to command. The other battalions were commanded by their lieutenant-colonels, and they asked that the fourth not be an exception.

Lord Loudoun did not reply. The other colonel-commandants were all serving in important capacities. Colonel Prevost had to remain with his battalion because Loudoun refused to promote so incompetent an officer. Also, he could not spare Sir John St. Clair, who was in Philadelphia serving as Quartermaster-General. Loudoun had few officers who understood the problems of moving supplies in a country with no decent roads. However, Loudoun put in a request for another lieutenant-colonel for the fourth battalion, which was to be posted to Halifax as part of a summer expedition against Louisbourg. That fortress had to be taken before the commander-in-chief could move on Quebec.

By the end of April, thirty transport vessels were riding at anchor in the harbour, being loaded with supplies and destined to carry six regiments. To the dismay of the officers and men of the fourth battalion, the War Office did not send a new lieutenant-colonel. Disheartened, Allan, the Mackays and Lieutenant Van Ingen prepared to depart.

On 12 May 1757, the regiments were ordered to embark, but confusion reigned in the fourth battalion of the 60th Regiment. While Major Prevost did his best, Colonel Prevost countermanded his orders, barked his own which no one understood, and swore that his was the finest battalion in the British army.

" Finest indeed!" Allan snarled under his breath as he watched the men of his platoon climb into ship's boats for the ride out to the fleet. " And God knows what that lunatic will do under fire!"

On 30 June the six regiments reached Halifax, a small community enclosed within a stockade and five wood and earth forts. The soldiers were to stay in tents, but Allan found that none had been sent for his battalion. Fortunately, Major Prevost got some from the stores in Halifax. Allan, Lieutenant Van Ingen and the Mackays found quarters in an inn, a miserable log building below the hill where the middle fort stood. Major Prevost informed them that they would have to wait for a fleet from England. The six regiments from New York, and the third battalion of the 60th, raised in Nova Scotia, were not sufficient to deal with the Louisbourg garrison. Meanwhile, Colonel Prevost had the rank and file planting cabbages.

" I hope we're not here to harvest them," Lieutenant Van Ingen remarked.

On 9 July the fleet arrived, and the troops were brought ashore to exercise after the long voyage. More delays followed as the wind was contrary or non-existent. Finally, on 1 August the battalion was ordered aboard the transports.

For the next four days the enlarged fleet stood offshore, but the wind refused to blow. Then, in a light breeze the fleet turned and after drifting some hours regained the harbour. Major Prevost soon explained that Lord Loudoun had cancelled the expedition. A spy vessel off Louisbourg sent an oared cutter to inform him that a French fleet had arrived there with reinforcements a few days before the British reinforcements reached Halifax.

Allan felt outraged. The season was well advanced, and there would be no campaign, therefore no promotions in the field until next year. Major Prevost found a way of solving his problems with his cousin. He transferred to the second battalion, which would remain in Nova Scotia, and his place in the fourth battalion was taken by Major John Rutherford from the third battalion. Major Rutherford was then the commander of Allan's company. Ironically, excellent winds took the ships back to New York harbour. As the transports moved to their anchorages, ship's boats were coming towards them to carry the troops. The first to reach Allan's ship brought appalling news.

When he learned that Lord Loudoun had detached many troops from the northern frontiers of New York for the Louisbourg venture, the Marquis de Montcalm had attacked Fort William Henry, at the foot of Lake George, which had surrendered on 9 August. As at Oswego the Indians had massacred civilians and wounded troops, to the fury of the British officers. Allan shuddered, both at the grisly details, and at the thought of another disastrous setback.

The dreary autumn and winter of 1757-1758 began. Late in December, Allan received a letter that raised his spirits. It was from Lauchlin Macleane, the friend from his Edinburgh days, who had emigrated with his wife Elizabeth and set up a medical practice in Philadelphia. John Stuart, now a qualified physician, had come with them as a partner.[4] Lauchlin invited Allan to apply for leave and visit them. Allan sighed longingly, but leave was out of the question. He must keep watch over his platoon to prevent any of his men coming before Colonel Prevost.

Spring brought dramatic changes in the administration. Lord Loudoun, held responsible for the failure to take Louisbourg, was recalled, and the new commander-in-chief was General James Abercromby, Loudoun's second-in-command. As soon as Loudoun was on the high seas, Abercromby took further steps to alleviate the tensions that plagued the fourth battalion. Abercromby also superseded Loudoun as the colonel-in-chief of the 60th Regiment, and despite what the Duke of Cumberland might think, he relieved Colonel Prevost of his duties. Sir John St. Clair, who would be the quartermaster for an expedition against Fort Duquesne in Pennsylvania, was moved to the third battalion that was in Nova Scotia. John Young, the major of the first battalion, was promoted to lieutenant-colonel of the fourth. Allan felt immensely relieved.

Orders posted at Fort George informed the officers that the fourth battalion would take part in an expedition northwards along Lake Champlain against Carillon, the French fort on the Ticonderoga promontory. Before these plans were well advanced, Lieutenant-Colonel Frederick Haldimand arrived from Philadelphia escorting part of the first battalion, which had also been assigned to the Ticonderoga expedition. Then, to Allan's satisfaction, Haldimand traded places with Lieutenant-Colonel John Young and assumed command of the fourth battalion. Haldimand agreed to the change when Abercromby informed him that Colonel Prevost was " hors de combat." [5]

In May the battalion embarked in small sloops for Albany, a slow journey for the ships had to battle the current, constantly tacking in the narrow Hudson River. The farther north they moved, the more enclosing became the dense strands of trees. Albany was little more than a fur fort in the wilderness. The forest stretched endlessly around the wooden stockade, and the place was swarming with troops who outnumbered the civilians, the latter mostly Dutch. For the first time Allan saw Britain's Indian allies, members of the Six Nations or Iroquois Confederacy, many in bright war paint, paddling along the Hudson in their elm bark canoes. Here indeed was the America of his dreams, a land vast and untamed.

The battalion soon proceeded to Fort Edward, at the great bend in the Hudson, where Lieutenant-Colonel Haldimand's task was to receive the bateaux of supplies and arrange to forward their contents north to Lake George. Abercromby's expedition would comprise some 15,000 men, of which 7,000 were regulars, the rest provincials, which required incredible quantities of food, clothing, medicines, heavy guns and ammunition. Some ten miles, Allan reckoned, separated the Hudson from the lake, and Haldimand was organizing enough wagons to cover that distance, and making certain that a huge fleet of bateaux and whaleboats was in readiness at the foot of Lake George.

The fleet of oared, lateen-sailed bateaux that left Albany was enormous, enough to carry the fourth battalion and its supplies, with more supplies for the troops who would follow. Some of the provincials went along a path close to the shore, driving oxen and horses needed for the wagons. The battalion disembarked at Fort Edward, a tiny village with a small, stockaded fort, where the men pitched tents because the barracks were inadequate for the garrison already there. Allan's company was occupied searching the few farms in the vicinity for wagons, or in building them from boards cut at a sawmill on a tributary stream.

Provincials with the necessary skills soaked long, thick strips of wood and bent them into wheels, and cut spokes while blacksmiths from the companies of artificers fitted iron rims. As soon as a few wagons were ready, detachments of regulars set off along the rough track for Lake George.

Allan's platoon formed one detachment. Along the trail, he found that trees blotted out the sun; clouds of stinging insects tortured him in a manner far worse than Highland midges. At the end of the trail he came upon the charred remains of Fort William Henry, where more detachments of regulars and provincials were busy constructing bateaux and whaleboats.

By mid-June the entire expedition had gathered at Fort Edward. General Abercromby's second-in-command was the popular Lord George Augustus Howe, commanding a battalion of the 55th Foot but when the expedition was over, Howe was to assume command of the third battalion of the 60th Regiment. A battalion of the 42nd Foot arrived, and Allan made enquiries about his cousin Francis, but learned that Francis was serving in a battalion that had been sent to the West Indies. Meanwhile, more supplies were brought from Fort Edward and forwarded to Lake George. When the entire force set out over the trail, the men were in marching columns and the officers on foot because all available horses were needed to haul the supply trains.

On 4 July the expedition was moving into a new encampment at the site of Fort William Henry, where the following day, the men embarked on 800 bateaux and 90 whaleboats. The artillery pieces rode on wooden rafts. Allan's platoon was crowded into one whaleboat with Major Rutherford, near the front of the flotilla.

" Do you know French strength at Ticonderoga, sir?" Allan asked the major.

" Montcalm is supposed to have eight battalions in Fort Carillon," Rutherford replied. " And many Canadians and Indians. We'll have to dislodge them but we have enough artillery to pound their fortifications into pieces."

To Allan the flotilla made a stirring sight. Flags were flying, fifes and drums sometimes playing, and to his joy the pipes of the Highland regiments. Not far off he could see companies of green-coated rangers — provincials skilled in the art of fighting in forests — who would serve as advance troops and scouts. On either side of the long, narrow lake rose forested mountains. He wondered if the hills of Mull had once resembled them.

On 6 July the army disembarked in a cove and began setting up camp. All women and servants were to remain there, and the advance prepared to move at once on Fort Carillon. Lord Howe was to command it, and Haldimand was to lead his own battalion and the light companies of all the regiments. The rest of the regulars would form three columns to follow. The advance column formed up, the light companies following parties of rangers, with Allan's battalion bringing up the rear. The advance moved towards Carillon by a circuitous route along Rivière des Chutes, which joined Lake George to Lake Champlain, to avoid having to portage this river. Far ahead Allan heard firing. The column came to a halt, and Major Rutherford walked back to Allan's position at the head of the platoon.

" We've been ambushed," he reported. " But we're to press on."

The column began to move again, then Haldimand ordered an open formation and the companies spread out. The French—soldiers from an outpost, Allan suspected—were being driven back, their white coats flashing amongst the trees. His platoon advanced, firing, reloading, and pushing on, a few falling. As they drew their bayonets, Allan thought the situation was deteriorating. Redcoats were firing from every direction and he feared his men might be killed by their own side. Drummers sounded the retreat. The French had vanished and Allan ordered his men to bring back the wounded. By early evening the advance column had returned to base camp, and Allan heard that in the skirmishing Lord Howe had been killed.[6]

On 7 July the troops portaged across Rivière des Chutes, for Abercromby had changed his plans and wanted a more direct approach to Fort Carillon. Allan's company camped beside a sawmill close to the French position. The next morning Sir William Johnson, the Superintendent of Indian Affairs, appeared with 400 native warriors, terrifying in their war paint. They took up a position on nearby Sugar Hill, and commenced firing their muskets, which Allan thought was accomplishing very little. Now many provincials forded the river, to act as a screen for the main attack. Allan's battalion followed, holding their rifled carbines and cartridge cases above the water, and formed up along the opposite shore.

Allan advanced with his company towards Carillon's outworks. To his dismay his platoon was soon floundering into a line of abatis — felled trees with their branches facing them that had been placed well in advance of the fort's stone bastions — while the French kept up a withering fire from their outer line of defence. A wild yell rising from the light company of the 42nd sent him crawling over branches, echoing the Old Jacobite shout, voice hoarse from the blue smoke he was inhaling. Around him men were writhing in agony among the tangled branches; others tried again and again to surmount the abatis and attack the outer breastworks. Suddenly Major Rutherford appeared out of the smoke.

" Where the devil's the artillery?" Allan shouted over the guns

" Some blockhead engineer told the general we would not need it," the major shouted before his voice was drowned by another explosion of grape shot.

By mid-afternoon the regulars were still trying to push past the outer defences, officers and ranks suffering grotesque casualties. Allan expected to hear drums sounding the retreat, but no signal came. The branch-strewn defences now resembled Culloden after the Jacobite line had been broken. Another hail of bullets and grape shot fell all around him. Allan collapsed in a heap, a searing pain wracking one of his thighs. Then he lost consciousness.[7]

Chapter Six

The Third New York Independent Company 1760-1762

The wound that Allan sustained on 8 July 1758 would plague him off and on for the rest of his life. In later years he developed causalgia — a burning pain and wasting of the lower leg. The bullet that struck him in the thigh had damaged a peripheral nerve.[1]

After he was stricken he was carried back to the base camp and placed with the other wounded officers, among them Lieutenant-Colonel Haldimand who was not seriously hurt. Later in the day General Abercromby gave the order to retreat, and the attempt to take Carillon that season was over. The wounded were sent ahead in bateaux to the hospital in Albany, where Haldimand, recovering rapidly, was a frequent visitor at Allan's cot. From Haldimand, Allan learned that General Abercromby had gone to New York, bewildered over his failure. Allan voiced no such astonishment. Whoever would have believed that a general could attempt a frontal assault without first demoralizing the enemy with a long artillery barrage? Haldimand, dutiful, did not criticize his superior's tactics, but he admitted that he could not understand why Abercromby had withdrawn after that two-day attempt. True, there had been 1,600 casualties, but Abercromby still had 5,000 able-bodied regulars, and his 8,000 provincials had scarcely been bloodied. He could have brought up his artillery and tried again. Allan fumed but Haldimand urged discretion.

" It's easy for a junior officer to criticize," he said. " Yet how can you know you would have done differently if you had the responsibility of thousands of men?"

The campaign of 1758 was not a total disaster. Word soon arrived that a small expedition under John Bradstreet had captured Fort Frontenac, at the foot of Lake Ontario. Strategically this was a significant prize, for the British now controlled the supply line to France's inland posts. Then great news came from Halifax. Louisbourg had fallen to a combined British military and naval force under Jeffrey Amherst. Allan worried that his wound might prevent him from taking part in next year's campaign, for it might well be the last of the war.

Towards the end of September the wounded were taken down the Hudson to the more comfortable hospital at New York City. When Allan was able to leave the hospital he moved to an inn where other convalescent officers were staying. Lieutenant-Colonel Haldimand, who had rented a house nearby, often invited the officers of his battalion to dine with him. At one such party, in January 1759, Haldimand told Allan that he had recommended him for a field promotion. There was no vacancy in the fourth battalion of the 60th Regiment, but the captain of the Third New York Independent Company had resigned, leaving a vacancy there. The ranks of the independent companies were filled by colonials, but they were part of the British regular army. For Allan this was important to know. Officers of provincial regiments were not part of the British establishment and were not entitled to half-pay when the regiments were reduced. Allan was delighted with the appointment, and his commission as captain of the Third New York Independent Company was signed on 10 January by General Abercromby.

The company, of light infantry, was stationed at Schenectady, and Allan would join it in the spring when he expected to be fit again. His junior officers were three lieutenants, and he noted the dates of their commissions. Lieutenant Archibald McCauley's was 25 December 1756; Henry Farrant's was 31 March 1758. Walter Butler's was dated 25 December 1725 — the year Allan was born. Having a subordinate old enough to be his father was disconcerting. Besides, what sort of man would be content to remain a lieutenant in the British army for thirty-four years?[2]

In February the newspapers reported that the British had captured Fort Duquesne, driving the French from another important base. Then Allen received a letter from Lauchlin Macleane, who had been a surgeon under Lieutenant-Colonel Henry Bouquet on the expedition. Montgomery's Highlanders had also been with Bouquet, and Lauchlin bragged that he had met Sir Allan Maclean of Maclean, their chief. The men had set out late in the season, and the winter march back to Philadelphia, Lauchlin claimed, had almost finished him. He had not been well since.

When the winds of March were melting the snow, Allan felt much better and was eager to be back on duty. A mood of contentment swept over him. His pay, retroactive to the date of his commission, was now ten shillings a day, and he was able to cover his expenses while in New York City and repay his battalion in the 60th Regiment the debt he had incurred while recruiting in 1756. In mid-April, accompanied by his servant, he went aboard a sloop for Albany, and from there he planned to acquire an army horse for the ride to Schenectady.

Upon landing at Albany, Allan heard that General Abercromby had been recalled, and the new commander-in-chief was General Amherst, the victor of Louisbourg. Allan had a tailor change the blue facings on his coat for the green ones of the independent companies. From the commissariat department he got a horse and left Albany, his servant riding pillion behind him.

Schenectady, on the Mohawk River, was another Dutch-looking town. Everywhere, he saw Iroquois Indians of the Mohawk nation. A stockade enclosed the older part of the town, with more dwellings outside it than at Albany. Beyond stretched the grainlands of the Mohawk Valley, interspersed with swamp and forest. Supplies were stockpiled in readiness to be moved westwards to the newly-built Fort Stanwix, at the portage between the Mohawk River and Oneida Lake. A river from that lake emptied into Lake Ontario at Oswego, still empty since Montcalm's destruction of the post nearly three years before.

Allan rode to the fort beside the Mohawk, where his new company was stationed, and met his three lieutenants. Archibald McCauley was a fellow-Scot. Henry Farrant was a German-speaking settler from the Palatinate, in the Rhineland of Germany. Walter Butler, who spoke with a lilt, was, as Allan feared, a gnome of a man who appeared to be in his seventies. Immediately Butler invited Allan to make his headquarters at his house in Fonda, on the Mohawk a short way to the west, where Captain Maclean, so recently convalescent, would be more comfortable than at the fort.

Butlersbury at Fonda N. Y. Described as a typical New England saltbox, the house was built in 1742 by Walter Butler Sr., a lieutenant under Allan Maclean in the Third New York Independant Company. Butlersbury was the home of Walter's son John when the revolution began.

Gratefully Allan accepted the offer. The company would be occupied moving supplies to Fort Stanwix, and Allan could supervise this operation as well from Fonda as from Schenectady.

After ordering his servant to return to Albany and bring his baggage in a bateau to Fonda, Allan rode with Lieutenant Butler for his new quarters. He was anxious to be better acquainted with the old officer. He trusted the younger lieutenants instinctively, but he had doubts as to whether so elderly a man as Butler would be able to pull his weight. They forded the Mohawk to the north shore, and at the village of Fonda climbed a steep hill away from the river. On top they came to a track leading eastwards to a neat, symmetrical, square-timbered house, small but larger than most of the log dwellings they had passed. Butler was a man of some standing in the neighbourhood.[3]

After a servant took their horses, Butler smiled broadly. " Welcome to Butlersbury, Captain Maclean."

" A fine farm, Lieutenant," Allan rejoined. " How many acres have you?"

" Sixty thousand, Captain," the other replied, and he ushered Allan into the house and towards a hearth over which a plump woman of like vintage was bending. " And this is Mrs. Butler. Captain Maclean has come, my dear. May we have some rum?"

Gratefully Allan accepted the rum and a seat beside the fire. The ride had warmed him but the interior of the house was rather chilly.

" The war has reached a turning point," Butler said as they sipped their rum, each sizing the other up. " Bradstreet's capture at Fort Frontenac was a start. My son John, a captain in the Indian Department, was with the expedition. The only clever thing Abercromby did was send Bradstreet to deal with the Frenchies."

" Not quite," Allan argued mildly, thinking of Colonel James Prevost. " But he certainly blundered at Ticonderoga. I hope you are right about a turning point. First Frontenac, then Louisbourg and now Fort Duquesne."

" Nasty," Butler said. " A winter campaign, great suffering."

" Sir," Allan asked, raising the matter that troubled him most. " I hope you will not think me impertinent, but may I enquire why you have never been promoted in the army?"

"Never needed a promotion," Butler replied with a grin. " Never had the opportunity to win one in the field, and purchase would have been a waste of good money. However, I am the lieutenant-colonel of our militia, and I've commanded forts in this district. I'm as strong as an ox, and you'll find me useful."

Allan grew to have a healthy respect for Lieutenant Walter Butler. He seemed very much a laird with his vast acreages and substantial number of tenants, although much of the land had yet to be taken up. He had been born in Ireland, and had come to America in 1711, settling first in Connecticut. In 1733 he had obtained these lands and brought his family here. His son John, whom Allan learned was born in 1725, the same year as himself, was serving under Sir William Johnson. He had been with Sir William at Carillon when he arrived with his Indian warriors, and was on the earlier expedition along Lake Champlain in 1755. At that time the lieutenant's other son Walter Jr., had been killed. Allan suspected that part of the father's motive in remaining active was to make certain that his namesake had not died in vain.

Early in May, as Allan was watching the loading of boats for Fort Stanwix, a fleet of bateaux reached Schenectady. Lieutenant-Colonel Haldimand was in the lead boat, and Allan recognized many men from his old battalion. He pulled off his hat and waved.

"Where are you going?" he shouted.

In one of the later boats Samuel Mackay stood up. " to occupy Oswego," Mackay shouted back.

On the last day of May, orders came. Allan's company was to go to Oswego to take part in an expedition against Fort Niagara. The commander was Colonel John Prideaux of the 55th Regiment. The company would go in bateaux up the Mohawk, over the carrying place at Fort Stanwix, and descend to Oswego. Then they would move along the shore of Lake Ontario to the French post where one Captain Pierre Pouchot, of the Regiment of Béarn, commanded a garrison of 600 men, and no one knew how many Indians.

Schenectady hummed with activity. Colonel Prideaux arrived with some men of the 44th Regiment, and a whole regiment of New York provincials was busy filling supply bateaux. A detachment of the 46th Regiment arrived, bringing the expedition to 3,000 including Allan's company.

At Fort Stanwix, a log wilderness fortress, the men pulled their bateaux over the dry ground to Wood Creek, which emptied into Lake Oneida, using oxen belonging to the garrison. From there the going was easy, a matter of floating across the lake and down the Onondaga (now the Oswego) River. Allan found his former fourth battalion of the 60th hard at work restoring three forts after the depredations of 1756. A week later, Sir William Johnson, Prideaux's second-in-command, rode in on a fine stallion, a swarm of Indians in his tail. Lieutenant Butler hurried forward, greeting the Indians in their own tongue, and returned with a short, sturdy man in a buckskin shirt and leggings and a slouch hat, who was clearly his son John.

" Captain Butler," Allan said, extending his hand.
" Your father has told me of your services."

Allan thought John Butler could be an Indian, with his dark hair and leathery brown face. He watched as father and son moved easily among the warriors, clasping their arms. Here were two white men who seemed more at home among the " savages" than among their own kind. Allan was also intrigued by Sir William Johnson, tall and broad, behaving like a highland chief to these brown men in their feathers and paint.

Sir William was attended closely by four youths — his son and heir John, his nephew Guy Johnson, and two Mohawks, Joseph Brant and William of Canajoharie. John Johnson, seventeen years old, to Allan resembled a Dutch peasant, fair-haired and stalky. Guy, born in Ireland, was small, slender and fragile-looking. The two Mohawks were slender and unusually tall, and Allan was not surprised when Lieutenant Butler told him that William of Canajoharie was Sir William's son by a Mohawk woman. Allan detected a likeness in Joseph Brant, and he wondered whether this seventeen-year old, too, was Sir William's natural son.

The expedition, in bateaux, whaleboats and canoes, left Oswego on 1 July, a swell causing the waters of Lake Ontario to rise and fall. Allan might have been on an ocean, for the opposite shore was invisible. Each night the men camped on shore. On the evening of 6 July, they disembarked a short distance east of Niagara, and before dawn the following morning Allan led one of the detachments that surrounded the stone structure and captured the outposts. Sir William Johnson sent war parties to deal with the French's native allies, but all had decamped, deserting a lost cause.

Prideaux sent Allan to a position close to the shore on the east side of the fort, where his men erected a barricade. Niagara was now invested, and the expedition prepared to move in by stages, digging forward positions at night. The French were not idle, shelling the British positions but not doing much damage. Officers of the Engineering Department directed artificers to dig trenches closer to the fort, and on 20 July Prideaux ordered Allan's company to occupy one. The trench proved to be at the wrong angle and French guns raked it, killing five privates and wounding others.

" Get out of there," Allan shouted. When the survivors were safe he confronted Prideaux, temper blazing. " Those engineers are fools and blockheads," he stormed. " God damn them!"

On the 23rd a British cohorn exploded, and part of a shell struck Prideaux on the head. The colonel never regained consciousness and Sir William Johnson took command.[4] Later in the day, Indian scouts reported that a French relief force 1,200 strong, of troops from the upper posts, had gathered at Detroit and sailed down Lake Erie. Soon they would be marching along the road that led from the landing place above the great falls of Niagara. Sir William ordered an ambush set up on the road. He selected two companies of grenadiers, part of his light infantry and parties of Indians. Allan was to lead a detachment of his company, of men wise in the ways of forest warfare, and join the Indians. Lieutenant Butler chose the men, and they hid with some Seneca warriors in thick bush beside the road. All night they lay in wait.

About nine o'clock on the morning of the 24th, the ground vibrated with marching feet. The main body of regulars waited some yards to the rear. When the French vanguard appeared, Allan was about to give the signal to attack, but Butler put a hand on his arm and shook his head. " Strike the rear," he counselled in a whisper.

As the last of the guns rumbled by, Butler nodded and Allan barked the order. Muskets popped, a field gun back with the regulars boomed, firing, Allan guessed, grape shot. Then he collapsed in a heap, wounded again, and lay in the woods until the skirmish ended. French soldiers were fleeing towards the British blockade, to surrender before the Senecas could use their scalping knives. Some of his men carried Allan to a hospital tent behind a British barricade. Fortunately this wound was not serious and he would not be laid up for long.[5] Over Lieutenant Butler's objections Allan insisted on attending the funeral service for the men lost on the expedition, conducted by a chaplain of the 44th Regiment.

Dawn of the 25th brought a welcome sight. A white flag was flying over Fort Niagara. Drums sounded *reveille*, and the little army prepared to march into the fort, with orders to prevent atrocities by the Indians. Although he was feeling faint, Allan resolved not to miss this show.

The troops entered the gate in the bastion by the Niagara River, and on the parade ground the French garrison, pitifully small, Allan noted, was drawn up. Captain Pouchot, the French commander, short and dapper, surrendered his sword to Sir William Johnson, who returned it. The French officer, in halting English, invited the officers to dine with him that afternoon, and Sir William accepted.

The regulars and provincials set up camp on the parade ground, keeping the Indians outside as they came and went. At two o'clock the officers went into the mess, in a substantial stone building on the north side of the parade ground, where a table was spread with fine linen and silver. Captain Pouchot was all politeness, as were the French and British regulars. The Canadian militiamen and New York provincials were surly, glaring at each other while the professionals carried the conversation, Allan speaking with Captain Pouchot in French, to the other's delight. As always, a Frenchman had a soft spot for a Highlander, even one in the service of George II. After the meal, Sir William allowed his provincials to loot. Allan was horrified, and he protested to the baronet that his men were behaving as badly as the French had at Oswego and Fort William Henry.

" Never," Sir William retorted. " I've kept my Indians from massacring anyone. Letting my men take a few things is only justice."

The oldest part of Fort Niagara The Indians who came to trade named this stone building the "French Castle." Maclean was at the capture of the fort in 1759 and during the revolution he was its governor.

On 28 July, Lieutenant-Colonel Haldimand arrived in a whaleboat to take command, his right as the highest ranking regular officer in the vicinity. Allan hastened to report Sir William's infraction of the rules of war, and to congratulate him on taking over.

"I am not in command, Captain Maclean," Haldimand said gravely. "Sir William has refused to accept me. I have written to General Amherst, who is at Fort Edward, for instructions. I dare not offend Sir William, for he is a hero to the provincials and Indians. I am only a foreigner."

Haldimand remained at the fort awaiting Amherst's reply, and on 1 August Sir William agreed to guide him to the falls of Niagara. He ordered an escort from Allan's company and two other companies of light infantry for the short journey, because he was expecting a flag of truce from the Chevalier Portneuf, the commandant of the French outpost at Presqu'ile, on the south shore of Lake Erie. The men marched, Sir William, Haldimand, Walter Butler and Allan on horses, Butler in deference to his age, Allan because he still felt shaky from his wound. Allan was astonished at the deafening roar the huge cataract made, and the height to which the spray rose long before the little force came within sight of the white waters. There the flag of truce met them. Sir William placed Allan in command of the escort that marched to the shore of Lake Erie where the Frenchmen had left their boats.[6]

The following day the men returned to Fort Niagara, where Haldimand soon sent for Allan. General Amherst's reply had come, and he approved of Haldimand's discretion in not challenging Sir William Johnson. A small garrison would remain at the fort with Sir William, and Haldimand was to return to Oswego. Allan was to take all the men who could be spared, including his own company, and proceed to Ticonderoga to reinforce that post. The French had abandoned Fort Carillon, which was now in British hands under Amherst, who hoped to reach Montreal before winter set in.[7]

A few days later Allan set out with Haldimand, and from Oswego, with the reinforcements he retraced his steps back to Albany. He paused so that the reinforcements could be supplied with new equipment, where needed, and the warm clothing for the autumn campaign, and he insisted that

Lieutenant Butler go home to Fonda. The march for Montreal might be too much for him.

When he reached Fort Carillon, which the British had renamed Fort Ticonderoga, one of the first people he recognized was his chief, Sir Allan Maclean of Maclean, for Montgomery's Highlanders, now the 77th Regiment, was part of the garrison. Maclean of Maclean informed him that General Amherst was being thwarted by a French fleet on Lake Champlain, and was away building his own fleet farther up the lake. Everyone was disappointed, for Amherst was not likely to reach Montreal that season.

Allan reported to Lieutenant-Colonel William Haviland, the commandant of Ticonderoga in Amherst's absence, who assigned the reinforcements to work on a restoration of the fort. In October the garrison learned that Quebec had fallen to a force under General James Wolfe, but the troops were in mourning, for Wolfe had been killed. A few days later Amherst brought his force back to Ticonderoga and began sending most of the regiments south for the winter. Allan's company would remain at Ticonderoga to continue the restoration. As winter set in, the garrison was housed in a new barracks, a blessing, for the bitterest cold Allan had ever experienced descended upon the wilderness fortress as the year 1759 drew to a close.

Chapter Seven

The 114th Regiment Royal Highland Volunteers 1761-1763

Allan spent a bad winter at Ticonderoga, plagued by illness and suffering and the after-effects of his wounds. Lieutenants McCauley and Farrand fussed over him, downright motherly in their concern. Early in March, Allan wrote to General Amherst asking for a leave of absence so that he could have medical treatment in London from the best physicians available. His decision was a bitter one. He desperately wanted to be on the next campaign, certain to end with the capture of Montreal and the collapse of New France, or he would miss a further chance of a promotion in the field.

A month later a letter arrived from the commander-in-chief's secretary, granting the leave, and Allan prepared to set out for New York City. Once there, he took a room at the inn where he had convalesced and went to enquire about a passage home. He could not get one at once, for the ships were heavily booked. Back at the inn he reflected that four years had passed since he had set foot in this city to begin his service with the 60th Regiment. In all that time he had had only one promotion, not exactly a brilliant record. Perhaps while he was in London he might find a way to better himself. Meanwhile, General Amherst was planning his attack on Montreal, from three directions, and moving reinforcements from Philadelphia. Early in June, Lauchlin Macleane arrived at the inn, temporarily a surgeon in Agnew's Grenadiers, a special corps created by uniting the grenadier companies of several regiments.[1] Agnew's was assigned to the army commanded by the Lieutenant-Colonel Haviland that was to go by Lake Champlain and would include Allan's own company. A second thrust would be from Quebec City, led by Brigadier James Murray. Amherst himself would lead an expedition from Oswego down the St. Lawrence.

On learning Allan's reason for taking a leave of absence, Lauchlin examined him and recommended that he see Dr. John Hunter, one of the best men in London. Then he asked Allan to do him a favour.

"Of course," Allan replied without hesitation.

Lauchlin gave him a draft of seventy pounds to take to Archibald Maclaine, the merchant in Cheapside who already had Allan's account. Next he gave him a bulky packet wrapped in brown paper which he was to deliver to a printer, Henry Woodfall, at the newspaper office of the *Public Advertiser*, at the corner of Ivy Lane and Pasternoster Row, near St. Paul's. Afterwards the two old friends prophesied that Montreal would almost certainly fall before the end of the year. Wolfe's victory had made this possible.

"I hope to return in time to see action before the French posts in the interior are taken," Allan said.

Lauchlin did not seem to be listening. "That rascal Townshend. Do you know what he's done?"

"Brigadier Townshend, one of Wolfe's officers?"

Lauchlin fairly spluttered in indignation. "He's spreading a story that the credit for the victory at Quebec belongs to the three brigadiers under Wolfe. That's a damn lie, and the man should be horse-whipped. The final plan was Wolfe's, and the people should know the truth."

"You think Townshend is taking advantage of Wolfe's death, spreading lies about a man who cannot respond?" Allan asked him.

Lauchlin nodded. "Damn unfair."

A few days later Allan got a passage on an armed vessel in a convoy destined for Portsmouth. Before he was to sail, a letter arrived from his elder brother Hector, dated six months ago that had been forwarded from Albany. Hector had moved his law practice to Glasgow and bought a small house near the Trongate. Glasgow was thriving on overseas trade, and Edinburgh had too many solicitors. Allan resolved to write Hector as soon as he reached London.

The convoy had fair wind and he was in London towards the end of July. He found a cheap lodging house and sent for Dr. Hunter, who pursed his lips in disapproval as he studied Allan's scarred thigh. He prescribed massage and cold compresses to ease the burning pain, as well as complete rest for a fortnight. An assistant would call daily and give the treatments. After the fortnight Allan could take short walks, but if he was going any distance he should take a sedan chair.[2]

By chair, Allan delivered Lauchlin Macleane's packet to the office of the *Public Advertiser* as he had promised, and the money to Archibald Maclaine. He also went to the War Office in Whitehall to enquire about the possibility of resigning his commission in the Third New York Independent Company and raising a regiment of his own in the Highlands. At the Secretary at War's office, he found that new levies were contemplated, and that he had a very good chance of being chosen to form a regiment.

In late August, feeling much better, Allan again called at the War Office, this time to enquire about a return passage to New York. A secretary advised him to take a ship bound for Quebec. The capture of Montreal was expected daily, and once that city was in British hands, the Independent Companies were to be posted to the Quebec garrison. The day before he was to sail, Allan was taking a stroll when he heard a street vendor shouting that he had a new pamphlet. "Read the debunk of Townshend," the man called. "Find out how he tried to slander General Wolfe."

"Here!" Allan called. "How much is the pamphlet?"

"A mere shilling, sir," the man replied, running towards him.

Allan paid him and returned to his lodgings where he began to read the pamphlet at once. It was anonymous, and no printer's name was appended to it, yet the style seemed familiar, with phrases not unlike Lauchlin Macleane's letters. He thought of calling on Printer Woodfall to sound him out, but the stage-coach was leaving for Portsmouth in the morning and he had to pack.

At Portsmouth only one ship was waiting. The British and French fleets were locked in combat around the West Indies, where Francis Maclean's battalion of the 42nd Foot was serving. A convoy was no longer necessary on the northern sea route. The crossing took six weeks, delayed somewhat by September storms, and the ship dropped anchor off the rock of Quebec in late October.

Ashore, Allan hired a caléche to take him with his

baggage to the Chateau St. Louis, the headquarters of the military governor, Brigadier James Murray, to obtain his orders. The driver, whose French Allan found almost unintelligible, guided the horse towards the steep hill to the Upper Town and deposited him at the gloomy-looking two storey residence inside the citadel. Allan told the driver to wait, and a footman ushered him to the office of one of the governor's secretaries, a red-coated captain in the blue and silver of the 60th Regiment. The secretary told him the Third Independent Company was quartered at the barracks on Buade Street, while his officers had rooms on St. Anne Street, close by. Next Allan asked about the war news.

"General Amherst entered Montreal on September the 8th," the secretary said. "Major Rogers, of the American Rangers, has gone inland to accept the surrender of the French upper posts."

"I'm sorry I missed it," Allan said as he was leaving.

He had the driver take him to the Buade Street barracks, where he found Lieutenant Henry Farrant on duty, delighted to see him, but with sad news. Lieutenant Walter Butler had died at his home in the Mohawk Valley back in June, when he was preparing to set out to join the company at Ticonderoga. To please Sir William Johnson, Governor Murray had appointed the baronet's nephew, Guy Johnson, as the third lieutenant for the company.[3] Allan was displeased for he had formed a low opinion of that languid youth.

Lieutenant Farrant offered to share his room with Allan, for the city was crowded. Many houses had been destroyed during Wolfe's bombardment before he landed his army upriver from Quebec and scaled the Heights of Abraham. Lieutenant McCauley was delighted to see Allan, but Lieutenant Guy Johnson was aloof, a man with an overly high opinion of himself, Allan concluded, because of his kinship with Sir William.

Allan found the winter tedious, although the officers did their best to create a social life, assisted by the few wives who had come with their husbands. Late in February the members of the garrison were issued with black crepe for their hats. King George II had died on 25 October, soon after Allan landed at Quebec. Since the Prince of Wales had predeceased the King, the new monarch was his grandson who, after a year of court mourning would be crowned George III. Allan's mood of gloom deepened. The *Quebec Gazette* heralded the new King as the first truly English sovereign of the House of Hanover, but the death of the old King would have been a fine time for the restoration of the Stuarts. If Charles II had succeeded, why had James III failed?

With the spring fleet of 1761, Allan received a letter from the Secretary at War's office. New levies were being raised, and he had permission to resign his captaincy and return to the Highlands to raise a regiment, to be numbered the 114th Foot. He also received a letter from his brother Hector, who had had a visit from their cousin Francis Maclean of Blaich. Francis had been severely wounded at Guadeloupe the year before, and had resigned from the 42nd Regiment in order to raise a regiment of his own, the 97th Foot.

Perturbed, Allan sent a letter to Hector asking him to see that Francis stayed away from Mull. Many men would be disappointed if they joined him then discovered that one of their own was also raising a regiment. He received a letter from Governor Murray's secretary. Allan's resignation would be effective at the end of the year, when Captain John Gordon would take command of the company.[4] However, Allan was free to depart for London as soon as he had moved his company to Fort Ticonderoga, where the men were to resume work on the restoration of the fortress.

He embarked the company on whaleboats for Sorel, turned up the Richelieu as far as Fort Chambly and left the whaleboats. Above the rapids they procured bateaux for the rest of the journey up Lake Champlain. Once the men had settled in, Allan left with a brigade of bateaux for the head of Lake George, crossed the portage by wagon and found a bateau bound for Albany, where he caught a sloop for New York City.

By mid-September he was in London, and at the War Office he received his new commission, which empowered him to raise ten companies, each of 100 rank and file. Initially he would have five captains; the other four would be appointed when the first six companies — one of them his own — were completed. He could draw public funds, but he must have an agent to advance him money to purchase the equipment the regiment would need.

Little did he realize that he was falling into a financial trap, and that raising a regiment was not an undertaking for a man with no private means, especially if, as Allan intended, he wanted a crack unit, properly equipt. The only way a commander could profit from his regiment was by selling officers' commissions, and he could only make such sales after a regiment was at full strength, and was not considered a "new" one. An unscrupulous commander might get his profit earlier by skimping on equipment and buying poor quality food and the cheapest of cloth for the uniforms. Picturing himself at the head of a first-rate unit, Allan never entertained a notion of choosing anything but the best for his men. The public money Allan was empowered to draw was not quite sufficient for the most basic of his expenses, but he never considered that he would have to find some other source of funds before the regiment was at strength.

With never a thought on how he would repay any money, Allan went to see Archibald Maclaine, the agent both Lauchlin Macleane and his brother Hector used, and from whom he had borrowed when he first joined the 60th Regiment. The Cheapside merchant agreed to purchase uniforms — red coats, silver accoutrements, and kilts and plaids, for Allan's was a Highland regiment, and Highland dress was permitted for military use. He arranged for the purchase of arms and footwear, and hired a sutler to supply the provisions.[5] Allan wrote to the Edinburgh garrison to arrange for barrack space.

At the War Office he interviewed several officers eligible for captaincies, wanting if possible men who had seen some service in America. He selected the Honourable William Boyd, George Sutherland, James Stewart, John Forbes, and Robert Campbell, and appointed James Gray his captain-lieutenant to command Allan's company.[6] His own commission was dated 17 October 1761.

Allan hired horses and with his officers rode off for Glasgow to see his brother Hector before going on to Mull. At Hector's house he found his second brother Lachlan, recently back from Jamaica. Lachlan was engaged to marry Margaret Smith, who lived in the city.[7] Allan did not linger. Newspapers reported that France's Indian allies were making trouble along the frontiers, and he was determined to complete the regiment and return to America. With his officers he rode along the Clyde and turned north at Dumbarton. As they crossed the Highland Line, a welcome sight raised Allan's spirits. People were openly wearing bright tartan again, although the proscription had not been lifted officially. At Crianlarich the officers separated, each to look for recruits among his friends. Once each captain had 100 men, he was to muster them in Edinburgh.

With Captain-Lieutenant Gray, Allan rode on to Mull. He found that practically everyone was wearing the beloved Highland dress again, and a feeling of peace overcame him. At Torloisk he found few changes, except that more cattle and small horses were on the hills, and flocks of chickens pecked about near the cottages. Now he began recruiting in earnest, and without a sergeant and drummer to attract attention. He did not need them, nor did he need to worry about encountering hostility.

He found no shortage of willing recruits. Apart from the odd day of fishing, the women still did most of the work, and the chance to go to war in the fighting tail of a son of Torloisk had great appeal. He visited the islands of Coll and Tiree, and the Maclean settlements on Morvern, until he had promises from the 100 men he needed. By early April of 1762, Allan was ready to muster his company for the march to Edinburgh, where he would train the recruits. For junior officers he searched among literate recruits, preferably lairds' sons who already had commisions. Initially he assigned two lieutenants and one ensign to each company. For his staff officers he chose George Douglas and John Duncanson, with John McArthur as his adjutant. Then he wrote to Archibald Maclaine in London, asking for a letter of credit to meet his expenses.

Uniforms, officers' side arms and silver accoutrements arrived and Allan drew muskets and bayonets from the quartermaster's stores in Edinburgh. In May, all six companies were filled, and in training. The men were taught the skills needed for backwoods fighting in America, but also parade ground drill. The regiment might be used in Europe, where the war was still going on.

Allan wrote to the War Office requesting four more captains to raise the other companies, and continued a strenuous programme for the recruits and officers of the existing six companies. By the end of August he had the makings of a fine fighting unit. Several of the other new regiments had arrived in Edinburgh, among them the 97th, and Allan was reunited with his cousin Francis. Allan's four new captains were in the Highlands looking for recruits, progressing slowly because so many men had already enlisted. Yet Allan was confident that by the spring of 1763 his regiment, the Royal Highland Volunteers but more popularly called Maclean's Highlanders, would be ready to embark.

Then in December, to his alarm, he heard that preliminary articles of peace had been signed on 3 November, and the war might be over before he could complete a full battalion. Until he did, he could not sell commissions to officers wanting promotions — the only way a lieutenant-colonel had of making a profit out of his regiment. Trying to control his inner turmoil, Allan began settling the regimental accounts. He drew the funds to which he was entitled from the Paymaster's Department, and forwarded a draft to Archibald Maclaine to cover his debts.

Towards the end of February the axe fell. The Treaty of Paris was signed on the 10th, and the war had ended. Allan still hoped that he would be needed against the Indians in America, but at the end of the month he received word from the War Office that his regiment was to be reduced. Since he had only raised six companies he would be allowed a major's half-pay of seven shillings and sixpence a day. This was hardly enough to keep up appearances, let alone marry and support a family. Worse news soon followed. Archibald Maclaine wrote from London that the funds Allan had sent were a staggering 1,900 pounds short of meeting his debts.[8]

He wrote at once to the Cheapside merchant for an accounting, and very worried awaited the reply. Meanwhile, he disbanded the regiment. He sought out Francis, whose regiment had suffered the same fate, and they commiserated with each other. Francis, too, was deeply in debt, for he had not had time to sell any commissions either.

"Some commanders cheat, " Francis said glumly. "They buy unshrunken flannel for uniforms and inferior rations.

They make a profit without selling commissions, but the men suffer cruelly. I could not bring myself to do that."

"I would never have though of such a thing," Allan rejoined.

"I'm going to put myself out of reach of creditors," Francis said.. "I've accepted a commission in the Portuguese service."

The accounting arrived from Archibald Maclaine, and it made sense, which was cold comfort to Allan. He sent Maclaine's bill to Hector in the hope that he could pay it, and decided to retire to Mull. Before he was ready to depart he received a letter from his sister Betty, saying how proud their mother was that Allan was a major like their father. Allan moaned, thinking of the predicament that commission had caused. Then Hector wrote summoning him to Glasgow, where he explained gently that he could not settle Archibald Maclaine's bill. He had not been well of late, and was turning away clients. Besides, he was sending money regularly to Torloisk, more than he could afford.

"What should I do?" Allan asked, panic welling inside him. "Even if I live cheaply at Torloisk, my half-pay will never repay so much money."

"You can't stay here, Allan. If Archibald Maclaine finds out where you are, he can imprison you for debt. You must go abroad, to Paris, where prices are low and your half-pay will stretch farther. Maclaine can not touch you if you are out of the country."

Allan's shoulders slumped dejectedly. "That's why Francis went to Portugal."

Hector nodded. "After you've gone, I'll try and arrange a loan with someone else and pay Archibald Maclaine. That will buy us time."

Two days later, in civilian clothes and travelling under a false name, Allan rode out of Glasgow bound for London, the first stage of his second journey into exile.

Chapter Eight

Paris 1763-1765

Allan found a cheap pension, and set about meeting Jacobites in Paris, who were prone to swagger through the city in Highland garb, or half-pay officers like himself, in exile to escape creditors. He passed hours in cafés discussing the world in general, the Jacobite cause in particular. In September he received a letter from Hector. Una Maclean, the wife of their chief, had died, and Sir Allan had taken his three daughters to Inch Kenneth, a small isle off the coast of Mull, where he was building a house. Francis Maclean was now a major-general in the Portuguese army, stationed in Lisbon. Hector had not been able to raise a loan, and Allan must remain abroad for a while yet.

That Hogmanay of 1763, Allan attended a party given by one of his new Jacobite friends. Later in the evening, to his astonishment, in walked Lauchlin Macleane, followed by John Stuart and a third man Allan did not recognize.[1]

"Allan!" Lauchlin shouted in his hesitant brogue. "I didn't know you were in Paris."

"I thought you were in Pennsylvania," Allan said, smiling.

Now the tale came tumbling out. Lauchlin had had enough of the Quakers in Philadelphia. He had been fined twenty-five pounds for kissing a lady in the street, a mere peck on the cheek, Lauchlin maintained, but from the fuss anyone would think he had lifted her skirt and seduced her. Allan knew that Lauchlin's wife Elizabeth must have been humiliated. He asked if she was in Paris,too, but Lauchlin had left her in London to her own devices. He now introduced the third man with him as Andrew Stuart, a Scots lawyer and kinsman of John Stuart, although they were still arguing over the exact relationship.

In the early hours of 1 January 1764, the four men left the party and went to Lauchlin's house, in the Rue de l'Echelle. John Stuart lived with him, and Andrew Stuart made the house his headquarters when he was in Paris. Over the wine Allan, a little tipsy, talked about his private affairs, and he told Lauchlin the reason for his exile. Lauchlin did not regard a debt as a serious matter. Creditors were fair game.

Now that Lauchlin was in Paris, Allan's days became more interesting. Lauchlin drew people about him like a magnet, and there was always plenty of gossip. Despite his present stay in Paris, Lauchlin was full of plans to advance himself soon, taking advantage of the corrupt system of politics then in vogue. Back in London, Mr. Pitt, the great Reformer, was superseded by Lord Grenville, the King's favourite. Not long after this change, two of Pitt's most vocal supporters in Parliament, John Wilkes and Colonel Isaac Barré (who had served under Wolfe at Quebec) arrived to await the collapse of the Grenville ministry. Wilkes had published his *Essay on Women* which was speedily labelled obscene. He was expelled from Parliament, and threatened with imprisonment, the reason he had left England on what would turn into a four-year exile. Neither Lauchlin nor Allan met Wilkes in Paris, but they heard many juicy stories about his debauched private life. In due course, in London, Lauchlin and Allan would have further dealings with John Wilkes.

Meanwhile, John Stuart was busy becoming acceptable to the men of letters in Paris. He had met Adam Smith and David Hume while they were visiting the city, and had arranged to be introduced into the Literary Society where Voltaire was the star attraction. While Stuart pursued cultural matters, Lauchlin chased women. For once, Allan seemed to be inspired by Lauchlin's example, for he became intimate with a French woman who craved him for her lover.

He accepted her advances, stressing that while he was of noble birth, he was very poor and she could expect nothing more than transitory sexual pleasure. In his writings he was the soul of discretion. That Allan had such an affair was revealed only once, and only through certain circumstances.[2] Somehow, the hint that he was capable of this conduct makes Allan a more complete human being, the career soldier who could not yet think of marriage because he had so little to offer a woman.

In July Lauchlin came to Allan's pension with a startling offer. He wanted to settle Allan's debt to Archibald Maclaine, who was also his agent. Allan hesitated. For all he knew, Lauchlin was living on credit, but his friend was very persuasive. That Irish tongue could turn the head of the naive man from Torloisk and hold him in a spell. Allan agreed to Lauchlin's offer, but warned him he might not be able to repay him for some time. Lauchlin furrowed his heavy black brows and stared solemnly at Allan.

"I don't expect to be repaid in cash," he said."One day I will need a man like you to stand behind me. I intend entering politics, a very corrupt business but fascinating, being at the seat of power, able to make things happen. A professional soldier, especially a tall one, would be indispensable to me."

"I will serve you any way I can," Allan promised him.

Lauchlin suggested Allan leave his pension and come to share his house. Allan was happy to accept, knowing how much money this would save. On 9 July he moved his belongings to the house on the Rue de l'Echelle and Lauchlin sent a draft to Archibald Maclaine.

In the summer his mistress gave birth to a son. As his mother did not want to keep him Allan arranged for the baby to be cared for by some of his Jacobite friends.

Late that autumn of 1764, John Stuart fell ill with rheumatism. Lauchlin sent for an English doctor, Samuel Musgrave. After seeing the patient, the doctor was closeted with Lauchlin for some time. When Musgrave left, Lauchlin told Allan an amazing tale. The doctor claimed that France bought peace in 1763 by bribing three people with a million pounds. Half went to the King's mother, the Dowager Princess of Wales; the other half was divided between Lord Bute, the Prime Minister at the time, and Lord Holland, the paymaster general of the armed forces.

Allan was thunderstruck. If the story was true, he had lost the chance to complete his regiment and sell commissions because of corruption. "Do you believe him?" he asked Lauchlin.

Whether the story was true was not the point, Lauchlin maintained. The King thought he had won an honourable peace, and had no inkling that France would find a bribe cheaper than continuing the war. What a scandal there would be if the Dowager Princess of Wales was accused of taking the money. Lauchlin told Musgrave he should keep quiet unless he had iron-clad proof, but his only evidence was hearsay, a conversation with a French minister.

Allan was angry, but his Jacobite instincts suggested this information might be turned to advantage. The British people could be aroused against the House of Hanover and persuaded to restore the Stuarts. Lauchlin scoffed at the idea. He knew of at least a dozen men in high places who would suppress Musgrave, and not one voice, except Wilkes' who was in exile and had lost his citizenship, would be raised on Musgrave's behalf. Lies would be told to discredit Musgrave's evidence, if he could produce any.

"I don't see why," Allan said impatiently.

"That's why you're a soldier, Allan, while I'm going to become a devious politician," Lauchlin said, gently, so as not to offend him.

That winter all three men led quiet lives. Lauchlin suffered from heavy chest colds, a legacy, he thought, from the campaign of 1758 to Fort Duquesne. John Stuart's rheumatism continued to plague him, and Allan's old wounds ached during the cold weather. In the Paris spring all were feeling more lively. Lauchlin acquired a new mistress and set her up in a house on the Rue de Rivoli.

In April, Allan received a letter from one Donald Maclean, a merchant in Glasgow and a member of the Brolass branch of the clan whom Allan had never met. Donald urged him to come as soon as possible. Hector was seriously ill with pneumonia and asking for Allan. Their brother Lachlan, now married to Margaret Smith, was postponing his next voyage to Jamaica until he knew how Hector fared. Appalled at the thought that he might lose his favourite brother, Allan took the letter to Lauchlin Macleane.

"I'll come with you as far as London," Lauchlin said. "It's time I made some friends there. We'll hire horses and leave tomorrow."

They caught a packet at Calais, crossed over to Dover, and took the stage-coach to the capital, arriving on 2 May. Allan rode away to Glasgow, leaving Lauchlin house-hunting, for he had no intention of living with his wife Elizabeth. His mind in turmoil, Allan changed horses at inns along the Great North Road so that he could ride faster and longer.

At Hector's he found his two unmarried sisters, Mary and Betty, nursing their brother, aided by two strange women — Mary Maclean, the wife of Donald, the merchant who had summoned Allan, and his new sister-in-law, Lachlan's wife, Margaret. Allan could not help gazing at Margaret with admiration and envy. She looked every inch a Celtic lassie, with fair skin, freckles over her nose, deep blue eyes and long dark hair. Lachlan was a lucky man. Now his two sisters took him to Hector's bedside and left him alone with his eldest brother. An ashen-faced, emaciated Hector opened his eyes and a thin smile came upon his white lips.

"Allan," he whispered. "Come to bid me farewell."

"No," Allan said, managing a smile. "Soon we'll ride to Torloisk."

Hector ignored him. "Lachlan has a good head for business, but I want you to be my executor, Allan. Settling is in Lachlan's best interests, but I don't want him to neglect the rest of you."

"I'll do my best ", Allan replied. "But that day is far off."

Hector turned his head away, exhausted, and Allan slipped out of the room. The 6th laird of Torloisk died in his sleep during the night of 29 May 1765. The family set out for Mull from Port Glasgow in Lachlan's ship *Mary*, since they could not carry Hector's coffin over the narrow tracks on the island by wagon. When they went ashore at Torloisk they buried Hector in the churchyard at Kilninian, near the graves of their parents.[3] (The date of Allan's father's death is known, but not that of his mother, except that she predeceased Hector.)

Afterwards Allan and Lachlan began settling Hector's affairs. Lachlan had many plans, now that he was the 7th laird. He decided to sell the *Mary* so that he could invest the profits in improvements and build a decent house for Margaret. Mary and Betty could live in the old cottages, and he would give their youngest brother, Archibald, a croft for his livelihood. Leaving Lachlan to continue revitalizing Torloisk, Allan returned to Glasgow to sell Hector's house and furnishings. He stayed with the Donald Macleans, and the more he saw of them the better he liked them. Furthermore, Donald was Sir Allan Maclean of Maclean's heir, since the chief had no son to inherit the title. Donald had several daughters and one son, Hector, who in 1765 was three years old.[4]

One of Donald's daughters was Janet, and although she was barely into her 'teens, Allan felt strongly attracted to her.[5] She was just the kind of girl he longed to have as his wife, with her dark hair and creamy skin, the blue eyes and freckles he admired in his brother Lachlan's wife Margaret. Yet what would such a lass see in a forty-year-old career soldier with a bastard son in Paris and a lame leg? Perhaps he was not building castles in the air. He would not be the first elderly officer to marry a young woman and raise a large brood of fine children. If, by the time she was twenty-one, he was back on the active list, he resolved to ask her father for her hand. In so many other respects they were well-matched, she so closely related to the chief, he the son of an important cadet branch of the clan.

Once Hector's belongings had been sold, Allan returned to Torloisk. Lachlan and Margaret were settled into the little cottage his parents had used. Archibald had moved to Laggan croft, where Mary was housekeeping for him. Allan stayed in the second cottage with Betty, to allow Lachlan and Margaret some privacy. In September he received a letter from Lauchlin Macleane, from a house on Holles Street, London. Lauchlin had a scheme to develop estates on the Island of Saint John (Prince Edward Island) in the Gulf of St. Lawrence.

This island, from which most of the Acadian French had been removed, would soon be available for settlers. and Lauchlin had hired a government surveyor, Captain Samuel Holland of Quebec, to lay out 20,000 acre lots. Once the survey was completed, Lauchlin proposed that Allan and some of his friends apply for these lots and found estates. Money was to be made from the tenants' rents — tenants from the Highlands. All that the proprietors must pay was a small quit rent to the government. Lauchlin suggested Allan send letters to friends who might be interested in becoming proprietors.

Allan thought of his cousin Francis, still in Lisbon, and of his sister Elizabeth in Jamaica, for her husband Lachlan might want a share. Others worth approaching were Dr. Richard Huck, now in London, and the two Mackay brothers, who had settled in Montreal. As the months passed, he received many replies, most of them favourable. His sister Elizabeth wrote that her eldest son, Lauchlin, was a merchant in Baltimore, Maryland, and he was close enough to visit the island.

Late in January 1766 a Jacobite messenger arrived from London, bringing word that James, the old King, had died in Rome on the 1st of the month. The King o'er the water was Bonnie Charlie, now an unhappy man much given to drink and loose living. Yet he was the true sovereign whose conduct could not be held against him after the severe disappointment he had endured.

Lauchlin Macleane wrote again towards the end of February. He appeared to be deeply embroiled in London politics and enjoying the intrigues. He would soon depart for Paris, to see John Wilkes. The Grenville ministry had collapsed, and the new Prime Minister was Lord Rockingham, who did not want Wilkes to return to England. Lauchlin was to offer Wilkes an annuity of 1,000 pounds a year to remain in France. Isaac Barré had returned to London and was trying to keep Dr. Samuel Musgrave from stirring up a scandal over the way France supposedly bought the peace of 1763. Lauchlin's mistress in Paris was pregnant, and he was delighted that he would soon be a father — something his wife Elizabeth had failed to do for him.

Captain Holland had completed his survey of the Island of Saint John, but the proprietors might not be named for some time. Meanwhile, Lauchlin was hoping to find a way to invest in the East India Company, and he had persuaded John Stuart to leave Paris and take a house near his in Holles Street. Stuart would look after Lauchlin's interests in London, and they would soon need Allan's help. If all went according to plan, Lauchlin expected to be appointed the lieutenant-governor of the West Indian island of St. Vincent. Allan only half understood what he read, and he was not particularly interested. His only thought was his obligation to Lauchlin for settling his debt to Archibald Maclaine, and he resolved to obey the summons when Lauchlin sent one.

Allan's brother Lachlan's wife was pregnant, and the prospect of an heir to Torloisk delighted the family. Allan dreamed of Janet Maclean in Glasgow, and wondered if he could become a laird himself once he secured acreage on the Island of Saint John. He would populate it with impoverished Highlanders on forfeited estates that had lost their true lairds and chiefs, but not with people from

Torloisk. Lachlan would need his tenants to build up the estate and to join his fighting tail if the Stuarts should return.

In April, Allan received another letter from Lauchlin Macleane asking him to come to London, and he packed his belongings with a sense of relief. His brother Lachlan was fully in command at Torloisk, and Allan was glad of an excuse not to remain until the army put him back on the active list. As he rode across Mull he was looking forward to hearing more about Lauchlin's scheme to make money through the East India Company, and eager for a share in the profits.

He intended to stop a night with the Donald Macleans, since his fortunes appeared to be about to take a turn for the better, and he wanted to sound out Sir Allan's heir to see whether he would make an acceptable son-in-law. At the Maclean house, he thought Janet's greeting unusually warm, hoping he was not guilty of wishful thinking as she told him how much she missed him. After dinner, when the women had withdrawn leaving Allan and Donald alone with their port, he raised the question.

"Ach aye," Donald said dourly. "I know the lass is sweet on ye. I have to admit you're a might long in the tooth, but there's no denying you're well connected. You can have her when she's twenty-one, provided ye can care for her."

"By that time I should be able to," Allan assured him.

Riding on towards London he was elated. Donald had revealed what he suspected on meeting Janet during his brief visit. She was fond of him, and for him she was just what he had always longed for. Though she spoke hardly a word of Gaelic, in ancestry she was a true Highland lass.

Chapter Nine

The East India Company, Rise and Fall 1766-1769

When Allan reached the house on Holles Street, Lauchlin Macleane insisted on briefing him before he had time to brush the dust of the road from his clothes and boots. The appointment as lieutenant-governor of St. Vincent had been approved, and Lauchlin expected to leave for the West Indies in July, by which time he intended being a man of wealth. And everything depended on Allan.[1]

"I've no talent for making money," Allan protested.

Lauchlin ignored him, his mind full of the plan. He had worked out a triangular system. John Stuart was his man in London. Robert Orme, employed by the East India Company, was his spy in East India House. In Paris, at the second point in the triangle, was Thomas Foley, a banker. In Amsterdam, the third point, was Isaac Panchaud, of a Paris banking house. Allan would be their courier, to carry messages to Paris and Amsterdam.

Each ship from India brought dispatches which went straight to East India House. Robert Orme would let John Stuart know what news he received, information that went directly to the London Stock Exchange, but which was relayed by mail to the stock exchanges in Amsterdam and Paris. Buying and selling was therefore later in those cities than in London. Allan would take whatever information John Stuart received and carry the letters by express. That meant riding hard for Dover, hiring a packet boat, and seeing that the letters reached Paris and Amsterdam ahead of the regular mail. Thus Thomas Foley in Paris and Isaac Panchaud in Amsterdam would know what was happening in India before the news affected the market. If the news was bad, they would sell stock before the price dropped; if it was good, they could buy heavily before the price rose. If he was successful as a courier, Allan would receive 500 pounds in East India stock.

Allan accepted the job without question. His military mind, accustomed to taking orders, did not consider Lauchlin's ethics.

As the weeks passed, Lauchlin became more and more excited over the scheme. Daily, usually accompanied by Allan, he went to East India House in Leadenhall Street. Robert Orme had nothing to reveal, as no ship had come from the Far East. Lauchlin became so agitated that on 18 June he left for Amsterdam to be with Isaac Panchaud. John Stuart would be in communication with Robert Orme, with Allan standing by at Lauchlin's house.

Just two days later John Stuart arrived with a dispatch from Robert Orme, and Allan sprang into action. On an excellent horse hired in advance, he galloped to Dover, hired a fast packet and crossed the English Channel. At Calais he hired another fast horse and rode at breakneck speed towards Ghent, changing mounts often, cat-napping beside the road.

On he raced to Antwerp, Utrecht, and to the outskirts of Amsterdam, a distance he reckoned at 300 miles. Using his rusty Dutch he soon found the inn to which the letter was addressed.

Lauchlin was pacing up and down as though looking for him, and he grabbed the letter as soon as Allan had removed it from his saddle bag. Then Lauchlin's brow wrinkled in disappointment. The news was inconclusive, not something on which he could take action. Allan ate prodigiously and slept round the clock. Then, anxious lest important news reach London, Lauchlin asked him to return in all haste, and Allan was back in the saddle riding like the wind. By 29 June he was in London, reporting to John Stuart before going to Lauchlin's house in Holles Street to get some rest.

On 1 July, John Stuart arrived. Robert Orme had sent promising information, and Stuart had two letters for Allan to carry. He was to take one to Lauchlin in Amsterdam, and find a way to get the other to Paris, as long as the letter for Thomas Foley, like that for Lauchlin, could reach its destination ahead of the regular mail.

Away Allan flew, riding for Dover. At Calais he enquired at the port office when the mail boat from Dover was expected, which was not for two days. Confident Stuart's letter to Foley would arrive by an earlier post, Allan put the letter in the mail and hired a horse for the ride to

Amsterdam. This time, as he entered the Dutch city, he hoped that Lauchlin would not expect him to go posting straight back to London, for his strength was spent.

Again, as he reached the inn, Lauchlin was pacing up and down, and Allan wondered at the sixth sense that brought him out. The letter Allan brought was of great importance. Clive, the renouned military leader in India, was doing well, news that was bound to send the East India Company stock soaring. Fortunately Lauchlin did not want Allan to set out at once, and in the interval a letter came from Thomas Foley in Paris.Word of Clive's good health arrived in time for him to buy stock before the price rose. Allan's ride was paying off handsomely and he was content. Although he was sore from the ride, he was 500 pounds richer, money that would stand him in good stead in his suit for Janet Maclean.

On 15 July, with Lauchlin and Isaac Panchaud, Allan left for London in a carriage, at a more leisurely pace, not reaching the house in Holles Street until the 22nd. In London everyone was talking about the fall of the Rockingham ministry. Pitt was back in power, but he had a problem. He had accepted a peerage as Lord Chatham, and he could not sit in the House of Commons.

"I'll wager he'll find a way to bring Wilkes home," Lauchlin said.

"When do you leave for St. Vincent?" Allan enquired, for time was passing.

Lauchlin looked reflective. "I'm thinking of resigning. I may find something better if I stay here."

In August, Lauchlin went back to Amsterdam to see how well he had done at the Stock Exchange. When he returned he reported he had made a staggering ninety percent profit in East India stock. He was now a man of wealth, and he intended entering politics with a vengeance. First, he needed a better address and he bought a house at 52 Queen Anne Street, the same on which the Whig philosopher Edmund Burke lived. Lauchlin invited his wife Elizabeth to move in with him. A respectable politician needed to appear to be on good terms with his spouse. He gave Allan a room, and wrote to his younger brother, Henry Macleane, to join him from Dublin.

Henry was a well-educated, facile young man, as willing as Allan to do Lauchlin's bidding. For Allan, Lauchlin had taken the place of his chief, still hibernating on Inch Kenneth, as well as of his deceased brother Hector. Whatever happened, Allan had faith that Lauchlin would look after him, and he bestowed on him the kind of loyalty a Highlander traditionally gave his chief.

The summer of 1766 ended, and Lauchlin still had not arranged to take up his duties as lieutenant-governor of St. Vincent. In October, Allan learned the reason for his benefactor's delaying tactics. He was appointed Under Secretary of State to Lord Shelburne, the Secretary of State for the Southern Department, which comprised Southern Europe and all the American colonies. The salary was 1,000 pounds a year, and no doubt Lauchlin had paid someone to recommend him. Allan was not overly curious. As long as Lauchlin's star was rising, so was his.

Not long afterwards, an election was held for the Board of the East India Company. A shareholder who owned 500 pounds in stock was entitled to one vote, which was what Lauchlin had in mind when he gave Allan his block of shares. To ensure that the faction Lord Shelburne favoured won the election, Lauchlin split his own large block of shares into 500 pound portions, and looked for reliable men to whom these could be loaned temporarily, until after the election. Lauchlin's trickery worked, for the faction Shelburne liked won the election.

Allan received a letter from his brother Lachlan at Torloisk. His wife Margaret had given birth to a daughter Marianne. Margaret had had a difficult time, and a doctor warned Lachlan that she could not have another child. He had now sold his ship, and was starting to work on a new house. The letter was matter-of-fact in tone, but Allan could read between the lines. Lachlan regretted that Marianne was not a son to become the next laird. If either Allan or Archibald had a legitimate son, he would take precedence over Lachlan's daughter. Although the married sisters had sons, they could only inherit if there was no issue from the three brothers. Allan felt no malice towards Marianne, but he thought about Janet Maclean in Glasgow, and of his little son growing up in Paris. He could never marry the boy's mother, but some day he and Janet would have children, and perhaps a son of his would be the next laird of Torloisk.

Throughout the winter of 1766 and the spring of 1767, Allan wrote regularly to Janet, and received encouraging replies. They were now unofficially engaged, and Allan expected to receive a grant of land on the Island of Saint John. Then the next hurdle would be finding a way to move tenants there. He would need passage money, since very few Highlanders could afford to pay their own way. Meanwhile, he had received many replies from friends who wanted land grants, and one was from his nephew in Baltimore, Lauchlin Maclean, his sister Elizabeth's son. The Commission for the Lords of Trade and Plantations was expected to meet soon to consider applications. At length, Lauchlin Macleane and Allan received appointments with the Commission on 1 July.

At the interview, they found that quit rents were to be paid at the rate of two, four, and six shillings per 100 acres, depending on location, and would not be due for five years. Each successful proprietor must settle 100 persons per lot or township, within ten years, which meant one person for every 200 acres, and only Protestant settlers were eligible. Allan thought the terms reasonable.

The names of the winners were to be drawn from a ballot box, which alarmed Allan. Lauchlin, however, winked reassuringly. He would never have gone to the expense of having Surveyor Holland lay out the lots on the island if he did not know which ones he and his friends would receive; the outcome was already rigged. When they left the Commission, both men were confident, and their optimism was confirmed in the *London Gazette* on 23 July.

Dr. Richard Huck had received all of lot 55. The Mackay brothers and their friend, Hugh Finlay, the Postmaster of Quebec, had lot 53. Lauchlin and Henry Macleane had lot 21. Lot 22 was shared by Captain John Gordon, who had succeeded Allan in the Third New York Independent Company in 1761, and Captain William Ridge, who had served in the fourth battalion of the 60th Regiment with Allan. Lot 23 went to Allan and his nephew Lauchlin of Baltimore, while Francis Maclean of Blaich received half of lot 24.[2] The quit rent for Allan's lot was four shillings per hundred acres, and since the lot had 21,000 acres, he and his nephew would have to pay forty-two pounds in July 1772. By that time, Allan was certain, they would have found the settlers and the means to send them to the island. From the rents they would receive, they could easily find the forty-two pounds for the quit rents.

Once the matter of land grants was settled, Lauchlin Macleane went to Paris, to close up the house on the Rue de Rivoli and bring his mistress to London. Allan had him arrange small semi-annual payments for the maintenance of his three-year-old son.When Lauchlin returned, he installed his mistress in rooms at Lincoln's Inn Fields, whether his wife Elizabeth liked the arrangement or not.

Lord Chatham retired in October, and the new Prime Minister, Lord Grafton, dismissed Lauchlin from his post as Under Secretary of State. Grafton created a new Secretary of State for the Colonies, leaving Lord Shelburne with only Southern Europe in his department. Lauchlin, whose main worth was his knowledge of the colonies, Grafton declared redundant. Early in January 1768, enraged over the loss in income, Lauchlin sent Allan to the office of the *Public Advertiser* with a packet and instructions to drop it inside the door and hurry away before anyone could get a description of him.

A few days later a letter attacking Grafton appeared in the *Public Advertiser*, signed "Junius."Allan could not help wondering if his friend and benefactor was the author. If so, Lauchlin was playing with fire. While innocent where political intrigue was concerned, Allan was well aware of the military approach to treason. Government agents would watch the office of the newspaper, and letters posted to the printer, Henry Woodfall, would be opened before they were delivered.

Lord Shelburne still made use of Lauchlin, now as his private secretary. In February Lauchlin learned that the borough of Arundel was to elect two members to the House of Commons. Sir George Colebrooke, the proprietor, would stand, as was customary, but he agreed that Lauchlin should seek the other seat, and he recommended him personally, a guarantee of success. On 12 March 1768, Colbrooke and Macleane won the seats.

On the 22nd, John Wilkes was elected to the seat for Middlesex. Assured of support from London street mobs,

Wilkes slipped home from exile in Paris. However, he was expelled from Parliament, fined 1,000 pounds, and committed to King's Bench Prison for twenty-two months. Lord Shelburne wanted to support Wilkes indirectly, and he used Lauchlin Macleane for his purposes. When Lauchlin rose for his maiden speech in the House of Commons, he ridiculed the treatment meted out to Wilkes and called it illegal.

That summer Allan had plenty of time to amuse himself, going to coffee houses with friends, and to concerts and plays. Lauchlin employed two other henchmen on whom he could call, Allan suspected, as a way of confusing government agents. Both men were named John Stewart. One, always called Jack, was a wine merchant whose home was in York Buildings, on Buckingham Street, Westminster. The other was short, nicknamed Little John, and he had once been in King's Bench Prison for debt. While in prison Little John Stewart had acquired a mistress, Mrs. Anne Eastick, and when she was freed he took her to live in his house in Lincoln's Inn Fields, where she bore him a son.

In the autumn Allan went north to visit Janet in Glasgow and to pay a visit to Torloisk. The stay in Glasgow was everything he could have wished. At Torloisk he found the new house finished, three storeys tall, of stone with wooden floors imported from the mainland, a proper home for the laird of the estate and his family. Allan was impressed at his brother's success in making the estate prosper. Lachlan's secret was kelp, the seaweed so plentiful along the shores of Torloisk. The ashes of the kelp yielded iodine and soda, valuable chemicals for which there was a growing demand. Gathering and burning the kelp provided extra work and income for the crofters, and everyone was enjoying the good times the industry brought.[3] To Allan's astonishment, the old cottage where they had been born was still standing, and he asked Lachlan why he had not torn down the eyesore.

"I'll never do that," the sentimental Lachlan replied. "I need it to remind me how far our fortunes had fallen, and how hard I had to work to restore Torloisk to a bit of its old self."[4]

Lachlan now had time to indulge in his great loves, music and Gaelic poetry, some of which he wrote himself. The windswept outpost was becoming a tiny centre of culture as Lachlan pursued his objective. He sought out local people interested both in preserving the old Gaelic music and in learning the classics of other parts of Europe, especially the music of Italy, rapidly gaining popularity in the salons of London.

In April 1769, back in London, Allan again helped Lauchlin Macleane rig the election of officers in the East India Company to suit Lord Shelburne. Again they were successful, but in June a ship of the company arrived bringing news of unrest in India. A French fleet had left Mauritius bound for Madras or Bengal to attack the English trading posts. Company stock plummeted by fifty-three and three quarters points. Allan's loss was relatively modest, but Lauchlin's amounted to 90,000 pounds. Clive's reputation was temporarily tarnished, Lachlan's shattered.

Allan grieved for his friend, but he knew his recuperative powers. Lauchlin lived by his wits and would soon get back on his feet. He began with a pamphlet defending Clive, signed by himself and John Stuart, from an address in Berkeley Square, the home of Andrew Stuart, the Scots lawyer. Then Lauchlin began to retrench. He sold the house in Queen Anne Street, but kept a country retreat he had bought at Muswell Hill near Highgate Village. He bought a cheap house in unfashionable Lambeth, at 27 Bridge Road, near the south end of Westminster Bridge. His brother Henry Macleane leased 5 Brick Court, in the Middle Temple, and suggested Allan live with him. Allan agreed, for he did not want to remain with Lauchlin at present. The man had a new mistress, Penelope Agnew, who had been Elizabeth's friend until Lauchlin's wife discovered the liaison.

Elizabeth vowed she had left Lauchlin forever. Mrs. Agnew, a wealthy widow with a son, Patrick, moved into the house on Bridge Road and Lauchlin adopted her boy. The Bridge Road address was to be kept a secret, given out only to trusted friends. Others wanting to find Lauchlin were to be directed to Brick Court, where Henry and Allan would deal with their requests. That way Lauchlin hoped to dodge his creditors.

Archibald Maclaine, the Cheapside merchant, had died and his son Thomas had taken over the business, continuing to act as Lauchlin's agent. Suddenly Thomas Maclaine vanished. Since Lauchlin had involved Thomas in his financial muddle, Allan thought that the disappearance had been contrived so that no one could question the merchant. Allan paid scant attention to these financial entanglements. His duty was to do Lauchlin's bidding, to help him extricate himself from his present difficulties, and to elude government agents. He kept on delivering secret packets to coffee houses used as drops, and occasionally to newspaper offices.

Chapter Ten

Janet 1770-1771

Allan hired a sedan chair in front of a tavern on Fleet Street, so that no one could connect him with the house in Brick Court. Curtains closed, the chairmen carried him with to the office of the *Public Advertiser*, in the shadow of St. Paul's, a thick packet bulging his waistcoat. He hopped out, threw the packet into Printer Woodfall's door, and slipped back inside the chair. He left it near Charing Cross and went to report to Lauchlin Macleane at Bridge Road. The mission was completed, and Allan was confident no one had glimpsed him long enough to identify him later on.[1]

On 19 December 1769, under the heading "A Letter to the King" and signed "Junius", was a piece very critical of Lord Grafton's ministry. The Prime Minister and the German monarch both viewed the letter as downright treason. Lauchlin grew perturbed when the newspapers reported that one of the printers had noticed a tall, dark man who wore a sword at the office a week before the letter appeared, and he came to Brick Court to confer with Allan. "The description fits any number of half-pay officers," Allan said, unruffled.

"You should go to Torloisk till this blows over," Lauchlin suggested.

"Was that your letter, Lauchlin?"

"Of course not," Lauchlin scoffed. "But you could be subjected to disagreeable questions if the King's agents decide you fit the description."

Allan refused to take him seriously, and remained at Brick Court. In January 1770, Lauchlin told him of rumours suggesting Henry Woodfall, of the *Public Advertiser* was about to be arrested.

Next, on the 28th, the Grafton ministry fell, and Frederick Lord North, a Tory, became the new Prime Minister, which Lauchlin viewed as a welcome development. Despite the change in ministry, Henry Woodfall was arrested on 14 February, but since several tall, dark men had been suspected of leaving the manuscript for "A Letter to the King" at Woodfall's office, Lauchlin began to breathe more easily. Allan had never been seriously worried, and he knew he could bluff the government agents if necessary.

Besides, Allan had more pleasant things to occupy him. Janet came to London to stay with relatives in order to become better acquainted with her betrothed. The couple spent every moment they could together. Although her father now allowed their engagement to be official, and in just another year she would be twenty-one, Allan felt self-conscious and had not told any of his London friends. Meanwhile, Henry Woodfall was released on bail and was back in his office. However, no more letters of "Junius" appeared in the *Public Advertiser*. John Wilkes, released from King's Bench Prison despite Lord North's disapproval, was living quietly in Prince's Court. Then suddenly Lauchlin was scheming again, and making more demands on Allan's time.

Not only that, Lauchlin was living with Anne Eastick in a house on George Street. Penelope Agnew was pregnant, and Lauchlin was using Anne until she was available, which rather disgusted Allan. How could Lauchlin bear to have relations with a jailbird? He felt revolted when he received a summons to the George Street house. Lauchlin, looking very much at home in gown and carpet slippers, allowed the Eastick whore to drape herself over him. Allan was relieved when Lauchlin dismissed her from the parlour so that they could chat in private.

Lauchlin had decided to give Allan all of lot 21 on the Island of Saint John. He had many other plans and did not have time to develop the land, nor was his brother Henry, who owned half of the lot, interested. Allan looked gloomy. "I can find plenty of people in the Hebrides who want to emigrate, but I can not raise money for passages across the Atlantic, Lauchlin."

"And I can't help," Lauchlin said. "Penelope is badgering me to divorce Elizabeth so I can marry her. Yet my creditors could claim her fortune if she were my wife. To protect her we must go on living in sin."

Early in June, Henry Woodfall's case came up for trial in the Court of King's Bench in the Guildhall. The jury's verdict was "guilty of printing and publishing only." In effect, Woodfall was not guilty of treason, and he had to pay a modest fine.

On 29 June 1770, Penelope Agnew gave birth to a son whom Lauchlin named John Macleane, and since he could soon make love to Penelope, he left Anne Eastick. On 1 July, Lauchlin sent for Allan to come to Bridge Road. "Henry tells me you are spending most of your time with a lassie," he said, after showing Allan his new son and being every inch the proud father.

"Aye," Allan replied guardedly, and fell silent.

"Won't you at least tell me who she is?" Lauchlin asked him.

"She's Janet, a daughter of Donald Maclean of Brolass."

Lauchlin whistled in admiration. "True quality. A daughter of Sir Allan's heir. I almost envy you, Allan."

"I suppose she'll have a dowry," Allan said, frowning. "But we'd invest that and make do on my half-pay."

"There may be something I can do," Lauchlin volunteered. "I'm trying my best with Lord North and have hope of a sinecure. Once that is secured, I'll try to have you returned to the active list. A lieutenant-colonel's full pay should suffice."

Indeed it would, Allan thought., wondering how Lauchlin could arrange that. Lauchlin, hitherto pulling strings for Lord Shelburne, had switched sides without a qualm to ingratiate himself with Lord North. Politics was a fickle business, but he would leave that to Lauchlin, content to serve him well.

A few days later, when Henry Macleane had gone to Muswell Hill with Lauchlin and Penelope for a holiday, someone rapped on the door at Brick Court. Allan responded and found Anne Eastick there. She had called at the house in Queen Anne Street and been given this address, and she wanted to see Lauchlin. Tears streamed down her face. She was pregnant and although Lauchlin had given her five guineas, she had spent them and needed more.

Forbidden to reveal the Bridge Road address, Allan asked her to come back when Henry Macleane was in, and he would advise her. Two weeks later Anne again knocked at Brick Court. This time Henry opened to her, and Allan, in the parlour, heard angry voices and hurried into the hallway.

Henry was pushing Anne backwards outside the door, shouting, "I have nothing to do with my brother's connections."

Allan went to Bridge Road , and in private told Lauchlin about Anne's visits to Brick Court. Despite the woman's blowsiness, he felt sorry for her. Thanks to Lauchlin she was pregnant and in dire straits. "If she calls again, give her the Bridge Road address," Lauchlin told him.

The following morning Anne Eastick again rapped at Brick Court, and Allan sent her to Bridge Road. In the afternoon a messenger arrived with a request for Allan to come at once to Bridge Road. Anne Eastick was there and kicking up a fuss. Allan fairly flew along the mud flats of the Thames and across Westminster Bridge. He found Lauchlin's hallway in an uproar. A maid, Margaret Satterthwaite, was beating Anne, while Lauchlin's cook was trying to intervene. Allan bellowed for order and the others stopped in amazement. Down the stairway came Jane Satterthwaite, the maid Margaret's sister and little John Macleane's nurse.

"You're wanted upstairs, Major Maclean," Jane said.

"Don't any of you leave till I come back," Allan ordered the three women as he followed Jane upstairs.

He found Lauchlin in a bedroom alone. "I can't see Anne here," he muttered. "Penelope is upset with me for letting her know where we live. I'll meet her at Brick Court. Bring her by boat, to give me time to cross the bridge and be there ahead of her."

Back downstairs Allan spoke kindly to Anne, explaining that Lauchlin was expected shortly at Brick Court. All the fight had gone out of her, and he led her towards a wharf on the Thames where boats were for hire. "What's wrong with the bridge?" she asked, eyes wary.

"Mr. Macleane wants to spare you the walk," Allan said soothingly.

When they reached Brick Court, Lauchlin was sitting in the parlour smoking a pipe, trying not to breathe heavily. "What do you want?" he asked sharply.

"Money, of course," Anne said sulkily.

"I owe you nothing," Lauchlin said sternly. "Little John Stewart told me you miscarried. I want you to leave at once."

Anne flew into a rage and flung herself at Lauchlin. Allan intervened and received a blow for his pains. The woman had the strength of two men! Someone was knocking on the door, and with Allan's help Lauchlin dragged Anne to the back of the house and locked her in a closet. The visitor was Joseph King, a large, brutish man who had been in King Bench's Prison with Anne and Little John. Over the howls coming from the closet, King offered to take Anne to a constable.

"It will take three of us to drag her there," Allan warned him.

That was not necessary. While Lauchlin and Allan were skilled swordsmen, Joseph King was a bare-fist fighter of note. Twisting both of Anne's arms behind her, her marched her out of the house, and Allan went along as a witness. The constable charged Anne with assaulting Major Maclean, but the magistrate let her off with a caution. The next day Anne charged Margaret Satterthwaite with assault, and the judge who presided called her a whore. Anne made many visits to Bridge Road, and finally Lauchlin threw her out bodily and ordered his footmen to get rid of her in future.

Towards the end of July, Lauchlin dropped in at Brick Court. Anne had threatened to shoot him and he wanted to lay a trap for her. "I'm going to invite her to Bridge Road," he told Allan and Henry. "We'll leave the door ajar, and she's bound to come inside. The servants will be hiding and they'll jump out and shout 'Robbery.' Then, since no one admitted her, I can charge her with breaking and entering."

A few days later another messenger arrived from Bridge Road. Anne Eastick had called, but a carpenter working in the house interfered when the servants tried to subdue her. She had escaped from them and locked herself in the parlour. Grimly Allan set out for Bridge Road, where he tried to reason with Anne through the locked door. Unsuccessful, he climbed through a window into the parlour and confronted her, begging her to leave the house peacefully, wary lest she attack him again. Persuasion failed, and Allan climbed out the window. Accompanied by the maid Margaret Satterthwaite, he went in search of a constable, who escorted Anne to a magistrate in St. Margaret's Hill, Lambeth. When Allan and Margaret returned to Bridge Road, Lauchlin emerged, having hidden himself during the fracas.

"I hope they lock her up and throw away the key," he said.

Allan was of two minds about Anne. He could not help pitying her, and yet he tended to agree with Lauchlin. Anne certainly was far from sane and in need of a keeper. Yet Lauchlin had treated her rather shabbily, using her when it suited him. Allan was obliged to serve as Lauchlin's courier, but being involved in a sleazy domestic squabble was beneath his dignity. For some time peace settled upon Bridge Road. Anne was so incoherent that the magistrate ordered her confined in the County Prison until she was fit to stand trial.

On 14 November 1770, another letter signed "Junius" appeared in the *Public Advertiser*. Henry Woodfall had got his nerve back, and other newspapers were following his example, testing to see whether anyone would be arrested. Three newspaper proprietors were, but the magistrates dismissed all charges. Lauchlin was jubilant. The battle for freedom of the press had been won.

Since Allan would soon marry Janet, Lauchlin suggested he move into better quarters, a suite of rooms belonging to Jack Stewart at York Buildings, Buckingham Street, Westminster. Allan was happy to make the move, for Buckingham Street was a better address than Brick Court. When Lauchlin had signed the lease, Allan took his belongings to the house beside Jack Stewart's wine shop. The rooms were large and airy and he visualized Janet in them, adding her own touches, her presence a joy.

The wedding date was set for 4 February 1771, and beforehand some of Allan's family came to London. The unmarried ones, Archibald, Mary, and Betty, arrived from Torloisk. Lachlan did not come, fearing delays from winter storms that would keep him away from the estate too long, but he sent his piper, Rankin. The pipes were still banned, but the authorities would look the other way when the groom was a soldier. The Donald Macleans came from Glasgow with Janet's sisters and brother Hector. They stayed with relatives, and Allan had beds put in his suite for Archibald, Mary, and Betty and Piper Rankin.

On 23 January, Lauchlin sent for Allan and asked him to write to John Wilkes, claiming that Wilkes owed Lauchlin 1,350 pounds, and threatening to sue for payment of half this sum. A Bill of Rights Society, founded to help Wilkes, had agreed to cover half his debts. In fact, the debt to Lauchlin was only 1,200 pounds, money he had loaned Wilkes during his exile in Paris. Lauchlin had Allan alter the amount to confuse the issue. Wilkes was enraged by Allan's letter and bewildered, too, which was what Lauchlin intended.

On the 26th, Lauchlin sent for Allan again, and dictated a challenge to a duel, which he was to deliver to John Wilkes' house in Prince's Court. At that Allan questioned Lauchlin's motives. His benefactor had long been a champion of Wilkes, and so, incidently, had "Junius." Lauchlin's motives, he told Allan, were threefold. First, he needed the 600 pounds. Second, Lord North disliked Wilkes, and Lauchlin would never get a sinecure if the Prime Minister thought he favoured the man. Third, a duel was good publicity.

"Dangerous and illegal, too," Allan remarked.

"Wilkes will refuse me," Lauchlin said complacently. "He had to post a bond of 1,500 pounds to keep the peace for seven years as a condition of his release from prison. He can't afford to accept."

At noon on the 27th, a Sunday, Allan presented himself at Wilkes' house. When the ugly man had read the letter, Allan told him that as the go-between he was to arrange the time, place, and choice of weapons. As Lauchlin predicted, Wilkes, looking confused, declined the challenge and returned the letter to Allan. He left Prince's Court, and to ensure that he was not alone with Lauchlin in the intrigue, he went to a coffee house in the Strand. There he met a brother officer, Captain Alexander Maclean, a native of the Isle of Islay. The captain wrote down Allan's version of the challenge to Wilkes and promised to keep it in a safe place. Afterwards, Allan returned to Bridge Road.

Lauchlin wrote a covering letter and sealed it with the challenge. Allan took the package to the office of William Woodfall, the proprietor of the *Morning Chronicle* and Henry Woodfall's brother, for publication in the Monday edition. The letters appeared as Lauchlin hoped. On the

Tuesday evening, Allan dropped a packet at the office of the *Public Advertiser*, and on Wednesday that newspaper carried Wilkes' reply to the challenge, as well as a letter from "Junius" supporting him. Allan found the coincidence remarkable. Could Lauchlin be "Junius" using the *nom-de-plum* to express his true sentiments on Wilkes?

On Thursday, Lauchlin asked Allan to write his own version of the Wilkes challenge for the *Public Advertiser*. When he had it ready he was to take it to Henry Macleane at Brick Court to have the language tidied up for his prose usually read like translated Gaelic.

Allan's account appeared in the *Public Advertiser* on Friday, 1 February, and he showed only a passing interest in it. Some of Janet's belongings arrived at York Buildings, and he had to arrange them. He was feeling overawed at what he was about to embark upon. He was now in his forty-sixth year, and Janet was just twenty-one. Yet many career officers were in the same situation, unable to marry until middle-age because they could not support a wife earlier. In fact, Allan was taking a chance, putting his faith in Lauchlin's ability to get him a promotion and return him to active duty. Until that promotion came through, he and Janet would have to live frugally.

Monday, 4 February dawned clear and frosty. After breakfast, Allan dressed in his regimentals, arranging the pleats of the kilt, tying the plaid round his waist and pulling it up to pin on his shoulder. With his sisters on either arm, followed by Archibald and Piper Rankin, he marched along, kilt swinging, ignoring certain hostile glares from passers-by. At the Monkwell Presbyterian Meeting House, he was joined by his cronies—Jack Stewart, Andrew and John Stuart, Captain Alexander Maclean, also in regimentals, Lauchlin and Henry Macleane.

Allan passed the rest of the day in a trance. Janet, in her white gown, was beside him while the minister, Dr. Fordyce, intoned the service. Janet's brother Hector, in a kilt, stood with his parents and sisters. Leaving the church Piper Rankin struck up Maclean's March as the little procession wound its way to the Strand, proud and defiant. With so many stout friends in his tail, Allan knew they could chase away anyone wanting to start trouble. They halted at a coffee house where Allan had ordered dinner, but he barely tasted the food, his mind on the wedding night ahead.

Their love-making was subdued, owing to the presence of four guests in their suite. Yet both felt satisfied with their first experience together, as they lay in each other's arms, half dozing throughout the night. They were barely awake when they heard footsteps outside their bedroom door, and the front door open softly. Their guests were going out for breakfast to allow the newlyweds some privacy.

Janet smiled up at him. "We'll have thousands of mornings like this, though I hope, before too long, we won't be alone. Oh, Allan, I want lots of babies to love."

"You shall have them," he assured her, clasping her in his arms as their lips met. Fleetingly he thought of the son in Paris, the symbol of his fertility.

Chapter Eleven

Who is "Junius?"
1771-1775

Only days after the wedding a letter signed "Regulus" appeared in the *Public Advertiser* which stated that the challenge to John Wilkes was unworthy of Lauchlin Macleane, and that Major Maclean was "highly culpable in every part of his conduct of the affair." Allan was perturbed, Lauchlin undeterred. The campaign to discredit Wilkes and curry favour with Lord North was working. "We can survive a little abuse," Lauchlin remarked. "it's very fashionable."[1]

Allan did not probe. He suspected Lauchlin was referring to a recent letter by "Junius" in which the anonymous author had attacked Lord North for being too conciliatory towards Spain over the Falkland Islands. In 1770, the Spanish had occupied these islands, and after some negotiations had returned them to Britain, but North had left the question of ultimate sovereignty up in the air. Lauchlin had written Lord North, pointing out that many of Spain's American colonies were on the verge of revolt, and by threatening to support Mexico, Britain could settle the sovereignty question forever. North, aware of unrest spawning in the King's own American possessions, had refused to play a game that he feared might misfire.

Since his move to Buckingham Street, Allan had carried many letters for Lauchlin, but had not dropped any packets furtively at newspaper offices or coffee houses. Yet he knew of mysterious happenings at Brick Court. Henry, Lauchlin, and Andrew Stuart were often in conference, and other henchmen were leaving letters to be picked up by persons unknown. Coffee house owners had approached him with overt warnings that government agents were watching outside. Allan was carrying Lauchlin's public correspondence, while others were delivering top secret letters. Lauchlin's various henchmen had one thing in common—all were Jacobites.

Allan could not fathom his benefactor's motives. Was Lauchlin's underworld intrigue directed at power for its own sake, or power one day to topple the German monarchy? Was the ultimate aim of these manipulations the restoration of the Stuarts? Dabbling in treason was a deadly game, and Allan felt the less he knew the better. He could not reveal anything incriminating.

In March, Lauchlin resigned from Parliament. A sinecure, the Superintendent of the Lazarettos, was available, and Lord North could not reward a sitting member. The Lazarettos were hospitals which the government maintained abroad. The sinecure entitled the Superintendent to a salary of 1,000 pounds a year, with no duties—simply a form of patronage. Lauchlin began to contrive that whoever won his seat would be pliable, and agree to give it up should he want to return to Parliament.

The candidate Lauchlin recommended was Jack Stewart, the wine merchant and Allan's landlord at York Buildings. Early in May, Lauchlin sent a message to Allan that he would soon need him in Arundel, and went to his constituency to soften up the electorate. He returned on the 9th, and on the 10th, a Friday, Allan left with him, Jack Stewart in tow. That evening, Lauchlin and Allan went through Arundel with a cart, dispensing wine and punch to the populace in a great revel.

Meanwhile, at the Crown Inn, the rival candidate, Thomas Mackreth, was being toasted by his supporters. On Saturday morning, after hearing of the largess of the night before, Mackreth left Arundel, although the election was scheduled for Monday the 13th. In the absence of his rival, Jack Stewart won by acclamation. As they packed to return to London, Lauchlin hummed a little tune of satisfaction.

In June, Anne Eastick published a fifty-page pamphlet setting forth the sins of Little John Stewart, then on his way to India as Judge Advocate of Bengal, and Lauchlin Macleane. The latter was indifferent. "She's damned for all I care," he told Allan with a shrug.

"Where could she have got the money?" Allan wondered.

"Wilkes, probably," Lauchlin replied.

A month later, Lauchlin wanted Allan to move back to Brick Court with his brother Henry. Allan hesitated, thinking of Janet, but Lauchlin was reassuring. Henry would meet with anyone not respectable at a coffee house in the Strand. Mollified that Janet's sensitivities would not be offended, Allan agreed to the move. Janet looked chagrined when she saw Brick Court, but she never complained. She knew they lived rent-free, and since Lauchlin paid the piper he had a right to call the tune.

Lauchlin's appointment as Superintendent of the Lazarettos was confirmed by the government, but not without a flurry of objections from anonymous authors to the press. The lines of the battle were drawn. Some writers charged that Lauchlin was only an apothecary. Allan and Henry Macleane concocted a letter pointing out that Lauchlin had a medical degree from Edinburgh, and signed it "Aequus of the Middle Temple." The letter was published in the *Public Advertiser* on 9 October 1771.

On 4 February 1772, when Allan and Janet celebrated their first wedding anniversary, both were very subdued. Janet's mother had died in Glasgow, and she herself had failed to conceive a child.[2] Sorrow and disappointment cast a cloud over their happiness.

Late in March, two volumes of the letters of "Junius" were published. Allan was more than half convinced that Lauchlin Macleane was back of "Junius" and using newspapers to attack a government that was heaping favours on him. Soon after the volumes appeared, Lauchlin was appointed Commissary-General of the army in Bengal, a plum. He planned to leave for India as soon as Penelope had given birth to their second child, expected in May.

In April, Colonel John Burgoyne, Member of Parliament for Midhurst, Sussex, rose in the House and demanded an enquiry into the affairs of the East India Company, and on his motion a select committee was struck. Lauchlin survived the purge that followed, but Andrew Stuart, who had been appointed a supervisor to work in Bengal, was removed from that office. During the enquiry, Burgoyne declared that Lauchlin Macleane's associates were a pack of Jacobites, citing in particular Jack Stewart and Major Allan Maclean. Both men wondered whether their futures, one political, the other military, might be endangered.

On 2 May 1772, Penelope Agnew died giving birth to a daughter Lauchlin named Harriet. Allan attended the funeral at St. Mary's Church. Lauchlin sold the house on Bridge Road, and arranged for John Stuart and Robert Orme to care for the three children—Patrick Agnew, John and Harriet Macleane, whose nurse, Jane Satterthwaite, would remain with them. Then with his brother Henry, who had been hired as a secretary in the office of the East India Company in Calcutta, Lauchlin planned to leave for Bengal. He did not arrange to pay the rent on Brick Court, where Allan and Janet did not want to live.

Their financial problems were solved on 25 May, when through Lauchlin's influence, Allan was appointed an active lieutenant-colonel in the army with full pay of one pound a day.[3] Since he was not assigned a battalion, he had no duties. He went to see Jack Stewart and leased the rooms Janet loved in York Buildings, Buckingham Street, which he could now afford to rent himself. He also hired a maid, for he had never approved of Janet's doing her own work.

In June, Allan accompanied Lauchlin and Henry Macleane to their ship, the *Egmont*, lying in the lower Thames. He promised to look in on the children, a prospect he thought would delight Janet. Seeing John and Harriet would, he hoped, pave the way for her to view illegitimacy with tolerance. He was thinking of the son growing up in Paris, who should have a good education as a British subject. For this he would need money, and he sold the two lots on the Island of Saint John. The quit rents were due, and he refused to touch Janet's dowry to meet them. At times he had toyed with the notion of selling his major's commission to raise the passage money, but he abandoned all dreams of an emigration scheme when his promotion came through.

In Glasgow, Janet's father remarried a woman named Margaret Wall, from Castle Clonea, Waterford, Ireland. When their son Fitzroy Jeffreys Grafton Maclean was born, Hector, now twelve, decided to make his home with Janet and Allan in London. This gave Allan the opening he sought to inform Janet of his son in Paris. He dreaded confessing his indiscretion, and he was both astonished and relieved when he found Janet enthusiastic at the prospect of raising the boy. A son that was half theirs was better than no child at all, and he would be company for Hector. They decided to tell their friends that the boy was a foster child, and Allan hoped that the resemblance would not be so strong as to make the story implausible.

The nine-year-old boy he found in Paris was tall and sturdy, but otherwise he looked more like a Maclean of Blaich than of Torloisk. Allan was certain no one would suspect the boy's true parentage, even those who remembered his sojourn in France of the 1760s.

By July 1773, Allan was back in London and turning his attention to advancing his military career, while Janet took charge of his son and helped him adapt to a new life. Allan sent a memorial to the East India Company, offering to raise a regiment of Highlanders for service in Bengal. Ten years had passed since he had had a posting, although he felt that his work for Lauchlin had kept him from growing rusty.

The East India Company refused his offer, and he went to see Robert Orme to find out why. "If Lauchlin were still here I would have got a warrant," he told Orme, positive his friend's magic would have worked.

Orme disagreed. The Indian army belonged to the Company, and as a high-ranking regular officer Allan might not be eligible. He suggested Allan contact Mr. Matthew Lewis, the Deputy Secretary and First Clerk at the War Office. Allan went to Whitehall and made an appointment, and when he kept it Mr. Lewis took him to see the Secretary at War, Viscount Barrington.[4] Allan said he wanted to resign from the army in order to join the East India Company, but Lord Barrington shook his head. He did not want to lose officers with experience in America.

"The colonists are outraged over the Townshend Acts and the Stamp Act, even though they have been repealed," Barrington explained. "Personally I think His Majesty and Lord North are foolish to maintain the tax on tea, and wish it were repealed. Otherwise I expect we shall have to increase the garrisons there before long."

"Have you a regiment for me, Your Lordship?" Allan asked.

"I think we will ask you to raise one. You completed your platoon in the 60th Regiment with dispatch, and the six companies for the 114th. You are a proper person to raise battalions in the colonies, where many Highlanders have been settling in the past few years. Most were Jacobites, probably still are. I am aware of your sentiments on that head, Colonel Maclean, yet you have shown remarkable dedication to the service."

"My duty, Your Lordship," Allan murmured.

After he left the Secretary at War, Allan mulled over what he had heard, especially the suggestion that he raise men in the colonies. The press favoured the colonists. "Junius" had advocated leniency, and many letters echoed him. Then a startling thought flashed through Allan's mind. There had not been a single letter from "Junius" since the publication of the two volumes of his letters, and not one letter that smacked of Lauchlin Macleane's style since his departure for Bengal. Now Allan was convinced that his benefactor was indeed the anonymous political journalist, and he resolved to take Lauchlin's secret to his grave.

In the spring of 1774, startling news arrived from Boston. The colonists had refused to allow ships carrying tea to unload. On 16 December 1773, a group of men dressed as Indians had thrown vast quantities of tea into the harbour in what the press was calling the Boston Tea Party. An indignant home government ordered the port of Boston closed.

Frederick Haldimand, now a major-general in the British army, was the commander at New York City. General Thomas Gage, the commander-in-chief in America, wanted to resign, and Allan thought that Haldimand would be Gage's successor. General Sir Jeffrey Amherst, knighted in 1761, had declined the job out of sympathy for the colonists, an emotion Allan could ill afford. As the months passed, the British army began to mobilize. King George arranged for the use of troops from Hanover and its dependencies because recruiting was going badly at home. The prospect of war with fellow-Britons was as unpopular among the masses as with Amherst.

In January 1775, Mr. Lewis sent Allan a letter recommending that he write a memorial to the War Office, offering to raise troops in the colonies. Allan set to work at once, and when the memorial had been sent, he began making a tentative list of officers. He had several nephews who were eligible, among them his sister Alicia's son, Lachlan Macquarrie of Ulva. His brother-in-law Hector, now thirteen, could be an ensign if his father approved. Donald Maclean did, since a military career would be fitting for a future chief of the clan. The boy was excited at the prospect, for like Allan he had been nurtured on tales of clan Maclean, and he took pride in having a brother-in-law who had been out with the Prince. If Allan could reconcile serving one master while dreaming of another, so could Hector.

Lord Barrington's reply, early in February, was favourable. Lord North would present Allan's proposal to the King, who, as Captain-General, must approve all new levies. Meanwhile, Allan should make all the arrangements he could in advance, and choose an agent to tide him over until bills could be submitted to the paymaster-general's office in Whitehall. Allan resolved not to repeat the mistakes he had made while raising the 114th Regiment. With so limited private means he could not afford to make up deficiencies from his own purse. As his agent he chose the firm of Cox, Mair and Cox, of Craig's Court, London, and he warned the partners of his financial limitations.[5] As his was to be a new regiment, commissions would not be purchased. He resolved to complete at least one battalion as soon as possible in order to be able to sell commissions, the only way he had of making a profit for himself. He was determined to emerge from this conflict with money in hand and no debts.

By 3 April 1775, when the King authorized the regiment, Allan was ready to sail for New York, with passage booked for the middle of the month for himself, Hector, and several officers. As majors, Allan had chosen Captain Donald Macdonald from the Isle of Skye, a half-pay officer in the Marines, and Captain John Small, an active officer in the 21st Regiment who wanted a promotion without purchase and a brother officer of Allan's in the Scots Brigade in the Netherlands in the 1740s.[6] Allan would receive his warrant from General Thomas Gage when he arrived in New York. As Commander-in-chief, Gage would also sign the officers' commissions.

The War Office sent the names of the half-pay officers in the colonies that Gage recommended, subject to Allan's approval. One man was Alexander Macdonald from the Isle of Skye,[7] who lived on Staten Island. In North Carolina was the Reverend John Bethune, a Presbyterian minister who had volunteered to be the regimental chaplain. In that same area, already actively recruiting was Allan Macdonald, also from Skye, who had served in Lord Loudoun's regiment in 1746. Although he had opposed the Prince's army, Allan Macdonald was the husband of Flora, the heroine who had helped Bonnie Charlie escape from his pursuers in the Outer Hebrides following the Battle of Culloden.[8] In Canada, scattered from Montreal to Murray Bay, were eight experienced veterans of the Seven Years' War who were eligible for captaincies.

Only the impending parting from Janet and his son dampened Allan's spirits. The boy was adjusting well to life in London, and Allan and Janet decided they would not disrupt his education by taking him to America. Although wives of high-ranking officers often accompanied their husbands, Janet agreed to remain at York Buildings for the duration, and Allan expected to be able to return each winter when campaigning ceased in the northern colonies. Because of the precarious state of his finances, while conferring with Lord North, Allan received the Prime Minister's promise, approved by the King, of a generous pension for Janet in the event of his death.[9]

The King named the new regiment the Royal Highland Emigrants, and authorized red coats faced blue, and gold lace and accoutrements. The kilts and plaids were to be of government tartan—the drab dark blue and green worn by the Black Watch—which the King had chosen for all his Highland regiments. However, the sporrans would be of racoon skin, which Allan knew could be bought for a song in the colonies, rather than the more costly badger pelt normally used. Allan arranged for Cox, Mair, and Cox to supply the uniforms, and he ordered his banners from a London firm. These colours were of lustrous, thick silk, the same design as the flags of the 60th Regiment of the Seven Years' War era. Allan ignored the regulations of 1768 since the Royal Highland Emigrants would not be a numbered regular regiment, but a Provincial Corps of the British Army. The earlier regulations permitted a riband bearing the regiment's name, rather than a number in the centre. When he sailed, Allan took only his regimentals and the colours. The rest of the uniforms would be shipped when he learned where he would be posted.

As the ship dropped anchor in New York harbour on 3 June, Allan noticed a ship's boat coming out from the wharves, a short, heavy man with thick red hair standing in the bow, shouting something. At length Allan heard "Colonel Maclean? Colonel Maclean?"

"Here," he shouted.

After the stranger scrambled up the ship's ladder, he introduced himself, in the broadest of Lowland Scots, as a half-pay officer, Lieutenant John Munro, come to warn Allan of dangers ashore. He should not be seen in his regimentals, for General Haldimand had taken the garrison to Boston to assist General Gage,[10] and the rebels had ransacked his house. In April, the rebels had skirmished with some regulars at Concord and Lexington, in Massachusetts. Now the rebels had the British army pinned down in Boston, and they had also seized Fort Ticonderoga. Officers in uniform were apt to be attacked in New York City, especially if word got about that they were looking for loyal colonists to enlist against the rebels.

Allan was furious. He had expected to deal with the rebels in many parts of the colonies, but for New York City to be unsafe seemed inconceivable. He had intended using the city as a base while his officers looked for recruits, but he would have to think again. Also, he had to see General Gage, who would sign his warrant before he could start raising his battalions. He confronted the captain of the ship, who agreed to take him to Boston after the New York passengers disembarked.

John Munro promised to wait in New York City in case he could be of any help there. Recruiting in colonies in a state of near-rebellion would be a clandestine business. Munro, who owned land and mills in northern New York, and who lived in Shaftsbury, a township in an area called the New Hampshire Grants, offered to act as Allan's pilot to reach Highlanders settled in the Mohawk Valley. Munro gave Allan the address of a friend in the city where he could be contacted. Allan accepted Munro's offer and suggested that Major Donald Macdonald go ashore with him, in civilian dress, to find out himself how things were. Attracted by the Lowlander's obvious zeal, Allan offered him a captain-lieutenancy in the Royal Highland Emigrants. Having a local man like Munro in command of the lieutenant-colonel's company might be a boon.[11]

Chapter Twelve

Quebec 1775

Allan's ship dropped anchor in Boston on 11 June, and he found billets for his officers, keeping Hector to share his own room. The following morning he met with General Thomas Gage, who signed a warrant empowering him to raise five battalions. A battalion would consist of ten companies, each of which would have one field officer or captain, two subalterns, three sergeants, three corporals, two drummers, and fifty privates. As an inducement, each recruit was entitled to fifty shillings bounty money.[1]

Initially Gage authorized only two of the battalions, the first to be commanded directly by Allan with Donald Macdonald as his major. For the second battalion, Allan chose John Small as the major-commandant, a younger but more experienced man than Macdonald. As Small's senior captain, Gage recommended Alexander Macdonald, the resident of Staten Island, who had already shown great zeal in recruiting among Highlanders living in northern New York, and who was also a half-pay captain-lieutenant from the old 77th Regiment.

Alexander Macdonald, Gage admitted, had hoped to raise his own regiment, and Allan's arrival was timely.[2] One large regiment of Highland emigrants was preferable over a lot of small ones commanded by half-pay officers hoping to become instant colonels. Gage signed provisional commissions for the two majors, sixteen captains, fourteen lieutenants, and six ensigns between 12 and 14 June 1775. Some were in Boston, but many were in areas where the regiment would be recruited, a task over which Allan wanted to waste no time. Gage approved, and suggested he make his way to New York City with all speed, to raise men amongst loyalists in the middle and northern colonies, areas where Allan had recruited and served in the earlier war.

Allan decided to send Alexander Macdonald to recruit in Nova Scotia, and to dispatch Major Macdonald and Captain Donald Macleod to enlist Highlanders who had settled in Maryland, including his nephew Lauchlin in Baltimore, in

Virginia, and in North Carolina. There, Allan Macdonald, a kinsmen of Major Macdonald as well as the husband of heroine Flora, was already at work recruiting. Highlanders in the more southerly colonies would, Allan expected, in time be formed into a third battalion.

General Gage arranged for Allan to leave on 15 June on a privateer bound for New York City. All the junior officers, including young Hector, would remain in Boston. In addition to Major Macdonald, still in New York, Allan would take only Captain Macleod, and Lieutenants Neil and John Maclean with him. All were veterans, Macleod and Neil Maclean from the 47th Regiment, John Maclean from Allan's old 114th. Allan was to muster his men on Lake Champlain and march to reinforce Boston, if possible. Since the rebels might still be holding the lake when he was ready to move, he might find such a march impractical. In that event he was to go to Canada, possibly by way of Oswego. With eight of his provisional captains residents of Canada, he might stand a good chance of completing one battalion from amongst settlers on the lower St. Lawrence River.

In the midst of his preparations, General Haldimand sent for him. Gage, more than sixty years old, had resigned, and the Swiss officer had been recalled. Haldimand was to return to London at once, but first he wanted to go to New York to retrieve some of his possessions. Like Allan and his officers, Haldimand would wear civilian clothes, in which few people would recognize him.

"I thought you would succeed General Gage, Sir," Allan said, surprised that the government did not see Haldimand as the obvious choice since he was on the scene and had seniority.

Haldimand shook his head. "I am still a foreigner, though I have become a British subject. Appointing a foreigner as commander-in-chief would be unpopular. The King has approved the appointment of Sir William Howe, a brother of Lord George who was killed at Ticonderoga in '58."

Two days after Haldimand and Allan departed, on 17 June, the British army in Boston fought the Battle of Bunker/Breeds Hill that was such a costly victory. At New York City, Allan parted with Haldimand who was going to his own house, and with his officers found the house where

John Munro could be contacted. Munro joined them later in the day with Major Macdonald. Allan dispatched the major and Captain Macleod to the southern colonies, and hired a horse for himself to ride to Philadelphia to seek out Jacobite friends of Lauchlin Macleane and enlist them as agents. Munro agreed to lead Lieutenants Neil and John Maclean to safe houses along the lower Hudson River and to be in the city on Allan's return.

Allan bought some medicines and a bag of instruments in order to pass himself off as a doctor. He took little baggage, and on Munro's advice sent his private papers for safe keeping to the warship *Asia*, offshore.[3] Now he began a summer of undercover work which he later summarized in a memorial he wrote to General Haldimand:

> The memorialist after travelling many journeys from Philadelphia to New York, thence to Boston, back to New York, and from thence to Canada in disguise and often without a Servant or Baggage, with great Expence, imminent danger and incredible fatigue....[4]

These adventures contributed to a fund of stories that delighted his niece Marianne, growing up at Torloisk, which she later passed on to her daughters. The eldest, Margaret Clephane, wrote to a friend, a Miss Stanhope:

> his history would make a novel; he once passed through the American Camp in the disguise of a quack doctor, and sold a whole box of physic to the Yankees, and reached the British headquarters.[5]

This ruse occurred when Allan slipped through the rebel army surrounding Boston, where he went to report to General Gage on conditions in the colonies he had visited. While there, he arranged for Major Small to take most of the

Lieutenaut-Colonel John Butler. This painting on wood is the property of the Niagara District Historical Society, Niagara-on-the-Lake. Maclean met Butler during the Seven Years' War, but their close association began in 1782 when Allan became commander of the upper posts.

officers of the Royal Highland Emigrants to Halifax, since they could not recruit many men in beleaguered Boston. Most of the loyalists had enlisted before Allan arrived. Major Small was happy to depart. He had been serving temporarily on Gage's staff and was anxious to complete a battalion.

By the time Allan left Boston, again on a privateer, General Gage was reconciled that he would never muster men on Lake Champlain. The rebels were building a fleet of armed vessels, and Allan should muster his men in the Mohawk Valley, where the powerful Johnson family was keeping people loyal, and find boats for the journey to Oswego and down the St. Lawrence to Montreal.

In New York City, John Munro was waiting for him. The lieutenants had not signed up many recruits, for getting them to Canada through unfriendly territory would be too risky. Munro, too, thought Allan should go to the Mohawk Valley, where men could escape easily into the country of the Iroquois Indians, who were friendly to Britain. Munro had left Allan's lieutenants at a safe house in Schenectady, and he proposed leading him there. Allan accepted, for although he was familiar with the area, he had travelled along established routes. Thus far his disguise had succeeded because he had been in populous areas where people were accustomed to strangers. Nearer the frontier a strange face might invite curiosity, and Munro knew which people could be trusted.

They went on foot, taking only small haversacks, razors, towels, and a change of linen. For the most part they followed trails through the forest, avoiding the towns and giving a wide berth to West Point and other sites which the rebels were fortifying. Skirting Albany they reached Schenectady after what Allan described as a march of 200 miles, and were reunited with the two lieutenants. There, Munro left them, fearful that his long absence from his farm at Shaftsbury might be noticed. A son of the house would lead them to Johnstown, where Allan would be among friends. John Butler, the son of his former lieutenant, Walter Butler, was the proprietor of Butlersbury, at Fonda. Sir William Johnson had died in 1774, but his nephew and Allan's onetime lieutenant, Guy Johnson, had succeeded him as Superintendent of Indian Affairs. Sir John Johnson, Sir William's heir, now occupied the family mansion,

E.Bartolozzi.RA.

Sir John Johnson. The 2nd Baronet of New York, Sir John raised and commanded the King's Royal Regiment of New York. The name is misleading for the regimental headquarters were in Montreal, not in any part of New York State.

Johnson Hall near Johnstown N. Y. This Georgian mansion, built by Sir William Johnson, was confiscated from his son Sir John. It is now a museum owned by New York State and open to the public.

Johnson Hall, at Johnstown. Allan had scant faith in Guy Johnson, but he placed confidence in his cousin Sir John, about whom he had had good reports.

Two days' march brought Allan's party to a stockade surrounding Johnson Hall, where they were stopped by a line of brawny Highlanders, bristling with broadswords, dirks and muskets, and supported by a few Indian warriors in bright paint waving tomahawks. Allan defused a dangerous situation by addressing Sir John's Highlanders in Gaelic, demanding to see their laird this instant, for he was travel-worn and out of patience.

Sir John made Allan welcome, but he had discouraging news. Many of the officers of the Indian Department had left the valley for Canada in May. Runners had brought Guy Johnson word that the rebels in Albany and Philadelphia were plotting to have him kidnapped, so that he could not influence the Iroquois against them. Guy, his family and 150 followers, including John Butler and his eldest son Walter, and Joseph Brant, had gone to Canada by way of Oswego. From Montreal, Guy and Joseph had gone to England. General Guy Carleton, the governor of Canada, had dispatched John Butler to Fort Niagara to take command of the Indian Department in the absence of the Superintendent.

Sir John was managing to stay put because he had turned his mansion, flanked by its two stone blockhouses, into an armed camp. Many of his tenants, staunchly loyal, were Macdonells from Glengarry, rescued by Sir William after huge rent increases imposed on them threatened them with starvation. They had moved into the blockhouses bringing their weapons. Outside the stockade, gangs of rebels roamed the countryside. Allan would undoubtedly find recruits as a Highland officer who spoke Gaelic, but attempting to march a large body of men, even into Indian country would be dangerous, to say nothing of provisioning them.

"I suggest you enlist as many men as you please, Lieutenant-Colonel Maclean," Sir John said. "But you will find you should leave them here until you can pilot them in small parties to Canada."

Depressed and frustrated, Allan knew he must follow Sir John's advice. With his two lieutenants he speedily enlisted 400 men, but he could not find a way of removing them safely from their homes. At Johnson Hall, Sir John did what little he could to help. His Mohawk warriors came and went at will, and he arranged to have canoes secreted on the shore of Lake Oneida for such men as could elude the rebels and meet Allan there.[6]

Early in August, Allan left Johnson Hall, guided by Ranald Macdonell, one of Sir John's warrior tenants. At the rendez-vous were a few Mohawks and a half dozen recruits, canoes and provisions of Indian corn and pemican made of dried venison. Allan was bitterly disappointed at the meagre turnout, but he could not blame men who dared not join him. He did not doubt their courage, and he knew that having them delay serving was better than risking near-certain capture. He wondered how long Sir John could hold out in his little fortress, and half expected to hear, on reaching Montreal, that a rebel force had attacked Johnson Hall and Sir John was dead or a prisoner in Albany.

With the recruits and Mohawks paddling, the canoes passed empty forts at Oswego and moved into the St. Lawrence. The party received provisions from the British garrison of the 8th Regiment at Fort Oswegatchie, where the commander was Captain George Forster. They shot the Galops Rapids, portaged around the raging Long Sault, Cedars, and Lachine Rapids, and reached Montreal late in the month. Allan did not arrive unheralded. On 20 July the *Quebec Gazette* had reported that he would be raising two battalions, and on 19 August the newspaper had published the terms of enlistment to attract recruits.

Leaving Lieutenants Neil and John Maclean in Montreal to enlist men, Allan wrote letters summoning his provisional captains to meet him in Quebec City, and set out himself on a hired horse to see the governor, Guy Carleton. Desperately short of troops, Carleton was relieved to see Allan when he called at the Chateau St. Louis, and appointed him second-in-command. In short order Allan enlisted 100 men, most of them volunteers who had come to Quebec City from their settlements downstream. On 9 September he sailed with his officers and recruits for Montreal.[7]

He had barely disembarked when a courier arrived from Governor Carleton ordering him to leave his men and return immediately to Quebec City. Rumours that a rebel expedition was moving down Lake Champlain had alarmed the governor, and he wanted to be on hand in case Montreal was threatened. The lieutenant-governor, Hector Cramahé, was a civilian, and Carleton wanted Allan in Quebec City lest the rebels menace that fortress in his absence. The British hold on Canada was fragile, for Carleton had sent two regiments of regulars to Boston at General Gage's request. Allan set up his headquarters in the Golden Dog Tavern, kept by a widow named Prenties, where he was joined by his new captains, William Dunbar, whom he made the town mayor, John Nairne and Malcolm Fraser from Murray Bay, as well as John MacDougall and George Lawes. All went to their homes to recruit.[8]

Towards the end of September, a message arrived from Carleton. Allan was to muster as large a force as possible and set sail for Sorel, and to march up the Richelieu River to Fort St. Jean, where one of his captains, Daniel Robertson, and nineteen Royal Highlander Emigrants were already on duty. A rebel force had encircled the fort and captured Fort Chambly, to the north of St. Jean. Carleton would join him from Montreal with reinforcements to retake Chambly and relieve St. Jean.

Allan worked fast, sending recruiting agents out, but to his disgust not all of his men were trustworthy. Seventeen who deserted and were recaptured elected to go to Britain and serve in Africa rather than face a court martial in Quebec City.[9] Nevertheless, by 14 October, Allan reached Sorel with 220 Royal Highland Emigrants, sixty of the 7th Regiment Royal Fusiliers, and some Canadian militia. At Sorel he added enough militia to bring his force to 400, and he marched at the head of his column for Fort Chambly, expecting Carleton to catch up with him shortly. Near Saint Denis, on the Richelieu, Allan's men skirmished with a small band of rebels, dispersed them, and continued their march.

Meanwhile, on St. Helen's Island, near Montreal, Carleton had assembled 800 Canadian militia, 130 Royal Highland Emigrants and Royal Fusiliers and 80 Indians. On 3 October he had an alarming encounter with the rebels— an ambush by 350 Green Mountain Boys as his boats were nearing Longueuil. Carleton sent a courier to warn Allan that he was returning to Montreal. Furious, Allan retraced his steps. The entire effort had been a waste of time and twenty of his own men were as good as lost. Off Trois Rivières a storm forced the ships to seek shelter, and Allan and his men marched the rest of the way, reaching Quebec City on 12 November.

He found a tremulous Lieutenant-Governor Cramahé talking of surrender, and Allan's temper, never far below the surface, erupted. Bellowing that all defeatist talk must cease, Allan was everywhere at once. Upon hearing that some civilians were in the Bishop's chapel discussing treating with the enemy, he burst into the meeting, pulled the speaker from the pulpit, and shouted, "Quebec must resist to the last able-bodied man!"

Calming down, he warned the citizens what to expect in the way of rapine looting if the Americans entered their city. "In future, your church bells will be rung only if we are attacked!"

He took inventory of his resources and had artificers strengthen the defences. Fortunately, a few days before his own return, the frigate *Lizzard* had reached Quebec bringing clothing and accoutrements for 6,000 men and 20,000 pounds in specie (coins) to pay the troops. On board was Captain Malcolm Fraser, whom Allan made the regimental paymaster, with 150 recruits from Newfoundland, men of Irish extraction from St. John's. Since his men had no uniforms, Allan ordered them to wear kilts if they had them, otherwise their own small clothes, and issued them with green jackets faced buff that had arrived on the *Lizzard* for the militia.

His own regimentals and the colours were with Major Small, but Allan resolved that the lieutenant-colonel would be dressed according to General Gage's warrant. He managed to find enough material in the government stores to outfit himself in a red coat faced blue, the proper tartan kilt and plaid, blue bonnet, gold gorget and sword hilt. He also had a seamstress fashion him a white cockade to place in his bonnet when he led men in battle, knowing how much the sight of it would delight the Jacobites in his ranks.[10]

On 14 November a ragged rebel army 500 strong led by Brigadier Benedict Arnold arrived on the Plains of Abraham after a terrible march along Kennebec and the Chaudière Rivers. After being provisioned by sympathetic Canadians on the south shore, they had crossed the St. Lawrence in all sorts of conveyances. Lacking artillery, the fiery Arnold

"Allan Maclean" prepares to command the battle, October 1975. The Brigade of the American Revolution staged the battle for Quebec 1775-1776, aided by a Canadian contingent that included Victor Suthren, curator of the Canadian War Museum, as Allan Maclean.

soon withdrew to Pointe aux Trembles upstream. Then on the 19th the snow *Fell* ran into the harbour and Governor Carleton came ashore. He had come alone, and Allan was distressed when the governor reported what had occurred. Carleton might be cautious to the point of disaster.

Fort St. Jean had capitulated on 3 November, and by the 13th the rebel army had occupied Montreal. On the 11th, Carleton had left the town aboard a fleet, with 130 Royal Highland Emigrants and regulars. Near Sorel the fleet was becalmed close to a gun battery the rebels had erected on the south shore. Although the ships sported thirty guns, Carleton had left the troops in command of Colonel Richard Prescott to surrender, and had had himself rowed away in a small boat under the cover of darkness. At Trois Rivières he found the snow *Fell*, which brought him the rest of the way. Allan wondered whether the garrison, some 1,200 men including 230 Royal Highland Emigrants, might not do better without the governor.

Carleton was impressed with Allan's preparations, but more had to be done. While Allan supervised the building of gun platforms and worked to weld the able-bodied men into a fighting force, Carleton concentrated on disposing of rebel sympathizers. On 22 November he issued a proclamation ordering all persons not willing to perform military duties to leave the city by 1 December or face being treated as rebels or spies.

Efforts by the artificers were redoubled when on 3 December spies informed Allan that General Richard Montgomery had come in the fleet captured off Sorel, and his men, and Arnold's, were dressed in uniforms stolen from army stores in Montreal. Two days later Arnold and Montgomery moved to the Plains of Abraham with their artillery pieces. Carleton set up headquarters in the Recollect Monastery, more central than the Chateau St. Louis, and Allan joined him from the Golden Dog. Now everyone slept fully clad, arms at hand.

Spies informed the governor that Montgomery would lead some men along the southern route into the Lower Town by a path called Près de Ville, while Arnold would lead a larger force along the northern route through the suburb of St. Roch. To meet the southern threat two strong fences had been built on Près de Ville, and Allan stationed Canadian militia under Captain Adam Barnsfare, and two 3-pounder guns, in a house belonging to Simon Fraser, a merchant. To guard the northern route, two strong barricades were erected, one at the entrance to Rue Sault au Matelot, the second at the exit where that street joined Rue de la Montagne, leading to the Upper Town. Allan had emptied the houses along Sault au Matelot, and had buildings near the St. Jean Gate pulled down so that they could not be used by snipers.

Carleton organized his forces into four brigades. Allan would command the most vital one, composed of his Royal Highland Emigrants and all the regular soldiers. Lieutenant-Colonel Henry Caldwell, a veteran of the regular army whose home was at Lévis, would lead the British militia, of English-speaking residents. Lieutenant-Colonel Noel Voyer would command the French-speaking Canadian militia, while Captain John Hamilton, the master of the *Lizzard*, would lead the seamen. As well prepared as they could be, Allan and Carleton waited at the Recollect Monastery for the rebels to make the first move.

On the night of 30 December snow fell, the wind rose and the storm became a blizzard, as Allan hoped. At four o'clock in the morning he was awakened by the roll of drums and the peal of church bells. He slipped the white cockade into the band of his bonnet and hurried to Carleton's office. The governor was there, and Captain Malcolm Fraser came rushing in after sounding the alarm. Making his rounds, Fraser noticed lights bobbing through the blizzard near the St. Louis Gate. Arnold's force was on the move through St. Roch, where the rebels had erected a gun battery, but as yet there was no sign of Montgomery's men.

Carleton ordered the Canadian militia to man the two barricades in Sault au Matelot, while Allan sent a runner to alert the defenders at the Fraser house in Près de Ville. Then they dispatched Lieutenant-Colonel Caldwell and his British militia south to the Cape Diamond battery, anticipating that Montgomery would be moving in that direction. Allan moved his own men and the regulars to positions from which they could reinforce the Canadian militia. He stationed half the Royal Highland Emigrants and the regulars with

The battle for Quebec was re-enacted on a bright October day in 1975 on the Plains of Abraham, rather than in the streets of the Lower Town where it actually took place. Many of the participants were from Gardiner, Maine, which decided to celebrate this American defeat as a bicentennial project. Others were Canadians from the Museum of Applied Military History.

Captains John Macdougall and George Lawes at the Palace Gate, on the northern approach, and sent the other half with Captain John Nairne to the head of Rue de la Montagne.

Caldwell returned to report that the Cape Diamond battery did not need reinforcement. He had led his militia past the St. Jean and St. Louis Gates, where the rebels were staging a diversion, but the troops there were sufficient to deal with them. Allan sent Caldwell and his men to the head of Rue de la Montagne, and hurried himself to the Cape Diamond battery. A militiaman who had scaled the height reported that Montgomery's force was in full retreat. The gunners in the Fraser house had opened fire on the vanguard, which had broken through the two fences in Près de Ville, and put Montgomery's force to flight.

The action switched to the Sault au Matelot, where the rebels broke through the first barricade and were milling about in the street. Allan sent reinforcements under Captain John Nairne to the second barricade from Rue de la Montagne and ran to report to Carleton. Both commanders agreed that the reserves waiting by the Palace Gate should go to the other end of Sault au Matelot, but not yet. By waiting they could bottle up all of Arnold's men in the narrow street. Towards six o'clock Allan hurried to the Palace Gate to give the order for Captains Macdougall and Lawes to advance, and to send a detachment to deal with the rebel gun battery in St. Roch. It was not bothering the gunners on the wall, but it might endanger the reinforcements after they left the Palace Gate.

Surprisingly quickly the firing died away, and Allan walked through the Palace Gate. As he slid down the icy hill, he saw that the blizzard had subsided. Inside the broken first barricade, rebels were surrendering everywhere, and Allan found a triumphant George Lawes. When Lawes stepped through the barricade, he was taken prisoner, but released when more men swarmed after him.

Allan had details of militia carry the wounded to the hospital in the Upper Town, while others laid out the dead. Questioning prisoners, he learned that Benedict Arnold had been wounded and taken to the rebels' hospital near St. Roch. At the battered second barricade he met a jubilant John Nairne, arms around the shoulders of two Canadians, François Dambourgès, a volunteer, and burly Charles

Charland. The latter had wrested a scaling ladder from the rebels and set it against the gable of a house. Nairne ran up, followed by Dambourgès and some Royal Highland Emigrants, and entered a second storey window. With bayonets they drove the rebels who had taken refuge there into the street. Allan promised to mention them in dispatches, and continued to Près de Ville. In front of the Fraser house was a pile of corpses half covered in snow, and he asked Captain Barnsfare if he had news of Montgomery. The defenders had brought in a wounded sergeant, but he would not say where the rebel general was.

"Damn," Allan swore, irate that both rebel commanders appeared to have escaped, but, he trusted, not for long.

Judging by the number of prisoners he had seen in Sault au Matelot, scarcely half of Arnold's and Montgomery's men had escaped back to the rebel camp. Allan turned towards the Upper Town, expecting to rally the troops for a sortie to finish the success of the early dawn. He broke into a trot, for Carleton must be anxious to start the last phase of the operation—the capture of the remaining rebels on the Plains of Abraham.

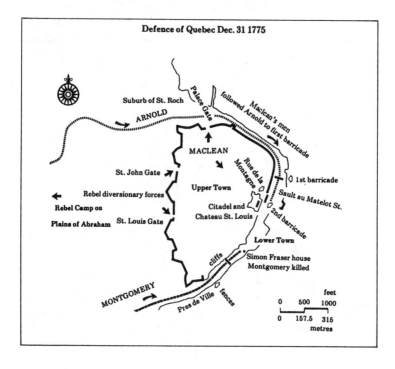

Defence of Quebec Dec. 31 1775

Chapter Thirteen

Canada Freed 1776

Outside the Recollect Monastery Allan found Lieutenant-Colonel Caldwell and Captain John Hamilton, coming to report. Both were as keen as Allan to begin mopping up operations as they entered Carleton's office.[1] "No!" Carleton replied coldly to Allan's request to marshall the division for a sortie.

"We've had so few casualties, General," Allan argued.

"One naval officer killed, five militia wounded, two of them mortally," Carleton recited. "The troops have had enough for today."

"They're not half as tired as the rebels, sir," Allan pressed on, a flush spreading over his face. "I hope you won't think me impertinent, but now is the time to strike and end this farce."

"We have 500 prisoners to put somewhere. More than forty are wounded, but the rest could make mischief if I emptied the city of troops," Carleton said impatiently.

"There can't be more than 700 in the rebel camp," Caldwell pleaded. "And some of them are wounded or sick."

"No!" Carleton repeated. "We have provisions to last until May, and we have no need to take risks."

The governor dismissed Caldwell and Hamilton, and Allan remained to work out arrangements for the prisoners. The officers would be sent to the seminary, the rank and file confined in the Recollect College and Monastery. Meanwhile, a soldier brought a message from Près de Ville. General Richard Montgomery's body had been identified among the corpses outside the Fraser house. Carleton ordered a coffin built for Montgomery. Funeral services for the rebel general, and for Captain Andrews, a lieutenant in the navy, were held on 4 January 1776. By that time Carleton had moved back to the Chateau St. Louis, and Allan had returned to the Golden Dog.

Soon Carleton moved the rank and file prisoners to the Dauphin Jail, and he presented Allan with a novel proposal. He wanted to allow prisoners of British birth to enlist in the

Royal Highland Emigrants. At first Allan was opposed, but Carleton insisted that the men were Britons who had been misguided by the colonists, who would themselves soon come to their senses. Reluctantly Allan accepted ninety-four prisoners, most of them Irish, as a means of helping complete his battalion. At Allan's suggestion, Carleton approved a lieutenancy in the Royal Highland Emigrants for François Dambourgès, the volunteer who had scrambled up the ladder after Captain Nairne in Sault au Matelot.

As the snow was beginning to melt, Carleton appointed Allan his adjutant-general, a reward for the fine work he had done preparing Quebec for the siege.[2] Allan was pleased, for the promotion meant a small increase in pay, but the job was an administrative one and he wanted a field command. However, since Carleton had no intention of attacking the rebels still on the Plains of Abraham, that did not matter. Melting snow also revealed that rebel casualties had been greater than assumed in January, for residents who returned to Près de Ville reported finding twenty more bodies outside the Fraser house.

Some of the prisoners who enlisted in the Royal Highland Emigrants proved untrustworthy. They tried to desert, and Allan had to take away their arms. Finally Carleton ordered certain ringleaders discharged and confined in the holds of ships in the harbour, as a warning to the rest to behave.

Now spies reported that rebel reinforcements were coming down Lake Champlain, and Allan fumed over Carleton's refusal to attack the rebel camp on 31 December. All told, some 4,000 fresh troops were reaching Sorel, Montreal, the outposts at St. Jean and at the Cedars Rapids west of Montreal. While Carleton had kept his little army inactive behind Quebec's defences, the rebels had strengthened their hold on Montreal, and might be more difficult to dislodge. To an unidentified friend, possibly Lord Loudoun, Allan wrote, "timidity in the field My Lord is a dangerous matter, for I am convinced few Generals are capable of waging a defensive war."[3]

Carleton also lost his chance to capture Benedict Arnold, who had moved to Montreal. Brigadier David Wooster had taken command of the rebel camp on the Plains of Abraham.

On 6 May, the frigate *Surprise*, the first of the spring fleet, reached Quebec with troops and provisions. At last Carleton felt he had the resources to take the offensive. With Allan and his Royal Highland Emigrants as the vanguard, Carleton's army of regulars and militia marched from the St. Jean and St. Louis Gates towards the rebel camp. The rebels, now commanded by Major-General John Thomas, offered no resistance. They fled, leaving masses of equipment and personal belongings. In the empty camp Allan found a meal laid out for the rebel officers, which he allowed his men to consume.[4]

Allan was eager to follow the retreating rebels, but Carleton was content to have them out of sight. As he led his men back into the city, Allan was disgusted. Carleton was deliberately letting rebels escape. War was war, and it needed to be conducted according to the rules. Carleton should be capturing as many rebels as possible and releasing them on parole, a condition that would keep them inactive until exchanged for a like number of British prisoners-of-war. The governor's leniency might mean that Britons would languish in rebel jails instead of being freed through prisoner exchanges.

Carleton lingered in the Chateau St. Louis, where Allan, scarcely able to contain his impatience, assisted him. Carleton was more concerned with French and English disloyalty in his midst than with the retreating rebels. Men who had left Quebec because of the governor's proclamation of 22 November were not to return, and he took pains to identify persons who had collaborated with the rebels. Not until 22 May did Carleton, with Allan and his regiment, and detachments of the 29th and 47th Regiments, embark for Trois Rivières. When the ships arrived, a messenger brought word that by 20 May, Captain George Forster, from Fort Oswegatchie, with some of his 8th Regiment and many Indians sent from Fort Niagara by John Butler, had captured the rebel outpost at The Cedars and taken 400 prisoners. Forster was arranging the exchange of some of these for the British soldiers captured last November with Colonel Richard Prescott. Allan would soon have those Royal Highland Emigrants returned to him.

He was cheered by the news, and desperate to have Carleton move on to Montreal while the rebels were off balance, but the governor hesitated. On 2 June a courier arrived to report that the rest of the spring fleet had reached Quebec the day before, bringing General John Burgoyne and 8,000 fresh troops. More than half were British regulars, and the rest were German regulars from George III's Hanover dependencies. The latter were commanded by General the Baron Friedrich von Riedesel. Carleton left Allan in command of the troops at Trois Rivières, and hurried back to Quebec to welcome Burgoyne and von Riedesel.

Allan disembarked the men and began setting up camp. On the 5th he was joined by Lieutenant-Colonel Simon Fraser, the commander of the 24th Regiment, with four battalions of regulars. Behind Fraser, Lieutenant-Colonel William Nesbitt of the 47th Regiment had embarked in ships with another brigade and would take up a position above Trois Rivières. Fraser brought a thick letter from Major John Small in Halifax, and eager as Allan was to open it, he first helped Fraser disembark his battalions and choose space for their tents. Once free, Allan broke the seal on Small's letter and studied its contents. Most of the news was bad.

In March, General Gage had evacuated Boston and brought the British army and some Loyalist refugees to Halifax. Worse, many of Allan's officers and recruits were prisoners of the rebels. Captain Duncan Campbell and Lieutenant James Symes, with twenty-three recruits, had left Boston on a privateer last October for New York, hoping to make their way to Canada. The privateer had been captured at sea.

Then on 27 February, in North Carolina, some 1,500 Highlanders led by Major Donald Macdonald, had set out for the coast on a rumour that a British fleet was approaching. At a bridge over Moore's Creek, the Highlanders had clashed with the rebels. Some thirty had been killed, among them Captain Donald Macleod, and 850 were captured. Among the prisoners were Captain Allan Macdonald and Lieutenant James Macdonald, the famous Flora's husband and son, and the regimental chaplain, the Reverend John Bethune. All had been taken to Philadelphia.[5]

Allan put the letter down, badly shaken. In North Carolina he had hoped to raise a third battalion, but the disaster at Moore's Creek bridge might rule this out. Major

Small's next disclosure raised Allan's blood pressure still more, for the royal governor of North Carolina, Josiah Martin, had flouted the King's plan to have all Highlanders serve in the Royal Highland Emigrants.

The treacherous Martin had given commissions to Allan's officers. He made Major Macdonald a brigadier-general and Captain Macleod a lieutenant-colonel, and had formed his own corps, the North Carolina Highlanders. The governor was empire-building, and had purloined Allan's officers and potential recruits. Major Small had saved a scrap of good news for the last. Allan's young brother-in-law Hector had the makings of a fine officer, and recruiting for the second battalion was going well. Small expected to have a complete battalion by the end of the year. Allan felt a twinge of envy, for the first battalion stood at scarcely 400 men—the 230 who had been with him at the siege of Quebec, the men captured with Colonel Prescott who would soon be exchanged, and the not too reliable American prisoners. Depressed, Allan put the letter away and returned to work.

Lieutenant-Colonel Fraser exercised his troops for they were out of condition after the long, cramped sea voyage to Quebec. Despite the weakness of the troops, Fraser's arrival was timely. On the morning of 7 June, Captain Landron, of the Canadian Militia, who had been scouting for Allan, reported that 2,000 rebels led by Brigadier William Thompson, were approaching from Sorel and might arrive in a few hours.

Landron had asked a local farmer, Antoine Gautier, to volunteer to guide them. If Thompson accepted him, Gautier intended leading the rebels through a vast swamp, rather than show them the road. Allan informed Fraser, who was delighted at the prospect of a scrap where little marching was involved. They inspected the terrain and formed a line of battle on open land that bordered the swamp. All went as Captain Landron predicted. Gautier led the rebels into the morass through which they stumbled, emerging exhausted to face Fraser's battalions. Rebel losses were 160 killed and 236 captured, including Brigadier Thompson. The rest fled into the swamp and some gained the road, where Lieutenant-Colonel Nesbitt's men, still aboard their ships, fired on them.

The following day Carleton sent an order for all troops at Trois Rivières to board transports and await further instructions, except 1,200 of Fraser's men, who would march by land. On the night of the 13th, Carleton returned, accompanied by Burgoyne, von Riedesel and the rest of the reinforcements. The fleet now numbered eighty ships, carrying some 7,000 men. At dawn on the 14th the fleet sailed and lay off Sorel by evening. The grenadiers and light infantry landed first, followed by Nesbitt's division. The rebels, commanded by Major-General John Sullivan, had already withdrawn up the Richelieu River towards Fort Chambly.

Carleton divided his troops into two divisions, each of 4,000 men. Burgoyne was detailed to lead one division up the Richelieu in pursuit of Sullivan. Carleton would lead the remaining 4,000 men, which included Allan's Royal Highland Emigrants, von Riedesel's Germans, and Fraser's men, to Montreal. The fleet arrived on 17 June, and was greeted by the Canadian Militia. Benedict Arnold had ordered a retreat. His scouts had reported seeing Fraser's redcoats downstream on the 13th, and on the 15th, when Arnold discovered that Sullivan had evacuated Sorel, he took only four hours to withdraw his troops from Montreal. Arnold had ordered the town put to the torch, but in their haste his men had set only a few fires, which the militia quickly extinguished.

Allan found quarters in a house rented by the government, which he shared with Lieutenant-Colonel Watson Powell, of the 53rd Regiment. Carleton stayed in the Chateau Ramezay, which had been Arnold's headquarters. The following day, the 18th, Carleton left to inspect Fort Chambly, and Sir John Johnson arrived with some 200 followers. The baronet was in a fiery mood, in rags, footwear worn through after a march from Johnstown over the Adirondack Mountains to elude pursuit. Not finding Carleton, he sought out Allan.[6]

"I left Johnson Hall when my Indians warned me a warrant had been issued for my arrest," Sir John said grimly. "We were subsisting on berries and leaves. The damn rebs disarmed all my tenants and we couldn't hunt along the way. The only weapon they left was a brass 3-

pounder. We took that up into the mountains, and abandoned it when the men grew too weak to drag it."

"How may I serve you, Sir John?" Allan enquired.

"Billets," the baronet replied briefly. "For myself and the 200 tenants who came with me."

"I'll be happy to arrange that," Allan assured him.

On the 19th, Sir John set out after Carleton, and when he returned from Fort Chambly he had a warrant to raise his own battalion, the King's Royal Regiment of New York, from among his tenants. This disconcerted Allan, and he worried that many of the Highlanders he had recruited in the Mohawk Valley might be pirated to Sir John's regiment. Completing his first battalion might not be easily accomplished. Not only that, one of Sir John's officers informed him that his captain-lieutenant, John Munro, who had guided him to the Mohawk Valley the summer before, had been taken prisoner and was in jail in Albany. Since Allan could not do without a captain-lieutenant indefinitely, he promoted Lieutenant Neil Maclean to take direct command of the lieutenant-colonel's company.

Recruiting in the rebelling colonies seemed almost out of the question, and the only safe places to look for men were Canada, Newfoundland, and Nova Scotia. Gloomily, Allan admitted that unless British authority could be restored quickly in at least some of the colonies, he would have to settle for only two battalions. Furthermore the regiment deserved to be made a regular one, not just a provincial corps that was inferior to the numbered regiments of the British establishment.

To achieve this end, Allan had to get to London, where he could exert pressure on Prime Minister Lord North and Secretary at War Lord Barrington, as well as the Secretary of State for the Colonies, Lord George Germain. He asked Carleton for a leave of absence when the governor returned after viewing the ruins of Fort St. Jean as well as Chambly. Both forts had been burnt by the rebels before they withdrew. Carleton was planning the capture of Fort Ticonderoga, but, he informed Allan, he would use only regulars. The Royal Highland Emigrants would remain in Montreal. Since the regiment would not see action, the senior captain, John Nairne, could command the men, and Carleton said Allan could go whenever he pleased.

Men representing the light and battalion companies of the King's Royal Regiment of New York. This re-created regiment appears at many demonstrations both in Canada and in the United States. The participants belong to the Museum of Applied Military History, a Canadian group.

Allan boarded a ship assigned to carry Carleton's dispatches on the successful expulsion of the rebels from Canada, and he reached London by mid-August. At York Buildings, Janet was overjoyed to have him home. She had been very worried when she had no news of him during the siege of Quebec. Then, in July, the newspapers had published glowing reports of Carleton's success, and had praised Allan's contribution as well as the exploits of his Royal Highland Emigrants. The King had bestowed a knighthood on Carleton for saving Quebec City. Allan thought of how much more Carleton might have accomplished; the governor really merited a court martial.

Allan found his twelve-year-old son thriving, but his landlord and crony, Jack Stewart, the wine merchant, was in poor health. He was living quietly and had resigned his seat in Parliament. Little John Stewart was still in India, and had become Judge Advocate General and Secretary to the Governor General, Warren Hastings, and to the Council of Bengal.

Henry Macleane, who had shared the house at Brick Court with Allan and Janet, had died in India in 1774, but Lauchlin was in London, and had taken a house in Berkeley Square. The children, John and Harriet, were with him, and their nurse, Jane Satterthwaite, was now the randy Lauchlin's mistress. At the first opportunity Allan went to see Lauchlin, who had returned from India in July 1775.

"I resigned as Commissary General of the Army in Bengal," Lauchlin said. "After a bit of trouble with one of the councillors, Sir Philip Francis, but that did me little harm. Clive's successor, Warren Hastings, approves of me, and I am his political agent, as well as agent for the Nabob of Arcot."

"Where's that?" Allan enquired absently, his mind on the favour he wanted to ask Lauchlin.

"Near Madras," Lauchlin replied. "Now, tell me about Quebec. There are those who think the battle honours were yours, not Carleton's."

Allan relayed a brief account of the siege and relief of Quebec, which gave him the opening he needed. After stressing how well his battalion had performed, he asked Lauchlin to use his influence to have the Royal Highland

Emigrants put on the British establishment. Lauchlin frowned, thought for a moment, then beamed. He often saw Lord North and he would see what he could do. Allan departed, confident that Lauchlin's magic would work. Meanwhile, he had much to occupy him.[7]

He sent a letter to headquarters in Halifax, requesting that his baggage, left in Boston in care of Major Small, and his private papers from the ship *Asia* be forwarded to the Golden Dog Tavern, as well as the colours of the regiment. He arranged to sail on 24 September for Quebec, and would take the uniforms for the first battalion with him. Those for the second battalion he arranged to have shipped to Halifax. He had thought of spending the winter with Janet, but changed his mind. He should use the time when campaigning was finished for the season to complete his battalion.

On that score Allan was disappointed. The ship was delayed by storms and what he called "contrary winds" and the captain found too much ice in the Gulf of St. Lawrence. Fearing that Quebec would be ice-bound, he sent a bulletin that the ship would make for New York instead. The British army under Sir William Howe had occupied the city in September. This was news to Allan and he hastened to the captain for more details. The message had come by ship's boat from an outward-bound vessel carrying Howe's dispatches home. Howe had sailed from Halifax in August, defeated the rebel commander-in-chief, George Washington, on Long Island, and taken Manhattan and part of Rhode Island.

On landing, Allan arranged to have his regiment's equipment stored and went to General Howe's headquarters in Fort George, in the city. To his astonishment, five companies of his second battalion had been part of Howe's expeditionary force, and Major Small had commanded them. Both Small and young Hector were staying near the fort. When Allan found Small, he learned that the second battalion was complete, and the major hoped to be promoted to lieutenant-colonel, to which Allan readily agreed. Once the first battalion was at strength, Allan wanted a new lieutenant-colonel so that he could become a full colonel. Of the second battalion, five companies would remain on garrison duty in

Halifax, while Small would take the other five on campaigns through the southern colonies.

Since he could not get to Quebec until spring, Allan reconciled himself to spending the winter in New York. One matter that had to be settled was a division of officers between the two battalions. During their deliberations, Ensign John Macdonell, who had received his commission in Montreal, arrived and asked to be promoted to lieutenant in the first battalion. As Allan had no vacancies, he offered Macdonell a lieutenancy in the second battalion. At a later date he might persuade one of his lieutenants to switch with him since Macdonell wanted to serve in Canada.[8]

In April 1777, not long before a ship was to try for Quebec, Allan's nephew, Lauchlin Maclean of Baltimore, joined him after a tortuous journey. Lauchlin had left Baltimore in the spring of 1776 on a ship bound for Europe, after being in hiding for a year because the rebels were after him. He then went to Halifax, but being unable to find a passage to Quebec, he had come to New York and joined Major Small in time to take part in the last stages of the capture of Manhattan. Then he sailed for England, convinced that getting to Quebec would be simpler from there. He returned to New York when he learned that Allan's ship was bound for that port. Now the two of them would go to Quebec together. Lauchlin had a double commission in the first battalion, signed by General Gage on 14 June 1775, as a lieutenant and the quartermaster.

They reached Quebec in mid-May, and Allan went to the Chateau St. Louis to receive his orders from the governor, now *Sir* Guy Carleton. Allan was feeling uneasy. His leg was troubling him, and he prayed that he would be fit for active duty in the coming campaign.

Chapter Fourteen

Governor of Montreal
1777-1779

Sir Guy Carleton told Allan that he had received a letter from Lord Germain, who stated that the Royal Highland Emigrants were being considered for the regular establishment. Lauchlin Macleane had not failed him. General Burgoyne, who had also spent the winter in England, had come back to Quebec on 6 May with a commission to command the British army in the field. He was to proceed up Lake Champlain, capture Ticonderoga, which Carleton had failed to do the previous autumn, and reach Albany. There he was to place himself under the command of Sir William Howe, the commander of the Central Department, based at New York City. Although Carleton knew the reason why he had been superseded, he was nevertheless affronted.

Since Carleton was senior to Howe, he could not be his subordinate, and thus Burgoyne, junior to both, had been given the field command, as a matter of military etiquette. Burgoyne would be taking four fledgling corps of provincials, recruited from among loyalists now in Canada, that would be augmented by loyalists in the colonies as the army marched south. The corps leaders were Ebenezer Jessup, John Peters, Daniel McAlpin, and Francis Pfister—all loyalists from New york. A small expedition was to move from Oswego through the Mohawk Valley to meet Burgoyne at Albany, and it would be commanded by Lieutenant-Colonel Barry St. Leger of the 34th Regiment. With St. Leger would go some regulars, Sir John Johnson's King's Royal Regiment of New York, and John Butler in command of a detachment of Indians from Fort Niagara.

The Royal Highland Emigrants would stay in Canada, for Burgoyne distrusted the American prisoners in the ranks, who would desert at first opportunity.[1]

"Damn!" Allan exclaimed, leaping to his feet. "I apologize, General, but I know that's not his real reason. He

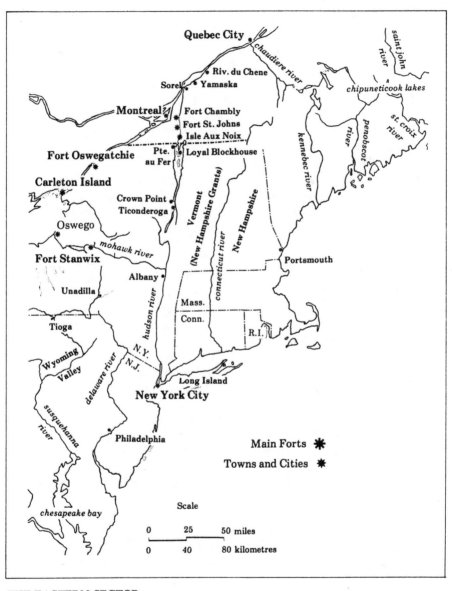

Quebec City

Riv. du Chene

Sorel • Yamaska

Montreal

Fort Chambly
Fort St. Johns
Isle Aux Noix

Fort Oswegatchie

Pte.
au Fer   Loyal Blockhouse

Carleton Island

Crown Point
Ticonderoga

Oswego

Fort Stanwix

mohawk river

Albany •

Unadilla

Mass.

Conn.

Tioga

R.I.

Wyoming
Valley

N.Y.

N.J.

hudson river

delaware river

Long Island

New York City

*susquehanna
river*

Philadelphia

Vermont
(New Hampshire Grants)

connecticut river

New Hampshire

Portsmouth

chaudiere river

kennebec river

*penobscot
river*

*st. croix
river*

*saint john
river*

chipuneticook lakes

Main Forts ✳

Towns and Cities ✳

Scale

0	25	50 miles
0	40	80 kilometres

chesapeake bay

THE EASTERN SECTOR

thinks we're a pack of howling Jacobites. That's why he won't take us."

"You're probably right, Colonel," Carleton said softly. "He detests Jacobites, I know."

"As soon as I can get enough reliable men, I want to retire those prisoners, if you will permit, sir."

"I will," Carleton promised him. "I'll have them exchanged or sent home on parole as soon as you no longer need them for numbers."

Carleton promoted Allan to brigadier-general in Canada, although he would remain a lieutenant-colonel in the army, and appointed him governor of Montreal. Allan had done such a fine job in organizing for the defence of Quebec, and as Adjutant-General that Carleton wanted him for the important task of defending Canada's second largest community, one that was poorly sited compared with Quebec City. The governor asked him to hurry to his new posting, for General Burgoyne would require his assistance in organizing the expedition. When Allan left for Montreal, he took the baggage that had been forwarded from Halifax with his private papers and the regimental colours, as well as the new uniforms he had brought from New York. His nephew Lauchlin went with him to take his place in the first battalion. Allan stayed in the house he shared with Lieutenant-Colonel Watson Powell before his leave.

Captain John Nairne reported that the regiment had received new recruits from Mohawk Valley. Captain John Macdonell, of Sir John Johnson's regiment, had arrived with 100 men, some for Sir John, the others for Allan.[2] The Royal Highland Emigrants captured with Colonel Prescott the year before were now back on duty.

The men of Allan's battalion were patrolling between St. Jean and Montreal, except for the prisoners, who were working as artificers and labourers in the town. Even at that, Captain Nairne had had to order his patrols to look for deserters, for some had managed to slip away.

Gleefully, Allan had the new uniforms distributed. The green and buff coats would not be disposed of, but kept for fatigue duty. On parade, however, the men would look splendid in red coats, Black Watch tartan and blue bonnets. If Burgoyne thought of them as Jacobites, they now looked the part, even though the tartan they sported was acceptable to the government. As a gesture of defiance Allan put the white cockade he had worn during the battle for Quebec back into his bonnet. The first time Burgoyne noticed, his eyes widened, but he made no comment. With a good grace Allan did all he could to help Burgoyne prepare his expeditionary force, which would number some 9,000 men, counting St. Leger's 1,000. With Burgoyne would go the Baron von Riedesel and most of the German troops although some would remain as part of the Canadian garrison.

In his spare time Allan befriended wives and children of loyalists who had been brought to Montreal for safety. By early June, Burgoyne was gathering his force at the foot of Lake Champlain, ready to embark in ships, gunboats and bateaux, his Indian allies in canoes. Allan persuaded his cousin, Lieutenant Archibald Maclean, to switch to the second battalion to accommodate Lieutenant John Macdonell, now back in Montreal and more eager than ever to be in the first battalion. Allan sent Archibald to Fort St. Jean with a letter to Burgoyne explaining that his lieutenant was joining Sir William Howe's army in New York.[3]

The supply situation was still not good, and much of Burgoyne's efforts, and those of his troops, would go into moving provisions to keep pace with the advancing army. The early news was cause for rejoicing. Burgoyne took Ticonderoga on 6 July, but then, like Carleton, he appeared to be too lenient with the enemy. He let the rebel garrison escape to the Hudson River without trying to intercept it. After that, all the news was bad. Burgoyne lost 1,200 provincials and Germain regulars at Bennington on 16 August. The first report indicated that John Peters and his eldest son had been killed at Bennington, and Allan hastened to the house the Peters family occupied in Montreal. Gently he warned John's wife Ann to expect the worst. Mrs. Peters raised her head and squared her shoulders.

"Thank God they died doing their duty for their King and country," she said bravely. "I have six sons left who as soon as they shall be able to bear arms, I will send against the rebels while I and my daughter will mourn for the dead and pray for the living."[4]

Colonel St. Leger was unable to drive the rebel garrison from Fort Stanwix, because he lacked heavy guns, and was now withdrawing to Oswego until guns could be sent from Fort Niagara. Soon St. Leger and Sir John Johnson arrived in Montreal, for Burgoyne had ordered them to come to reinforce him on the Hudson River. He could not expect much help from New York City, for Sir William Howe had taken most of his army by sea to capture Philadelphia.

Carleton was preparing to send part of his garrison, and John Butler called on Allan at the beginning of September. He was on his way to Quebec City to ask Carleton for a warrant to raise a corps of rangers to operate on the frontier with the officers and men of the Indian Department.[5] Allan was quick to notice that Carleton was not sending the Royal Highland Emigrants, no doubt because Burgoyne disapproved of them.

By October, Burgoyne's now poorly supplied army was badly outnumbered near Saratoga, and his only salvation would be a successful retreat. Carleton sent an order for Allan to take his battalion to Chimney Point, on Lake Champlain, to meet the army—fresh troops who could protect Burgoyne's rear from pursuing rebels. Allan organized brigades of bateaux filled with supplies, some for his men, some for Burgoyne's, and moved down the St. Lawrence and up the Richelieu, portaging the rapids near Fort Chambly. Five days later they were setting up camp at Chimney Point, and watching for troops from the south.

Couriers passed between Chimney Point and Ticonderoga, a day's march southwards, where Burgoyne had left a garrison under Watson Powell. To Allan, Powell reported that Captain Samuel Mackay, his old friend from the Scots Brigade and the 60th Regiment, had arrived from Saratoga with some provincials. Francis Pfister had been killed at Bennington, and Burgoyne had given the command of his men to Mackay. St. Leger returned with his reinforcements, having gone to the end of Lake George, and with him came provincials who said that Burgoyne had allowed them to escape from Saratoga. He feared that provincials would be regarded as traitors by the rebels if he surrendered, whereas regulars would be prisoners of war.

When a scout told Allan that some Canadian militiamen working near Ticonderoga were dying of exposure because they lacked warm clothing, he ordered a bateau to take him to the fort. Allan told Watson Powell of the plight of the men, but Powell had permission to supply only Burgoyne's troops. These men belonged to Canada, and Burgoyne's now belonged to the Central Department at New York City. Allan left his regiment under the command of Captain John Nairne, took a bateau to Montreal, ordered the clothing from some merchants, brought it to the militiamen and returned to Chimney Point.[6]

Early in November a courier arrived from Carleton. Burgoyne had surrendered on 17 October, and Allan was to relay an order to Brigadier Powell to destroy anything of value to the rebels and evacuate Ticonderoga. The Royal Highland Emigrants were to use scorched earth tactics from Ile aux Noix at the head of the Richelieu, to St. Jean, in case the rebels should move north, then they were to return to Montreal. Allan lay in a bateau sheltered by an awning while his men worked on the shore. The cold was too much for his bad leg, and he was lame and in pain.

Yet he felt optimistic about the war. Ultimately Britain would succeed, for he remembered the many reverses of the early years of the Seven Years' War, and the successes that followed. He wasted no sympathy on Burgoyne, but he was saddened and angry at the suffering the army had endured. Burgoyne had planned a summer campaign and his troops had no winter clothing. Among the dead was Simon Fraser, Allan's compatriot at the battle of Trois Rivières, whom Burgoyne had made a brigadier-general. Some 3,000 British and German soldiers were prisoners-of-war, and 300 provincials were unaccounted for. Allan cursed Carleton's idiocy in letting so many rebels slip through his fingers in 1776. Only the 500 taken in the Lower Town of Quebec, whom Carleton had sent home on parole in August, were eligible for prisoner exchanges, and the prisoners captured by Captain Forster at the Cedars who had not been returned in exchange for those taken near Sorel with Colonel Prescott. Allan feared that many British soldiers might suffer long terms of confinement.

He was soon busy finding billets for the provincials who had returned to Canada, which included John Peters and his son. All told, 468 were at St. Jean and around Montreal. Of these, 272 had escaped from Saratoga before the surrender, and 196 were on parole.[7] Despite Burgoyne's concern that his provincials would be considered traitors, the rebels had

The Brigade of the American Revolution re-created military units of the period, including British and Loyalist regiments. These men in the regimentals of the 84th Regiment Royal Highland Emigrants are from the Ottawa area and were associated with the Brigade during bicentennial celebrations of the 1970s and 80s.

agreed that all prisoners would be regarded as British subjects. Provincials still held were those that were captured earlier in the campaign and were not at the surrender.

Carleton ordered Allan to treat the provincials who had been with Burgoyne as refugees. Once Burgoyne crossed into New York, his army belonged to Sir William Howe and the Central Department at New York City. If Burgoyne's officers were allowed to recruit in Canada, which was the Northern Department, they might deprive Carleton's own provincial corps—Allan's Royal Highland Emigrants, Sir John Johnson's King's Royal Regiment of New York, and Butler's Rangers—of many recruits. Carleton wanted all potential recruits saved for his own regiments, not allowed to enlist under officers who might be called to New York by Howe. Allan approved of Carleton's order, for he was anxious to bring his Royal Highland Emigrants to strength without delay.

In November, with Carleton's permission, Allan set out for Quebec on leave to receive medical treatment in London. His leg had become so painful that riding was out of the question and he went by stage-coach. Reflecting, he admitted that his battalion had been lucky in not going with Burgoyne. His leg would never have held up, and the battalion would now be decimated, to no avail. Once he had been treated by Drs. Hunter and Huck, Allan resolved to return and start a recruiting drive to complete his battalion, and he hoped, when he saw his men, he could tell them they were British regulars. Carrying a pack of letters for Carleton, who had resigned but could not leave until a new governor arrived, Allan limped aboard a vessel for the journey home.

He was sorely disappointed, for again winter set in early. After viewing the ice in the Gulf of St. Lawrence, the ship's captain turned back to Quebec. Allan returned to Montreal in a sleigh, fairly comfortable under bearskin robes, hot bricks wrapped in flannel at his feet. He now had the house to himself most of the time, for Carleton had appointed Watson Powell commandant of Fort St. Jean with the rank of brigadier-general. A letter from Janet was waiting for him and he broke the seal eagerly. Lauchlin Macleane was back in India, having sailed in June, leaving two pregnant mistresses—Jane Satterthwaite at the house in

Berkeley Square, and a Lady Mary Walker, who lived near a country retreat Lauchlin had bought in Essex.[8]

The 1778 season was devoted to recovering from the loss of Burgoyne's army. Allan had officers out recruiting, mainly in Canada, but some had gone into the northern colonies. Four were captured—Lieutenants Neil Maclean, François Dambourgès and Alexander Stratton, and Ensign Hector Maclean, the latter a cousin with the same name as Allan's brother-in-law.[9] The rebels now held these officers, as well as those captured at sea out of Boston and in North Carolina. The rebels held the lion's share of the prisoners, a serious situation for few could be exchanged.

In May, scouting parties in quest of information on rebel movements, returned and reported that in February, in Paris, France had signed a military alliance with the Continental Congress. The rebels expected France to send troops, and some of Allan's brother officers maintained that the French could easily capture Canada. Allan disagreed. The French had been successful in the early phases of the Seven Years' War, mainly because of their Indian allies. This time the might of the tribes was mainly on Britain's side, for the mother country favoured restricting white settlement to the eastern seaboard. British policy of reserving the interior of the continent was keeping many Indians loyal.

At the end of June, General Frederick Haldimand arrived to succeed Carleton. Haldimand was a true friend, whose association with Allan went back to the Scots Brigade days. Allan wrote to Haldimand on 1 July, asking for leave as soon as convenient. The physicians had advised him that he must be treated by the best men in London if he was ever to recover the use of his leg:

> Give me leave to assure Your Excellency, that was it to save my Life, I could not walk over the walls of Quebec, nor am I able to ride on horseback by having a continual pain in the sole of my foot, and my leg is wasted & grown much smaller than the other.[10]

His preoccupation with this misery was interrupted by the arrival in Montreal of Lieutenant Archibald Maclean, whom Allan had sent with Burgoyne as a way of moving him to the second battalion. Archibald had been wounded, captured and taken to Boston where the rebels clapped him in irons and held him in the hold of a ship. He escaped and reached New York City, by which time he was owed considerable back pay, which he could not collect because Major John Small was on leave in England. After so many misadventures, Archibald no longer wanted to replace John Macdonell in the second battalion. Allan sent for Macdonell and explained that he would have to join the companies of the second battalion that were in Halifax, which displeased the junior officer. A fortnight later he learned that Macdonell had accepted a captaincy from John Butler, to serve at Fort Niagara. Allan was happy to be rid of the troublesome man, and he knew that Major Small would easily find another lieutenant for his battalion.[11]

Haldimand granted Allan leave, and promoted Captain John Nairne to the rank of major. Donald Macdonald, the original major of the first battalion, had been exchanged. He was made a major in the army and had accepted a staff appointment in Quebec City rather than return to the Royal Highland Emigrants. Allan sailed from Quebec in August, after conferring with Haldimand on the need for more prisoner exchanges. The prospects were poor, because the rebels held the lion's share of the prisoners still. Until the British had a like number of prisoners, few exchanges could take place.

At New York City, Sir Henry Clinton, who had replaced Sir William Howe as the commander of the Central Department, had opened negotiations for the return on parole of the Baron von Riedesel and other officers. When Howe took Philadelphia, he had expected to release many loyalists, but he found that they had been moved to remote parts of Pennsylvania as his fleet approached. Thus Allan might not receive the officers and recruits captured in North Carolina in 1776 for some time yet.

When Allan reached London, Janet told him that Lauchlin Macleane was dead. He was sailing home from India when his ship sank in the Bay of Biscay in February 1778 with no survivors. Robert Orme, Lauchlin's one time spy in East India House, was trying to untangle Lauchlin's finances and provide some security for his children.[12] Allan groaned, both at the loss of his benefactor and the thought that his regiment would never be made into a regular one that was part of the British establishment.

Janet also had news of his cousin Francis, whom Allan had not seen since 1763 when both men left Britain to elude creditors. Francis was now lieutenant-colonel of the Duke of Hamilton's Regiment, the 82nd Foot, and he had sailed for Halifax with his regiment in June. Allan felt a twinge of envy, and anxious to complete his battalion he wasted no time in sending for Drs. Hunter and Huck. Both men thought they could restore Allan's leg but it would take time. He should not think of returning to duty until the spring. He settled down to a restful winter with Janet, enjoying the company of his son, who was doing well at his studies.

About that time Allan and Janet adopted a child, but as with his son, Allan never identified this child by name in his written records .[13] The new addition to his family could have been one of Lauchlin Macleane's children. Jane Satterthwaite was taking care of John and Harriet Macleane, Lauchlin's children by Penelope Agnew, and her own child by Lauchlin, but money was scarce. Allan's obligation was to Lauchlin's dependents. Any needy child in his own family would have been the responsibility of his elder brother Lachlan, the 7th laird of Torloisk, who had become wealthy through the kelp industry, still flourishing on Mull.

Allan's household had grown larger as the years passed. None of Janet's sisters married, and some made their home at York Buildings. The main support of the household was Allan's pay, for apparently his father-in-law had died leaving his second wife and their son, Fitzroy Jeffreys Grafton, with only a small pension. On this leave Allan felt the pinch more than on the previous one, because he stayed longer, making do on a lieutenant-colonel's wages, not those of a brigadier-general which he enjoyed while in Canada.

Christmas brought Allan a welcome present from the War Office. As of 24 December 1778, the Royal Highland Emigrants were on the British regular establishment as the 84th Foot.[14] Even though Lauchlin Macleane was dead, he had done the spade work which influenced Lord North. Now Allan could hardly wait to return to duty, although his leg was responding slowly, as his doctors had warned him. This time they prescribed small doses of laudanum, a tincture of opium, for the pain, but cautioned him to use it sparingly.

"Some people think Clive of India committed suicide," Dr. Huck said. "I don't. Clive was taking laudanum for the pain of gallstones. I believe he did not intend to kill himself, but the pain was so great that he took too much."

"I'll do without it," Allan said, alarmed.

"You may while you're home, but," Dr. Huck added. "You will be glad of it when you return to Canada and the cold."

Stretching his means, Allan set aside 150 pounds for his brother-in-law Hector to purchase a lieutenancy in what he delighted in calling his 84th Regiment. This sum was the difference between the 400 pounds Allan would realize from the sale of Hector's ensigncy and the 550 pounds needed for a lieutenancy. The promotion would improve the morale of the clan. Sir Allan Maclean, still living on the Isle of Inch Kenneth, was in failing health, and Hector would soon be the 23rd chief.

Allan sent his son to the War Office frequently for news. In June, Sir Henry Clinton evacuated Philadelphia, but he arranged some prisoner exchanges. Many of Allan's officers and men, including Captain Allan Macdonald and his son James, had reached New York City. Major Small sent them to Halifax to recuperate and to train with Captain Alexander Macdonald. Butler's Rangers had raided Wyoming, Pennsylvania, in July and Cherry Valley, New York, in November. A British expeditionary force captured Savannah, Georgia, in December, and present were Major Small and five companies of the second battalion 84th Regiment Royal Highland Emigrants.

On the first day of March, a chair brought Allan's brother-in-law Hector to York Buildings. Allan and Janet were shocked at his appearance. He had become so ill that Major Small had sent him home, fearful the seventeen-year-old youth was dying. At first Allan agreed, but in a few days Hector was responding to the attentions of Drs. Hunter and Huck. He continued to improve, but the doctors warned Allan that the boy should not return to duty until the spring of 1780, to ensure a full recovery. Allan wrote Major Small telling him when to expect Hector.[15]

The young veteran regaled the family with tales of his adventures at the siege of Savannah before he succumbed. An ardent audience was Allan's fourteen-year-old son, who begged his father for an ensign's commission in the 84th Regiment. Regretfully Allan had to refuse the boy. "My battalion is nearly complete, son. More levies will soon be raised, and I may be able to procure a commission for you in a new regiment."

Allan wrote to his old commander, Lord Loudoun, still in his London townhouse. The following day, Loudoun sent a reply. He would look into the matter and see what he could do. He still detested the custom of purchasing commissions, which restricted promising young talent to the lower ranks.

By April, Allan was ready to sail, his leg much better although he would always have a limp. He could ride, and felt ready to "walk over the walls of Quebec." By 2 June 1779, he was back on duty in Montreal, writing Governor Haldimand to inform him that the militia at Sorel was being burdened with too many "covées."[16]

Chapter Fifteen

Montreal 1779-1780

He found only one company from his battalion in Montreal. During his absence, Governor Haldimand had been reinforcing Canada's weak spots. Sorel had been strongly fortified, and most of the first battalion was there, along with most of the provincial troops except Butler's Rangers, who were at Niagara. Haldimand had added a new base, on Carleton Island at the head of the St. Lawrence, where the new fortification was Fort Haldimand. To Allan's delight, all the officers and men of the first battalion who had been prisoners had been exchanged, and after the recruiting of the spring the battalion was close to strength. Haldimand had allowed one company to be formed of Canadians, which the officers called "the French company." Good workers, they had been employed on the defences of Fort Haldimand.[1] Allan did not retire the prisoners taken at the siege of Quebec, for by 1779 many provincial corps had allowed captives to enlist.

"They no longer keep us from looking respectable," Allan explained to Major Nairne and some other officers soon after his return.

He was responsible for many prisoners, most of them captured on raids by Butler's Rangers and shipped to Montreal for safe keeping. Allan arranged a secure compound for some, and he placed others on an island close to the Lachine Rapids, from which escape was difficult. Some were free on parole in Montreal when Allan thought they could be trusted. Refugee loyalists—old men, women, and children—were arriving in a steady stream, and Allan was sending them to Machiche, on the north side of the St. Lawrence, where Haldimand had set up a settlement for them. He wanted all refugees kept away from sensitive places. Machiche had few Canadian inhabitants, and rebel spies could do little harm among the loyalists, but Haldimand did not want any among his French-speaking subjects where they could spread republican propaganda. Allan gave the refugees emergency supplies and hired wagons to transport them to Machiche. Only a few of the officers' families were allowed to remain in Montreal.

In July, Haldimand appointed Major John Nairne the commandant of Fort Haldimand, and he left with his company to garrison Carleton Island. Because Nairne was now a major in the army, this left a vacancy in the 84th Regiment. Allan chose Captain John Adolphus Harris to succeed Nairne as the battalion's major, but Haldimand did not approve the appointment at once. By August the first battalion was complete, and on the 30th the governor signed a beating order, authorizing twenty extra privates to each company. Allan agreed, for he could never recruit enough men in Canada to form a third battalion.[2]

Rumours reached Montreal of a rebel expedition 5,000 strong marching on the country of the Iroquois Indians. At Niagara, John Butler, now the lieutenant-colonel of a full regiment of rangers, called for reinforcements, but Haldimand felt helpless. The first of his supply vessels, expected since the spring, did not come until September. By that time the rebels were ravaging the lands of the Iroquois to punish them for helping the British.

Once his supplies were landed, Haldimand ordered a reinforcement of the 84th Regiment and some other regulars to Niagara, while Sir John Johnson took his regiment from Montreal to join Butler in the field. Legend tells that some Royal Highland Emigrants joined the Indians in harrying the rebels, the Highlanders in Indian garb and war paint. No documentation supports the legend, but it could have been true.

In Montreal, bad reports were reaching Allan. Destitute Indians were fleeing to Niagara, where Colonel Mason Bolton, the commandant, was hard-pressed to feed them. In October, Allan wrote Haldimand, suggesting that many Indians be brought to St. Regis and Lake of Two Mountains, closer to Montreal and its stock of food. He was unable to move supplies beyond Carleton Island, where he had sent many bateaux of provisions, because Sir John Johnson had taken all the vessels to transport his men to Niagara. Until Sir John returned to Carleton Island with the fleet, little could be sent to Niagara to succour the Indians.[3]

Allan went to Quebec City, for urgent matters had to be settled. Bills could not be paid until Haldimand approved them, and several officers were ready to purchase higher commissions. Allan had too many junior officers, and Haldimand sent those who could not afford to purchase to John Butler, who needed experienced men for his companies. Allan parted with three ensigns, which made his brother-in-law Hector the senior ensign in the regiment. Allan delayed recommending Hector for promotion until he had word from Janet on the boy's health. At the end of the interview Haldimand authorized the payment of some bills.

Back In Montreal, Allan received a letter from Janet. Young Hector was somewhat better, and Allan wrote the governor's secretary, Captain Robert Mathews, explaining that seventeen-year-old Hector was ready to purchase a lieutenancy. While the boy had never been in Canada, he had seen service in the south, and he would soon be Sir Hector, the chief. Allan added, "This circumstance I believe would have no great influence on His Excellency who is a stranger to the Religious & Sacred kind of attachment Highlanders have for their Chief." He asked Mathews to explain that a promotion for Hector would confer favour on the whole clan.[4] The governor did not approve Hector's promotion, but he allowed Captain John Adolphus Harris to purchase the major's commission, left vacant by John Nairne, which cost 2,000 pounds.

On 2 November, a party of wounded men arrived from Niagara, sent to Montreal to recuperate, and the army doctors asked Allan to find billets for those who did not need to be in hospital. At three o'clock the next morning, a sentry aroused Allan and told him that one of the men, Private Michael McCabe of Butler's Rangers, had violated his landlady. The woman's husband was away, and neighbours who heard her cries had alerted the sentry. Allan summoned the provost martial, and ordered him to escort McCabe to him at once. By the time Allan was dressed, the provost was waiting for him. He eyed McCabe contemptuously, noting that the prisoner had an arm in a sling. "Where's your wound?" he barked.

McCabe did not reply, but looked down at his moccasined feet.

"The hand, Brigadier Maclean," the provost answered. "And there can't be much wrong with it. She's a strong woman. He couldn't have forced himself on her with just one hand, if you ask me, sir."

Allan ordered McCabe placed in irons and confined until he had orders from Haldimand. In a few days Captain Mathews replied. Since rape was a civil crime, Allan was to hand McCabe over to the magistrates, who would prosecute if the woman pressed charges. She decided not to, and Allan ordered McCabe held until he could be returned to Colonel Butler in the spring.[5]

Allan was vexed with McCabe, and almost as annoyed with the German troops. Officers and ranks alike were a plagued nuisance. The officers complained that their billets were inferior, while the men refused to carry their firewood or wash their shirts. Professional soldiers, the Germans complained, should not do the work of servants. Allan passed these complaints on to Haldimand, pointing out that the firewood was just outside the Germans' barracks, and wishing for an English garrison, so much more agreeable. Haldimand told Allan to discuss any differences with one of the German brigadiers, Ernst von Speth, and let the latter give orders to his own kind, as "Germans are Tenacious of their Rights."[6]

To Allan's distress, he received a copy of a memorial which John Macdonell, still a captain in Butler's Rangers, had sent to Quebec City. Despite Allan's efforts in 1777 to give him a lieutenancy in the first battalion by having Lieutenant Archibald Maclean trade places with him, Macdonell was accusing Allan of blocking a promotion, which was a blatant lie. Recounting his association with Macdonell, Allan pointed out that he *had* promoted him from ensign to lieutenant, but in the second battalion. If Macdonell would go to Halifax he could have his lieutenancy. Allan asked the governor for a court martial to clear himself of Macdonell's charges, but Haldimand suggested that the quarrel was a private one, and should be dropped.[7]

Late in November, scouts who had come overland brought news of Francis Maclean. Allan's cousin was now a brigadier-general in Nova Scotia and the governor of Halifax. Francis had led an expedition to the Penobscot River, in an area called Maine although it was part of Massachusetts. He built Fort George as an outpost for

Halifax because tall timber in the neighbourhood was needed for ship-building. In August, a rebel land force and fleet attacked the not fully completed Fort George. With the help of ships from New York, Francis repulsed the attack, left the fort secure, and returned to Halifax.

On 7 December, Captain Louis Bouteillet, of the Longueuil militia, arrived at Allan's house with a remarkable request. "Please put me in jail for fourteen days, General Maclean," the officer said in French. "I have come to you because the provost martial and the sheriff have refused me as I have no warrant. Please issue a warrant, sir. My life and property are in great danger."

"A warrant, Captain?" Allan enquired. "On what charge?"

"Of insulting Lieutenant-Colonel von Creutzburg, of the Hesse-Hanau Jaegers, General."

"Kindly tell me exactly what happened," Allan said, offering the captain a chair for his legs were trembling.

Bouteillet recounted a deed for which, Allan felt, only a German officer could have been responsible. The day before, by order of von Creutzburg, some soldiers had taken a good horse from Bouteillet's farm. Bouteillet was absent at the time, and when he returned he went to the barracks of the Hesse-Hanau regiment to retrieve the horse as he needed it for his own military duties. When the soldiers told him that Colonel von Creutzburg had allowed his servant to take the horse to La Prairie, Bouteillet lost his temper.

"I said, 'May the devil carry off the blackguard colonel, the servant and the horse!' sir."

Bouteillet returned home, but a few hours later a party of German soldiers arrived with orders to escort him to von Creutzburg's quarters. There the colonel ordered Bouteillet to spend fourteen days in jail, after which he was to apologize on his knees in front of the entire Hesse-Hanau regiment.

"Nonsense!" Allan exclaimed incredulous. "You would have insulted the colonel if you had called him a blackguard to his face, but you did not. The colonel is the aggressor. He had your horse stolen, and I can not issue a warrant unless you have committed a crime."

"But sir, if I do not go to jail the Germans will kill me,

and perhaps my wife and children also!" Bouteillet said, terrified.

Allan shook his head. "I can't put an innocent man in jail, but I can protect you. I will give you a pass to Quebec to put your case before His Excellency. While you are away, I will send some of my Highlanders to your house to intimidate the Germans."

"Will the governor see me, sir?" Bouteillet asked, fearful.

"I'll write and explain the matter," Allan assured him, confident that Haldimand would be as indignant as himself and reprimand von Creutzburg for such high-handedness.[8]

After the grateful Bouteillet left, Allan sent six of his men to Longueuil. Then he arranged for Major Harris to quarter 200 more at La Chénage. The rest of the battalion would be placed in the next parish. The move would be popular in both places, for the battalion had wintered there before and the local people liked his men.

Allan was frustrated over the conduct of many recruiting agents who were busy around Montreal, and worried that he might not find enough men to augment his companies, as Haldimand wished. The remnants of Burgoyne's provincials that had come into Canada were now considered part of the Northern Department, and Haldimand was allowing the commanders to complete battalions. Allan had to mediate disputes and decide which officers were entitled to which recruits. With competition so keen around Montreal, Allan received Haldimand's permission to send his new captain-lieutenant, Alexander Fletcher, to recruit in Newfoundland. Captain-Lieutenant Neil Maclean had retired in poor health. Allan's first captain-lieutenant, the long-imprisoned John Munro, had escaped from the rebels and had received a captaincy from Sir John Johnson.[9]

As the year 1780 opened, Allan was trying to put his accounts in order, both those for the 84th Regiment and for expenses which he incurred as governor of Montreal. One merchant had never been paid for rum he supplied to Burgoyne's expedition of 1777. Also, for the last six months the Barrackmaster-General had not paid the rent on the house Allan occupied. Allan asked that the rent be paid, as the owner of the house was a poor man. Replying for Haldimand, Captain Mathews told Allan that he must now pay the rent, as the government no longer needed the house for storage. Allan thought this grossly unfair, since Brigadier Powell lived rent-free at St. Jean.

Haldimand appointed Major Daniel McAlpin, a veteran of Burgoyne's campaign, his Inspector of Loyalists, in charge of the civilians, many of whom were the dependents of provincials who had served with Burgoyne. McAlpin came to Montreal to supervise the provisioning and movement of refugee families to Machiche, and Allan received orders to assist him.

On a bright February morning, Major Harris reported to Allan on a drunken brawl the night before, involving three officers of the first battalion, to the discredit of the regiment. In the fighting, Lieutenant James Macdonell, of the King's Royal Regiment of New York, had been badly hurt. The lieutenant was a son of Captain John Macdonell, of the same regiment. The attackers were Lieutenants Archibald and Ranald Macdonell—kinsmen of the victim—and Quartermaster Duncan Murray. Allan visited the injured officer, who wanted to forget the brawl and had no wish to press charges. A few days later, however, the lieutenant's father called on Allan. The three officers of the 84th Regiment had tried to murder his son, and Captain John Macdonell wanted them punished.

On the 11th, James McGill, a merchant and magistrate, came to Allan and reported that Captain Macdonell had asked him to issue warrants and hold a civil trial, a step the magistrate hesitated to take without consulting the officers' commander. Allan decided to hold a military court of enquiry. A civil trial was not appropriate since no civilians were involved. The court sat on the 14th, and found Archibald Macdonell innocent. Ranald Macdonell, who was also Allan's adjutant, and Duncan Murray were implicated, and Allan ordered them confined to quarters until Haldimand decided how they should be disciplined.

In the interval, Sir John Johnson wrote to Allan, describing the affair as a "nasty dirty disagreeable Drunken Squabble" that did credit to neither the Royal Highland Emigrants nor his King's Royal Regiment of New York and was best forgotten. Haldimand told Allan that he could dismiss the two officers, but as he knew their worth, he should use his own judgement. Haldimand regretted having such a trivial matter brought to his attention. Unwilling to part with his adjutant and quartermaster, Allan scolded them and put them back on duty.[10]

The quarrel was only an annoying distraction. Allan was fully occupied by the difficulties facing destitute loyalists. Major McAlpin had fallen seriously ill and was unable to carry on. A group of refugees brought Allan a petition for relief which he forwarded to the governor. McAlpin had been too zealous in denying provisions to deserving people, because of Haldimand's instructions to keep his provision list as short as possible. The expense of providing for the refugees was a heavy burden on the government, and Haldimand had to account for his expenditures to Lords Germain and North.

Knowing that Haldimand was as humane as himself, Allan recommended that many individuals be reinstated on the provision list. He cited a Mrs. Hicks, with six small children, whose husband had been killed serving with Butler's Rangers. An orphan child whose father, a private in the Royal Highland Emigrants who had been killed near Ile aux Noix in 1777, needed care. A widow from the Mohawk Valley with a young child was without any means of support.

Allan asked Haldimand to send an armed vessel to Newfoundland, where Captain-Lieutenant Fletcher had ninety recruits to transport to Canada. Haldimand replied that he had received an express from Halifax. Fletcher and his recruits had arrived there and would soon come to Quebec. The governor was also setting up a board of officers, to settle disputes over recruits that were claimed by more than one regiment. The board would relieve Allan of that responsibility for which he had no time.

The spring fleet of 1780 brought several letters from home. One was from Lord Loudoun, who had kept his promise concerning Allan's son. Loudoun had approached the Duke of Argyll, his chief and also the commander of the 1st Regiment of Foot. The duke contacted their kinsman, Sir James Campbell, who was raising the new Western Regiment of Fencible Men in North Britain. Campbell had given Allan's "adopted" son a subaltern's commission in the Fencibles. A letter also came from Janet, with the same news, adding that the boy had left for Stirling Castle, the regimental headquarters. Allan was grateful to the chief of clan Campbell. The commission was a small recompense from the duke (this was John, the 5th Duke [1723 - 1806]), who still owned Torloisk and was the family landlord.[11]

That spring of 1780 the first battalion of the 84th Regiment was more dispersed than before. Major Harris' company was at Carleton Island. Captain Daniel Robertson's was at Fort Oswegatchie, on the south shore of the St. Lawrence above the Galops Rapids. Captain John Macdougall died, and Patrick Sinclair purchased his commission for 1,500 pounds. Haldimand ordered Sinclair's company to the fort at Michilimackinac, the most westerly post in Canada's chain of defence. Fortunately the supply situation had improved. The home government was sending much larger supply fleets than in the early years of the war, and Haldimand at last felt able to undertake limited offensives into the rebelling colonies. On 20 April, Sir John Johnson brought Allan a letter from Haldimand's secretary, Captain Robert Mathews, that had come with a long one from the governor to Sir. John.

Johnson had Haldimand's permission to lead an expedition into the Mohawk Valley, to rescue distressed loyalists and to destroy rebel property. Halidimand asked Allan to give him every assistance, and to say nothing to anyone about the expedition. Spies were everywhere, and forewarning might result in a rebel ambush that could destroy Sir John's force. Allan was to see that 150 of Sir John's King's Royal Regiment of New York were properly equipped, and to arrange to have them transported as far as Crown Point, on Lake Champlain, in vessels of the Provincial Marine.[12]

Offensive Operations 1780-1781

"When do you hope to leave?" Allan asked Sir John.

"As soon as possible," the baronet replied. "The matter is urgent. A scout warned His Excellency that all the loyalists around Johnstown are to be formed into three companies of rangers. Any who refuse to join the rebel service will be sent to Albany in irons, their homes burnt, their property confiscated."

"We must move fast," Allan agreed. "But 150 men are hardly enough for such a task."

"In his letter to me, the governor authorized some 600 all told," Sir John explained. "Captain Leake's independent company, 188 men from the 53rd, 29th and 34th Regiments, and 21 of von Creutzburg's riflemen. Captain Thomas Scott will command the regulars, and we're taking 130 Mohawks and 80 Indians from Lake of Two Mountains."

Allan felt nettled but he remained silent. Why had Mathews mentioned only the 150 men of Sir John's regiment to him? As the commander of the district, he should have heard directly about the regulars and Indians.

"You're welcome to von Creutzburg's," he said shortly.

"They are temperamental," Sir John agreed. "My mother was a German woman. Perhaps that will help me understand them."

By 3 May, all the provincials and regulars were assembled at Lachine, about to leave in bateaux for Sorel, while the Mohawks were gathered with their canoes. The eighty Lake of Two Mountains Indians had gone ahead as scouts. As Sir John mounted an army horse for the ride from Montreal to take command of his force, Allan wished him Godspeed.[1]

On 1 June, Sir John returned, flush with success. His men had burnt 120 houses, as well as barns and mills, destroyed stored grain, stolen arms and cash, killed many cattle and removed seventy horses. They had rescued many loyalists—143 men fit for service, some women and children, and thirty black slaves. Of the latter, seventeen belonged to Sir John, his cousin Guy who was on duty at Fort Niagara, and his other brother-in-law Daniel Claus. As a consequence of his expedition, Sir John now had more than enough men to complete his battalion.

Allan found that forty of the rescued men did not want to enlist, and Haldimand ordered him to apply pressure. Neither Allan nor the governor wanted loyalists idle in Canada, consuming provisions, when they were needed in the service. On 13 July, Haldimand authorized Sir John to raise a second battalion, taking in the forty reluctant recruits and Captain Leake's company. As the major, Haldimand approved the transfer of Captain John Ross from the 34th Regiment to the King's Royal Regiment of New York.

Once the matter of Sir John's recruits was settled, Allan's time was taken up with his own regiment. He received a letter from Captain-Lieutenant Fletcher in Halifax, complaining that he did not yet have passage to Canada for his recruits. Desertion was a problem in Halifax, where there was a shortage of seamen. Merchants were paying men twenty-five guineas a voyage to England or the West Indies, and privateers paid even more. Three recruits had deserted to the merchant fleet, and the large rewards available "will debauch the best of men." Haldimand assured Allan he would soon get his recruits. In the meantime, Fletcher was making himself useful to Brigadier Francis Maclean, who was pleased to have the assistance.[2]

For quite different reasons Allan was disturbed over the recruits whom he had enlisted in the Mohawk Valley in 1775. Private John McDonald, of his grenadier company, had asked for forty pounds in back pay— from the actual date of his enlistment. Yet McDonald did not join the regiment until three years later, in June 1778, when two Indians guided him to Isle aux Noix. Agitated, Allan asked Haldimand to recommend a just settlement. He had other men in his battalion who had enlisted in 1775, but who had not joined him until some time later. Allowing all of them back pay would have a ruinous effect on the regiment's funds. The governor authorized ten guineas for McDonald, who willingly accepted this sum.[3]

In July, Major McAlpin died in Montreal, and Allan asked Haldimand to appoint a new Inspector of Loyalists to cope with the ever arriving refugees and to take charge of the provision list. Haldimand ignored Allan's letter, and instead ordered him to prepare a reinforcement of 260 men of the King's Royal Regiment of New York for Carleton Island. Allan was startled when one of that regiment's captains told him that this reinforcement was to be part of an expedition Sir John would lead through the Mohawk Valley. If the captain spoke the truth, the governor and Johnson were treating Allan shabbily. As commander of the district, he had a right to know what was going on.[4]

In a private letter to Sir John, Haldimand reduced the number of men from his regiment for the expedition from 260 to 150, and told him not to mention the expedition to anyone. On 11 September, Allan discovered that Major James Gray, of Sir John's first battalion, had left for Oswego from Coteau du Lac with only 150 men. Infuriated, Allan sent for Sir John, who ought to have informed him of any changes in plan, a serious breach of military ettiquette. At that Sir John admitted that the order had come from the governor. Fuming, Allan penned a letter to Haldimand's secretary, Captain Robert Mathews, over the impropriety of sending instructions to a junior officer without informing his superior. The governor seemed to imply that Allan was not to be trusted with certain information.[5]

Mathew's reply was a mild reprimand. "You should have co-operated as though you were privy to all the information." He ordered Allan to hold up the return of some rebel prisoners to New York State, whom Haldimand had agreed to send to their homes. The governor did not want them informing the rebel authorities of the forthcoming expedition to Mohawk Valley. To assist Sir John Johnson, Allan was to prepare a diversionary expedition of 100 men, to be commanded by Captain John Munro, who was to enter the Mohawk Valley from Lake Champlain. Allan set to work, limping, admitting that he was particularly short-tempered because his bad leg was paining him so. He was resorting more and more to the laudanum his London doctors had prescribed, and he informed Haldimand that he was getting "old and infirm."[6]

John Munro's force left Montreal as part of a larger diversion, Allan now discovered, again wishing that Mathews had been more explicit. Major Christopher

Carleton was to take an expedition to Crown Point to destroy the rebel outposts in New York. Carleton was Sir Guy's nephew and the commandant of the outpost at Pointe au Fer, at the north end of Lake Champlain. His force of regulars, provincials, and Indians, would include a detachment of Allan's 84th Regiment. Munro's men would travel with Carleton's by water to Crown Point and march inland from there.

On 28 September, Mathews wrote ordering Allan to seize a surgeon named Pillon who lived in the Quebec suburbs on the east side on Montreal, and to act in secret, choosing a discreet officer for the arrest. All Pillon's papers were to be confiscated, sealed, and shipped to Haldimand. The culprit was to be confined in irons incommunicado until he could be sent to Quebec City. Haldimand had proof that Pillon had been in contact with General Washington and his staff officer, the Marquis de LaFayette.

Allan had Pillon arrested, but when he looked through his papers before sealing them, he discovered that Pierre du Calvet, a prominent resident of Montreal, was one of Pillon's spies. On his own initiative Allan had du Calvet arrested, and informed the governor. To his astonishment, Haldimand was displeased. He had not wanted du Calvet taken just yet, as he hoped he might lead him to other members of Pillon's spy ring. However, now that du Calvet's arrest was fact, he, too, should be sent to Quebec City. While Allan had acted too hastily, the governor was pleased with his zeal.[7] Haldimand was very worried that French troops might invade Canada, and that many Canadians were plotting to support their former countrymen. If the French came, Haldimand did not think he had enough troops to hold Canada.

While Allan looked to internal security, Sir John Johnson's expedition, which included some regulars and a large detachment of Butler's Rangers from Niagara and many Indians, was destroying the 1780 grain crop in the Mohawk Valley. To the east Major Carleton penetrated as far as Fort George, at the south end of Lake George, burning rebel outposts and taking prisoners. John Munro struck as far west as Ballstown, a village north of Schenectady, and returned to Crown Point on 24 October with many valuable prisoners. The most important was Colonel James Gordon, of the Ballstown militia, and his family, kidnapped from their house.[8]

Allan was pleased with the results of the summer and autumn. The expeditions launched from Canada, as well as many small-scale raids by Butler's Rangers and the Indians, had changed the military situation in the north for the better. Newspapers brought to St. Jean by scouts carried reports that General Washington acknowledged the success of the raids of 1780. So much grain and livestock had been lost that shortages of provisions would hamper the efforts of his Continental Army for some time to come.[9]

Late in September, Brigadier Powell came from St. Jean to stay with Allan a few days. Colonel Mason Bolton, the commandant of Fort Niagara, was coming down on leave, and Haldimand had appointed Powell temporarily to take his place. Colonel Barry St. Leger would assume the command of Fort St. Jean during Powell's absence. In November, Allan received a letter from Powell. Colonel Bolton had sailed for Carleton Island aboard the *Ontario*, the newest vessel on the lake, on 31 October, but a sudden storm had struck. The *Ontario* sank with all hands. Butler's Rangers had gone looking for survivors but found none. Haldimand appointed Powell to command at Niagara.

After the navigation season closed, Allan received a copy of a letter his cousin Francis had sent to Haldimand from Halifax, brought overland by scouts travelling on foot. Francis warned Haldimand that France and the Continental Congress had designs on Canada, but the rebel commanders were divided. Some did not want Canada returned to France. Furthermore, France did not want Canada in rebel hands. A British presence there would keep the rebels dependent on the French. Francis also told Haldimand of the defection of Benedict Arnold to the British at New York City that September, and that Arnold's contact, Major John André, had been captured by the rebels. Sir Henry Clinton, in command at New York, was threatening retaliation if André was executed.[10]

The winter of 1780-1781 passed uneventfully. Seven companies of Allan's 84th Regiment were at Sorel, or at outposts nearer Lake Champlain. Sir John Johnson's regiment was billeted at Coteau du Lac and other outlying parishes. Most of the provincials were there or at two blockhouses on the Yamaska River, guarding that approach to the St. Lawrence. Allan expected his officers to visit him while in Montreal, but he was affronted to find that his kinsman, Lieutenant Archibald Maclean, had come at least four times without paying his respects.

Allan informed Captain William Dunbar, his brigade-major, of Archibald's rudeness and asked him to take the young man to task. Dunbar replied that Archibald had also been rude to Colonel von Barner, of the German light infantry, upsetting the "harmony between English and foreign officers." When informed, Haldimand asked Allan to see that all his officers were more polite to their German colleagues, advice Allan followed, although he sympathized with officers who showed their feelings.[11]

With the spring, work by provincials and the Canadian militia resumed at Coteau du Lac, where they were digging a shallow canal to bypass the Cedars Rapids. Haldimand was anxious to have the project completed, for the canal would improve the transport route to his inland posts. Allan sent Captain Malcolm Fraser to make a report, and on his return from Coteau du Lac, Fraser recommended sending a detachment of artificers from the 84th Regiment to help the others. While Allan was making these arrangments, a courier arrived with word of a prison outbreak at Coteau du Lac. Major James Gray was on leave, and his first battalion King's Royal Regiment of New York was temporarily under the command of Captain John Munro. Although some of the prisoners had been retaken, much valuable time had been wasted in the search.

As all prisoners were Allan's responsibility, he sent a stiff note to Munro, reprimanding him for negligence and for not reporting the outbreak himself. Munro took the letter to Sir John Johnson, who sent a copy of it to Haldimand. Sir John was upset because he felt that Brigadier Maclean had censured the entire regiment. Haldimand thought Allan reacted too quickly. Since Sir John Johnson was not an experienced professional soldier, he could not be expected to teach all the military forms. "Young Corps," the governor wrote, "stand in need of admonition & indulgence and naturally commit many errors which in old ones would be faults."[12]

He did admit that Munro had been remiss, which was precisely why Allan had written the captain in the first place. If the King's Royal Regiment of New York was young and inexperienced, John Munro was neither. He was a half-pay lieutenant of regulars before the war, and should have known better. Allan felt no remorse at reprimanding Munro, but he did recognize Haldimand's role as a pacifier. From the same motives the governor had wanted the officers of Allan's regiment to be more careful in their dealings with the German officers. Allan resolved to keep his temper, for he valued Haldimand as a friend and protector whose good will he might need. A bad report to Prime Minister Lord North could mean the eclipse of his military career. Haldimand had succeeded Lauchlin Macleane as the person Allan depended upon for advancement.

In June, a letter from Captian-Lieutenant Fletcher, still in Halifax, saddened Allan. His cousin Francis had died on 4 May 1781. Allan felt old and worn out as he recalled the young officer who had befriended him in his first days as a soldier in the Netherlands, thirty-five years ago. Still wondering when Fletcher would bring his recruits to Canada, Allan put aside the letter and resumed his many duties.

Throughout the summer he was swamped in a sea of prisoners and refugees. He had more prisoners than he could guard properly, and too many were on parole in Montreal. He received proof from informers that Colonel James Gordon, captured at Ballstown the autumn before by John Munro, had been passing intelligence to the rebels. Allan promptly sent Gordon to Quebec City. Haldimand ordered Allan to open a new prison camp on an island opposite Coteau du Lac, and to send an officer of the Engineering Department to supervise the building of the compound. Many of the prisoners were women and children, and Haldimand told Allan to send back those who could reach their homes easily from Lake Champlain. Some had been taken by Indians from the back of settlements of Virginia and Pennsylvania, and these would have to remain in Montreal. Haldimand felt that casting them adrift in the colonies to fend for themselves would be inhuman.[13]

The governor had Allan compile a list of "negroes" brought into Canada. Some, whose owners were in the province, should be returned to them. Escaped slaves, promised their freedom by recruiting agents if they would serve the King, would be allowed to enlist. A son of Colonel James Gordon was asking Allan for permission to go to Quebec City to be near his imprisoned father, but Haldimand wanted him kept in Montreal. Colonel Gordon would be certain to give his son messages for the rebels, and Allan was to see that he did not slip away.

Because he was so busy, Allan left the handling of the accounts of the 84th Regiment to his battalion paymaster, Captain Malcolm Fraser. Those for the period from 24 December 1778, when the Royal Highland Emigrants were put on the British establishment, were in fairly good order, but the accounts from June 1775 to December 1778 were in a muddle. Allan sent for Fraser from Sorel and they went over the figures, finding many discrepencies. Allan did not blame Fraser, who was clearly honest and incidently worried that the regimental debts might reflect on his good name. The difficulties arose from poor communication with the far-distant War Office. Allan's agents, Cox, Mair, and Cox, equally remote, had refused to advance any more credit, because the regiment owed the firm 4,500 pounds. This was awkward, for Fraser would need more money by autumn. Fortunately, the accounts for Allan's second battalion, still divided between the Nova Scotia garrison and British army in the southern colonies, were in good order. On 24 September, Allan asked Haldimand to grant him leave to go to London. Only there could he consult the Treasury, Lord North and the War Office, and arrange to settle the regimental accounts.[14]

Haldimand agreed to the leave, and he ordered Brigadier-General Ernst von Speth to take over as governor of Montreal. Before he left, Allan made a list of the arms and equipment needed by his battalion. He ordered jackets and waistcoats, but "Breeches we do not want." Then, thinking of the cold of winter and the biting insects of summer, he ordered some gaitered trousers, more practical for Canada. However, as men were fond of grumbling, he asked Haldimand to give the order for the issue of trousers, for added authority.[15]

After handing over his command to Brigadier von Speth, Allan left for Quebec City to sail on a vessel of the autumn

Butler's Rangers at Fort Niagara. The Corps had a fearful reputation at the time of the revolution. When the Brigade of the American Revolution was formed, it was one of the most popular units re-created. The regiment is represented at the birthday celebrations for George III held each June at Fort Niagara.

fleet. Before departing he conferred with Haldimand in the privacy of the Chateau St. Louis. The governor told him that another expedition to destroy the rebels' harvest was now under way from Oswego. It was commanded by Major John Ross, who was taking some of his own second battalion King's Royal Regiment of New York, as well as some of Butler's Rangers and thirty-six of Allan's 84th Regiment from Carleton Island. Haldimand was moving Major John Nairne, now in the 53rd Regiment, to Isle aux Noix as the commandant, and Major Ross would take over his command. The governor paused, a worried frown creasing his brows.

"We have won the war in the northern colonies, Brigadier Maclean," he said. "But I fear that Lord Cornwallis, campaigning in Virginia, is in trouble. Scouts from Niagara have brought word that His Lordship is withdrawing to Yorktown, and Sir Henry Clinton has sailed from New York with a reinforcement. General Washington and the French commander, the Comte Rochambeau, have Cornwallis surrounded. "

At that Allan's brows rose in alarm. "Where is Lieutenant-Colonel Small, Your Excellency?"

"He is still in Georgia, with five companies of your regiment," Haldimand replied.

Relieved, Allan begged Haldimand to advance the officers of the first battalion funds to carry them through the winter, until he could arrange for the arrears to be paid up while he was in London. Before they parted, Haldimand told Allan that Sir John Johnson was also on his way to London. Sir John was to look into the muddle his cousin, Guy Johnson, had made of the accounts of the Indian Department. Guy had been a poor administrator and Haldimand had recommended that he be replaced. Also, Sir John would try to have his King's Royal Regiment of New York put on the British regular establishment. Allan applauded the first, but was suspicious of the second.

"Sir John's men aren't ready to be regulars, Your Excellency," he protested. "They're frontier farmers, good raiders, and artificers, but they haven't much training."

"I have written to Lord Germain telling him I disapprove," Haldimand said.

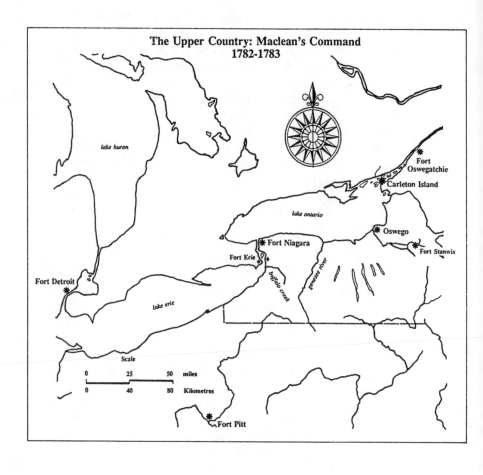

The Upper Country: Maclean's Command
1782-1783

180

Chapter Seventeen

Niagara 1782

At York Buildings he found Janet well and happy to have him home, especially as he had not come the previous winter. Hector was still with her, his health somewhat improved but he was not ready to rejoin the second battalion, even for service in Nova Scotia. Allan's son was with his regiment at Stirling, serving with the home garrison, which reminded him that Britain's own shores were being menaced by France, Spain, and Holland. He passed the first weeks of his leave having treatment from Drs. Hunter and Huck, still fashionable physicians, and in obtaining the latest war news.

In February, newspapers reported that Cornwallis had surrendered his army to Washington and Rochambeau on 19 October. A French fleet had blockaded Yorktown and kept Sir Henry Clinton and his reinforcements from relieving Cornwallis. Now Lord North's government came under fire and opposition politicians called for his resignation. A very worried Allan wrote to Lord North asking for an interview. In 1775 the Prime Minister had approved a pension of 500 pounds a year for Janet, should Allan die on duty, but he had never sent a warrant confirming the arrangement. Now time might be running out. If the government fell, its Whig successor would be under no obligation to honour the commitments of Lord North's discredited Tories. A secretary replied that Lord North was too busy to see Allan, and he wrote a second letter, reminding His Lordship of his promise. Again he received a reply from the secretary. Lord North would soon sign the warrant, but none came.

Newspapers appearing on 15 March reported that Lord North had appointed Sir John Johnson the Superintendent of Indian Affairs, Northern District, superceding his cousin Guy. Still Allan heard nothing from Lord North, and on the 19th the axe fell. North's government resigned, and the new Prime Minister was Lord Rockingham. The Whig ministry included Lord Shelburne— bad news for Allan. He could not expect patronage from a ministry where Shelburne had influence, not after the way his late benefactor Lauchlin Macleane had switched his support from Shelburne to North so long ago. Shelburne was certain to remember Allan's part in Lauchlin's games. Now Allan had few friends in high places.

Once his leg was better, Allan visited his agents, Cox, Mair, and Cox, armed with Captain Malcolm Fraser's pay books. The agents showed him their reckonings, and a very depressed Allan returned to Buckingham Street. Next he visited the War Office, and was granted enough bills to reduce the debt to 2,222 pounds, still a staggering sum, more than his debt of 1763 for the 114th Regiment. He had some 4,000 pounds saved from selling commissions, but he would need every penny to supplement the half-pay of a lieutenant-colonel once the war was over. His family now embraced nine dependents, counting his son, who could not equip himself solely on his pay. The others were one child and "seven helpless grown up women." Back in Canada the battalion debt was increasing as each pay muster came up. He was relieved that he and Janet had no children of their own, since he had virtually nothing to offer them. As his thoughts turned to his approaching departure for Canada, he admitted what he should have known years ago. A regiment was a rich man's plaything.

He went to pay his respects to Lord Loudoun, who although he was the military governor of Edinburgh, was at his town house because he was not well. His Lordship was resting on a couch before a roaring fire and pleased to have a visitor. Loudoun suggested that since fencible regiments were not regulars, and the officers were not entitled to half-pay on reduction, Allan should call on the Duke of Argyll, now in London. His Grace was the colonel of the 1st Regiment of Foot, the oldest in the army, and he might allow Allan's son a commission. The 1st Foot would not be reduced when the war was over. Allan thanked Loudoun and promised to follow his advice. He had scant wish to pay his respects to the chief of clan Campbell, but the duke had already done him a good turn. If there was a possibility of his doing more, swallowing Jacobite pride was a small price to pay. He sent a note to the duke's town house and received an appointment.

For the second time in his life, the third if he counted Mary Campbell, his late mother, Allan was impressed with a member of the despised clan. Argyll received "General

Maclean" hospitably, for he was intrigued by what he knew of this lame son of Torloisk. While poor as the proverbial church mouse, Allan had managed to rise high in an army where wealth and influence were so much more important than ability. The duke promised to do what he could to give Allan's son a subaltern's commission in his 1st Foot.

"Thank you, Your Grace," Allan murmured, elated. "To have my young gentlemen in the oldest regiment would indeed be an honour."

By April 1782, when Allan was ready to sail, Lord Rockingham had sent emissaries to Paris to open peace talks with representatives of the rebels' Continental Congress. Late in June Allan disembarked at Quebec, took a room at the Golden Dog, and sent a note to Haldimand. An hour later a soldier came with a note from Robert Mathews, now a major. The governor would see Brigadier Maclean the next morning. Allan spent an enjoyable evening with his brother officers, dreading a return to the dreariness of his Montreal command. The conversation dealt largely with the possibility of invasion. Now that Cornwallis' army had been captured, Washington and his French allies might turn their steps towards Canada. If they could occupy the province, the rebels at the peace talks in Paris would be in a stronger bargaining position.

When Allan saw Haldimand, the governor's talk, too, was of invasion. He had sent Major John Ross to occupy Oswego, with his second battalion King's Royal Regiment of New York, and a detachment of the 84th Regiment under Captain Lauchlin Maclean. Lauchlin was now in command of the grenadier company, and Allan agreed to allow his nephew to have the promotion from lieutenant without purchase. Captain-Lieutenant Fletcher and his recruits had come from Halifax, and Fletcher had purchased a captaincy. Haldimand approved the vacant captain-lieutenancy for Lieutenant Archibald Maclean, who was ready to purchase. Six companies of the 84th Regiment were now at inland posts. Captain Daniel Robertson and his company had been sent from Oswegatchie to Michilimackinac, where Captain Patrick Sinclair was still on duty with his company. From Sorel, Major Harris had sent one company to Oswegatchie, and one company was at Carleton Island. Half-companies were at Niagara and Detroit. Anxious to discuss the 2,222 pound debt to Cox, Mair, and Cox with Major Harris, Allan asked when he would be returning to Montreal.

"I do not need you in Montreal, Brigadier Maclean," Haldimand replied. Brigadier von Speth was getting on well with Sir John Johnson's first battalion and he did not want any more fireworks. "I would like you to stay here for a while, helping me with plans for defence. Brigadier Powell, at Niagara, has asked to be relieved, and I may decide to send you there. The security of my upper posts is of utmost importance. From Niagara you would be in command of all these posts—Oswegatchie, Carleton Island, Oswego, Fort Erie, Schlosser, Detroit, and Michilimackinac."

"A far-flung command, Your Excellency," Allan remarked.

"One that needs a man of ability," Haldimand said. "Herr von Speth is adequate for Montreal, and St. Leger for St. Jean, but neither would suit the Indians. You, who are so conscientious, would be right for Niagara. I may want you to investigate the conduct of the Indian Department, a great burden on the government. I have already recalled Colonel Guy Johnson, and as soon as Sir John returns from England, I want him to visit all posts where Indian agents are stationed. I have taken the precaution of making Sir John a brigadier-general, so that he will have authority over his cousin." Noting the frown on Allan's face, Haldimand added hastily. "You are, of course, senior to Sir John."

Allan remained in Quebec City all summer, doing administrative work in the Chateau St. Louis. Sir John Johnson returned in July, and accompanied by Lieutenant-Colonel Henry Hope, Joseph Brant, and an escort of native warriors, he left in canoes for the upper posts. A disgruntled Guy Johnson, relieved of his job as Superintendent of Indian Affairs, left for England. In September, Haldimand informed Allan that he was to replace Brigadier Powell at Fort Niagara. Allan prepared to leave for Montreal to collect belongings he had stored there. At a last conference with Haldimand, he learned that Prime Minister Lord Rockingham had died in June. Lord Shelburne was now the Prime Minister, cold comfort to Allan. Before he was excused he asked Haldimand to allow him to strengthen the Niagara garrison by taking Captain Lauchlin Maclean and forty-four grenadiers of the 84th Regiment from Oswego. The governor approved.

At Sorel, Allan left his vessel and saw Major Harris, who wanted a leave of absence in Britain. His parents were both eighty years old, and the major felt, if he did not return soon, he might never see them again. Allan granted the leave in the hope that Harris, more familiar with the battalion finances, might find discrepencies that would cover the debt to Cox, Mair and Cox. With Harris, Allan devised a plan. Peace might not be far off, and the 84th Regiment would be disbanded. Harris wanted to retire as a lieutenant-colonel and he was willing to purchase Allan's commission, worth 3,500 pounds. Allan was eager to sell, for that sum, carefully invested, would yield a higher income than his daily pay. Captain Malcolm Fraser wanted to purchase the major's commission for 2,600 pounds. Allan asked Haldimand for permission to sell his commission, in return for which he would serve as a colonel-commandant without pay.[1]

By 14 October, Allan was in Montreal, suffering from a very sore throat. He sent for an army doctor who drew off twenty-seven ounces of blood, after which Allan swallowed one and one half ounces of salts. The following day, he reported to Haldimand, he was feeling much better. Brigadier Powell had come to Montreal, leaving the upper posts in the care of Lieutenant-Colonel Alexander Dundas, of the 8th Regiment, until Allan could take up his duties. Powell briefed Allan on conditions along the frontier.

Rebel settlers were constantly encroaching on the country of the Western Indians in the Kentucky and Ohio Valleys. Since 1763, British policy had been to reserve the territory west of the Allegheny Mountains for the Indians, but the settlers had long ignored the government. All that season of 1782 small parties of Butler's Rangers had been in the Indian country, raiding settlements, endeavouring to help the natives against the settlers. The worst incident, Powell reported, had been the massacre of innocent Delawares known as Moravians because they had been converted to Christianity by Moravian missionaries. In March their village of Gnadenhutten had been attacked by a rebel force. Ninety-six men, women, and children were beaten to death. These Indians were pacifists who had not taken part in the war.

Allan's sympathies were aroused as he left in a bateau for Oswegatchie and Carleton Island. Raiding was all too familiar to a Highlander, whose own people had been subjected to brutal treatment by waves of Campbells and soldiers.

At Carleton Island, Allan found only sixty men, some of them old and infirm, for Major Ross had removed more of the 84th to Oswego. The garrison was too small to protect the large quantities of naval stores there. While he was still at Fort Haldimand, Major Ross arrived, and Allan ordered him to move seventy-four of Butler's Rangers then at Oswego to Carleton Island for the winter. Once the St. Lawrence was ice-bound, the island would be open to attack by rebels on snowshoes. He asked Haldimand for reinforcements and for provisions. Then, accompanied by Ross, he sailed for Oswego to continue his tour of inspection.

He was impressed with Ross' work in restoring the forts, which had been empty since 1763. He found 400 men fit for duty, but the barracks had space for 600. Ross, who feared an attack in the early spring, needed reinforcements.

"His Excellency has given me permission to take Captain Maclean and most of his grenadiers with me to Niagara, Major," Allan informed Ross. "Of course, I will not remove the grenadiers unless you receive more men from Sorel."

"I beg you not to remove them, sir," Ross said, looking worried. "And I do need Captain Maclean."

"I would like my nephew to assist me at Niagara," Allan repeated. "I will gladly send you Captain Fletcher in his place."

"Captain Maclean is my right hand man, General," Ross protested. "I don't know what I will do without him."

Sadly Allan abandoned his plan to have Lauchlin and more of his own regiment at Niagara. Ross was right in asking to keep Lauchlin and his grenadiers.[2]

He left Oswego on 31 October, and after a "disagreeable passage" of six days on storm-tossed Lake Ontario, he reached Fort Niagara on 5 November. Heavy rains had turned the road along the Niagara River into an impassable quagmire, which had prevented the movement of supplies to Fort Erie for shipment to Detroit. Writing to Haldimand, Allan asked him to send him old newspapers to help pass the time once winter had set in. At the fort, Allan met with Lieutenant-Colonel Dundas, who gave him a bundle of letters from the commandant at Detroit, Major Arent DePeyster of the 8th Regiment. A detachment of Butler's Rangers based at Detroit had struck two blows, in August at Blue Licks in the Kentucky Valley, and in September at Wheeling, Virginia, in an effort to protect the Western Indians—Shawnees, Delawares, and Wyandots mostly—from rebel frontiersmen. Now that the war had virtually ended elsewhere, the attacks on the western Indians had been stepped up as the frontiersmen sought to drive the Indians from their own country.

Allan was disappointed to find that Lieutenant-Colonel Butler, whom he had last seen in Montreal in 1777, was ill in his quarters, in the rangers' barracks across the Niagara River. Part of the cause, Allan suspected, was the death of his eldest son Walter, killed in action while on Ross' expedition the autumn before. Sir John Johnson had been at Niagara briefly in September, after travelling to Michilimackinac by way of the Ottawa River. With Sir John based in Montreal, Allan hoped that John Butler would have sole authority over the Indian Department. Until Butler recovered, he would have to watch over the expenses of that department, as well as the accounts for all the inland posts.

His responsibilities were heavy, Allan reflected as he inspected the fort and its surroundings. The old earthworks required repairs, and he organized parties of artificers to serve under an officer of the Royal Engineers. The garrison was barely adequate, with only six companies of Butler's Rangers on hand, and detachments of the 8th, 34th, and 84th Regiments. The other soldiers were a few provincials, some belonging to Joseph Brant's Volunteers, and some Loyal Foresters. The latter were to have formed a provincial corps at Fort Pitt, but when that fort had been captured by the rebels in 1776, some had come on to Niagara.

Allan was responsible for refugees, both Indian and white, who were in two places. Some had founded a temporary agricultural settlement at Buffalo Creek: others were across the Niagara River on land the government had purchased from the Mississauga Indians. There, a settlement the soldiers were calling a new Butlersbury was growing. Some civilians and men retired from the rangers were

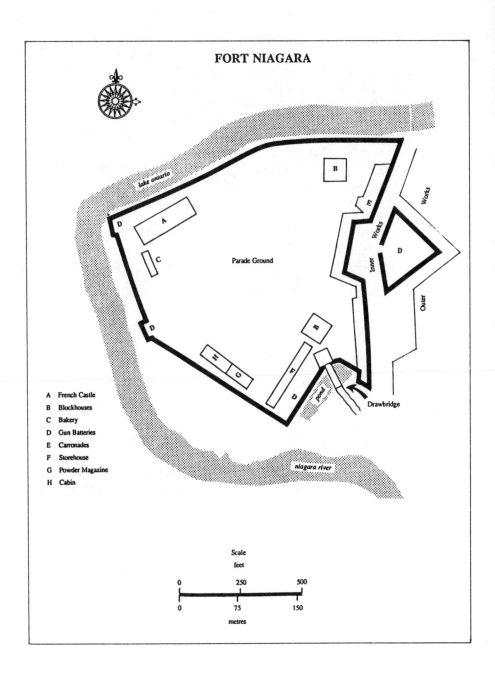

FORT NIAGARA

A French Castle
B Blockhouses
C Bakery
D Gun Batteries
E Carronades
F Storehouse
G Powder Magazine
H Cabin

Parade Ground

lake ontario

niagara river

Works
Works
Inner
Outer

Drawbridge

pond

Scale
feet

0   250   500

0   75   150

metres

farming, to relieve Niagara's dependence on provisions shipped from Montreal. Also present were some merchants, and James Secord, a retired ranger, kept a tavern. Captain John Macdonell was now the paymaster of Butler's Rangers, and Allan intended to ignore the presence of his onetime troublesome lieutenant in the second battalion.

As the headquarters of the Indian Department, Niagara was the main place of refuge for the Iroquois nations who had allied themselves with Britain. Most of the Mohawks, Onondagas, Cayugas and Senecas had done so, while most of the Oneidas and the small Tuscarora nation had sided with the rebels. Detroit was the place of succour for the Western Indians, especially the Shawnees, whose country was menaced by frontier settlers from Virginia, and the Delawares, who were being molested by men from Pennsylvania.

Only days after Allan's arrival, a stream of letters began coming from Haldimand, some by ship, others brought by runners. Allan was to devise a means of communication amongst all his upper posts, by water at present, in winter by runners on snowshoes. The governor had cancelled Major Harris' leave, to Allan's dismay. Instead, Haldimand had ordered two companies of the 84th Regiment to Carleton Island and had appointed Harris the commandant of Fort Haldimand.

Haldimand forwarded a copy of a letter he had received from Sir Guy Carleton, now in command at New York City. Carleton warned Haldimand that the rebels meant to attack his upper posts, as they wanted to be in possession of them before a cessation of hostilities could be arranged in Paris, Haldimand was ordering the rest of the 34th Regiment to Niagara, and Allan was to send a detachment of the regiment to Detroit. The governor also ordered Allan to send messengers to the Iroquois nations and their "younger brothers" the Shawnees, Delawares, and Wyandots, to persuade them to refrain from acts of hostility. Such acts would provoke retaliation. The Indians should stay in their own country, keeping scouts out. If rebel raiders approached any Indian villages, Allan was to send troops to help them, but troops were no longer to raid frontier settlements because a truce had been arranged between Britain and the United States. Haldimand ordered Allan to forbid native warriors serving in the Indian Department to attack white settlers in their own communities.

Traders and farmers at Niagara would be allowed to draw flour from government stores until a mill could be built. Indian corn grown at Buffalo Creek was to be purchased for winter provisions, but Allan was to distribute rum with "rigid economy" to avoid a shortage and because liquor was expensive. Haldimand had ordered the rest of the 84th Regiment to Carleton Island, to be ready to reinforce Oswego in March, when Major Ross thought the rebels would attack. Allan was not to send any of Butler's Rangers east of Oswego, to avoid separating them too widely. On his part, Allan sent an order to Major Harris, now at Carleton Island, to cover all his provision barrels with oil cloth to protect them from damp. Haldimand ordered Harris to have all his provisions under cover in barracks or aboard vessels wintering there.[3]

Although the companies of the 84th Regiment were widely dispersed, they were now all under Allan's command. Major Ross wrote from Oswego that British regulars were more suitable for his garrison, now that peace was in the wind, as his "colony troops have lost that relish for war" which they had shown while on the offensive. Ross, Allan assumed, would appreciate having Major Harris and most of the 84th Regiment supporting him.

The snow *Seneca* arrived at Niagara with a cargo of Indian presents for Detroit. Despite the muddy road, Allan had men moving the presents to Fort Erie, along with blankets and 300 stands of arms, ready for a ship of the upper lakes fleet to take to Detroit that season. He noted that some of the presents seemed damaged, and some items were inappropriate. Indians did not use sponges, so why had they been sent?

Among the letters brought on the *Seneca* was one from Janet. Lord Loudoun had died on 27 April 1782. Allan was saddened and alarmed. He had lost another friend who might have advanced him. Now he had only Haldimand. The Duke of Argyll had promised to help his son, but he placed scant faith in the chief of the Campbells.

To add to his bleak mood, a lieutenant in Butler's Rangers entered Allan's quarters escorting two women and a small girl, and an Iroquois warrior, John Montour, who was carrying four scalps.

"Fetch an interpreter," Allan ordered the ranger officer, and he turned to the women. "How old are you?"

"I'm twenty-one. My sister is eighteen, and this little one is just seven," a rather attractive but dishevelled one replied.

The interpreter arrived, and Allan began to question John Montour, angrily at first.

"He says he has only learned of the truce between Britain and the United States on coming here," the interpreter reported. Of his six brothers, five have been killed by the rebels since the war began."

"Small wonder he is bitter," Allan admitted, softening. "Explain the truce to him carefully. Tell him that he has greatly displeased his father, the King, by taking scalps now that we are trying to make peace."

As Montour and the interpreter left, the eighteen-year-old woman burst into tears. "Two of those scalps belong to the little girl's parents," she explained, mopping her eyes with the end of her apron.

Feeling nauseated, Allan made arrangements for the three prisoners to be accommodated among the wives and daughters of Butler's Rangers, who shared barrack space on the far side of the Niagara River.[4]

On the afternoon of 19 November, a vessel brought five companies of the 34th Regiment, and on the 20th another company came on the small sloop *Caldwell*. The remaining three companies would come from Carleton Island when the *Seneca* returned. Short of space, Allan sent Captain William Ancrum's company to Fort Erie and Captain Alexander Fraser's to Fort Schlosser, situated above Niagara Falls, for both companies were to go to Detroit. Ancrum's men would go on the *Angelica*, while Fraser's and the Indian presents would go on the *Wyandot*. At crowded Fort Niagara the troops would be housed "three and three in a berth." Allan had no blankets or cooking pots for the new arrivals, and he borrowed from the merchants so that John Butler could equip the Iroquois for the winter. He asked Haldimand to repay the merchants promptly so that they would be willing to make more loans.

One of Butler's officers, Lieutenant David Brass, a skilled millwright, had begun work on a dam at Four Mile

Creek. The mill would be a great boon to both the garrison and the settlers across the Niagara River. Allan asked Haldimand to be certain to send in the spring the iron work the mill would need. On 25 November the sloop *Felicity* arrived at Fort Erie with letters from Major DePeyster and Alexander McKee, the Indian Department deputy at Detroit. Both men reported a raid on the Shawnee village of Standing Stone. Allan was perturbed, after the warning he had sent them, that the Indians had been taken by surprise. If they had kept the scouts out, the attack could have been prevented.[5]

Just before Christmas the two companies of the 34th Regiment returned to Forts Erie and Schlosser for the winter. Contrary winds prevented the ships going farther west than Presqu'ile, and they had turned back. the *Wyandot*, loaded with Indian presents DePeyster desperately needed, would stay at Fort Erie until the spring. For the next few months Allan's contact with De Peyster would be the runners on snowshoes. Nor would the three companies of the 34th Regiment arrive from Carleton Island, for the bad weather had set in.

Chapter Eighteen

The Upper Country
1782-1783

On 10 December Allan attended a council of Iroquois—or Six Nations—chiefs. John Butler, now somewhat recovered, accompanied him. The Indian spokesman was the Seneca chief Toconando. At the Onondaga council fire near Buffalo Creek the chief explained that if the Iroquois did not go to war, the Americans would see this as a sign of weakness. Toconando recommended that the chiefs send a flag of truce to the rebels with the message that the Indians would in future "follow the Example set us by themselves seeing it is their intention to destroy the Indians and possess themselves of their Country."

The following day Allan addressed the chiefs, relaying Haldimand's policy in a speech he had prepared with considerable care. He spoke slowly, pausing after each phrase for the interpreter to translate his words.

"Brothers, I thank the Great Spirit for giving us this council fire, lighted by your late friend and brother, Sir William Johnson, by order of the King, your Father. It gives me pleasure that it has continued to burn bright since that time, and hope that by our continuing to act in a proper part, we shall not only preserve it, but make it burn still brighter. My orders from your brother, the General, are that nothing shall be wanting on my part for that purpose.

"Brothers, you have told me of your great misfortunes, and those of the Shawnees. General Haldimand wants you to cease going to war for very good reasons. He has repeatedly asked you to send out scouts. Had the Shawnees followed this advice, they would not have been surprised at Standing Stone. The General knows that many rebels are dissatisfied with the Congress for refusing to accept the generous offers made by King George III, and have not paid their taxes. Since so many rebels want peace, the General does not want the Indians to alarm them and harm them by making war.

"If the rebels come into your country, I have orders to help you. Your plight is similar to that of your loyalist brothers, refugees forced from their own country, their properties lost. I entreat you to keep watch. The enemy can not enter your country easily, and if they march they will quickly be discovered by your scouts. I beg you not to follow the example of the enemy, for that will anger your father the King and your brother the General. The humanity shown by Indians to rebel women and children they brought in as prisoners is more pleasing to the Great Spirit above than the cruelty committed by your enemies, who improperly call themselves Christians. I beg you to continue to act with the same humanity."[1]

Satisfied by Allan's promise to aid them, the chiefs departed, but on 16 December an infuriated Joseph Brant challenged both Allan and John Butler. The Mohawk war chief was distraught that the Iroquois leaders had departed so tamely after Allan addressed them. They should instead have resolved on war. Allan felt shabby at having carried out Haldimand's instructions, suppressing his own sentiments. Brant was right. King's troops who were captured were treated as prisoners-of-war, but Indians, and sometimes loyalists, were put to death cruelly. Revenge was justified, and he begged Haldimand not to "tie up their Hands." Now he was glad to be able to leave further meetings to John Butler and devote himself to his own military duties.

Nevertheless, Butler consulted him frequently. The records of the Indian Department were incomplete. Butler reported that a lad of eighteen named Clement had been in charge of the Indian store, and he had not kept any records at all. Clement, whom Allan found not very bright, had been made the store keeper by Guy Johnson, and Allan ordered the lad suspended. Next, Allan cut down the issues of rum, and ordered that artificers and labourers in the Indian Department be paid the same wages as those in the Engineering Department. Butler had been allowing five shillings a day to artificers and three shillings to labourers. The pay in the Engineering Department was fifteen pence and ten pence respectively.[2]

A runner arrived from Detroit with a letter dated 7 January 1783 from Major DePeyster. The major reported that the Congress was taking steps to restrain the rebel

Butler's Barracks, Niagara-on-the-Lake. Although named for the building erected during the revolution, this structure dates from the 1820s. Butler's original barracks were burnt by the Americans, along with most of Niagara-on-the-Lake, in December 1813.

frontiersmen. Some rebels had destroyed the Shawnee village of Chillicothe, but went no farther because the American garrison at Fort Pitt did not support them. Then on the 24th a runner reported that a rebel force was near Kanaghsaws, on the lower Genesee River. Allan suspected the report was exaggerated, but to hearten the Senecas he dispatched 210 men—regulars, rangers, and Loyal Foresters—to show his good faith. The men returned on the 28th, having found no trace of the enemy.

While the danger to the Senecas had been a false alarm, Allan soon learned of a genuine threat to Oswego. In February, Major Ross reported that 800 rebels in sleighs had approached his posts, but they turned back when scouts from the garrison discovered them and a surprise attack was out of the question. Although Ross had received reports of a preliminary peace treaty, he asked Allan for regulars from Niagara. His "colony troops" had behaved well, but he wanted a reinforcement of professionals lest the rebels try again.

At that Allan's fiery temper exploded. Ross dared to imply that the detachment of the 84th Regiment at Oswego was unreliable and prone to desert. If Ross was so dissatisfied with the men, he could send them to Niagara, and Allan would send him *Regular Troops* " in place of them. In the end Ross kept the men, and Allan sent him one company of rangers and twenty Indians, while Major Harris dispatched two of the companies of the 34th Regiment that had wintered at Carleton Island and ten rangers. Ross' garrison then numbered 600, while Allan had 750 men at Niagara.[3]

All through April, Allan had many scouts in the Indian country, convinced that the natives' lands were in more danger than his posts. Then four Delaware Indians who had been hunting since February returned from the neighbourhood of Fort Pitt with two scalps and a seventeen-year-old prisoner. Allan summoned Colonels Dundas and Butler as witnesses when he reproved the Delawares and ordered the scalps hidden. He told the four they had embarrassed Haldimand, and Butler could not give them any presents. Joseph Brant, too, castigated them for they might cause an invasion of the Indian country.

On the morning of 16 April, near the house of John Dease, Sir John Johnson's cousin and a medical doctor who worked as Butler's assistant, a Delaware Indian was found mortally wounded from an axe blow on his head. The Delaware had flopped down drunk, a common sight around the fort, Allan confessed, when he was attacked. The murder suspect was Jonathon Bray, a prisoner of the Indians who had been brought to Niagara in November, and who lived in the Dease house. Allan held a court of enquiry, with John Butler presiding, which ruled that Bray be sent in irons to Montreal for trial. If Bray was found guily, Allan wanted him hanged at Niagara, so that the Indians could see justice done.[4]

On the 28th, Allan wrote to Haldimand asking for a leave of absence. The war would soon be over, and his regiment reduced. If he had to use his savings from the sale of commissions to pay his battalion debts, he might have nothing to live on but his half-pay. This could not support his large family and he had to find someone who could influence the government to pay the regimental debt or raise his pension. While he was a brigadier-general in Canada, his rank in the permanent army was as a lieutenant-colonel.

A few days later Allan received a letter, forwarded from Oswego, signed by a Captain Tonge. With a Mr. Robertson, Tonge was travelling from New York City to Quebec City with a message from Sir Guy Carleton for Haldimand. At Albany, Tonge and Robertson met Colonel Marinius Willett, who complained that Indians sent by Brigadier Maclean had cut off the frontier settlement at Wyoming, Pennsylvania. Allan was puzzled, until three Oneida Indians arrived on 4 May with a letter from General Washington dated 14 April, which they had brought from his headquarters at Newburgh, on the lower Hudson River.

The rebel commander-in-chief had enclosed part of a letter Sir Guy Carleton had sent him, requesting passports for two messengers to travel to Haldimand's headquarters with dispatches announcing the ratification of preliminary articles of peace. Washington signed the passports and the two "Gentlemen" were now on their way to Canada. As the distance was great, to save time, Washington had written directly to Allan so that he would know that peace was "Official" before Haldimand could notify him from Quebec

City. Washington asked Allan to prevent wanton acts of cruelty by Indians on the frontier, "disagreeable to them and to inhabitants of the United States."[5]

That aroused Allan's ire. He retorted that if Washington truly wanted to "prevent disagreeable consequences to the inhabitants of the United States," why had he condoned some of the attacks on the Indians that had originated from Fort Pitt? Why had he alowed the expedition against Oswego? Furthermore, Colonel Willett's accusation that Allan had sent Indians to Wyoming was untrue. Why did Washington permit newspapers in Boston and Albany to print lies whose only purpose was to enflame ignorant people? Such lies were a disgrace to any nation. He promised Washington that he would abide by the cessation of hostilities, but he could not regard it as official until he received confirmation from Haldimand. He sent this reply with the Oneidas who had brought Washington's letter.

Shortly after the Oneidas left, four letters arrived from Quebec City. In the first Haldimand admitted that he was still waiting for official news, but he had received a copy of the peace terms from a friend in Philadelphia, which alarmed him. The boundary between Canada and the United States was to run along the 45th parallel to the St. Lawrence, then along the middle of the river and the Great Lakes. Haldimand was very distressed at the effect news of the boundary would have on the Indians. He cautioned Allan to be watchful lest resentful warriors wreak vengeance on any small post or detachment in the upper country. Otherwise he was to carry on, and to distribute provisions as usual. John Butler was to make plans to reduce the size of the Indian Department, and Major DePeyster could disband his Detroit Volunteers, a company of French-speaking farmers whose services were no longer needed.[6] Allan studied the letter, stunned. If the report was true, the Indians had been ignored under the peace terms.

A letter of 22 April directed Allan to investigate in secret certain expenditures made by Guy Johnson when he was Superintendent of Indian Affairs, and to take only John Butler into his confidence. The last two letters confirmed the disastrous boundary settlement and the signing of preliminary articles of peace. Haldimand ordered Allan to stop work on fortifications and other public works at all the upper posts. No more military stores need be sent to Detroit and Michilimackinac, but the Indian presents were to be distributed as planned. The governor was hoping that orders to compensate the Six Nations and other allies would soon arrive from England, and he instructed Allan to "pay your nicest attention to the Mangement and to the Conduct of the Indians."

Allan asked Haldimand to send Sir John Johnson to Niagara without delay. Butler had been doing an excellent job, but the Indians needed to see their Superintendent, who might be able to reconcile them to a boundary that placed their country inside the United States. Allan thought the situation might deteriorate at any time, for many of Butler's Rangers knew about the boundary. A sergeant and three men had been spying on Washington's army all winter, and had brought in newspapers. He was dispensing rum more generously to keep the Indians "in good humour."

Joseph Brant, whom Allan feared the most because he was well educated, confronted him and voiced his suspicions that his people had been deceived.

"England," the Mohawk war chief informed him, "has sold the Indians to the United States. To ingratiate ourselves with the Congress, we may have to attack the British in their posts."

Brant decided to go to Montreal to see Sir John, and he sailed on 7 May. Allan ordered officers of the Indian Department who resided in Indian villages to stay where they were, to avoid arousing suspicions. Reports sent by DePeyster showed that the Indians were quiet at Detroit. Writing to Haldimand on 10 May, Allan suggested he delay Brant's return. "Joseph knows too much and too little, tho' a good fellow in the main, he is a perfect Indian."

Allan did not want Brant coming to the upper country until after Sir John had visited the Indians. Major DePeyster asked Allan not to send any newspapers beyond Fort Erie, since knowledge of the boundary would mean trouble at Detroit. He was as disturbed as Allan over the way Britain had betrayed her Indian allies, and was equally aware of the need for secrecy, for the safety of the garrisons.

Allan carried out his private investigation of Guy Johnson's expenditures. John Butler was not much help, for he had no part in managing the affairs of the Indian

Department from 1779, when Guy had returned from England, until Haldimand had dismissed him. Butler did admit that two barrels of wine Haldimand had sent for sick Indians, which Butler wanted dispensed on doctors' receipts, had vanished. By making discreet enquiries of Captains John Powell and Gilbert Tice, Indian Department officers, Allan learned that Guy had ordered beef, which the Indians never received, and butter, which they did not like, as well as vast quantities of sugar, tea, and wine, and smaller amounts of raisins, almonds, and prunes. Guy had dispensed, on average, 465 gallons of rum each month, whereas Allan was handing out only 98 gallons. Furthermore, in April 1782, before his recall, many goods from the Indian store had been auctioned off as Guy's personal property. In short, Allan informed Haldimand, such records as Colonel Guy Johnson left were

Extravagant, wonderful and ficticious... that one may Exclaim with Hamlet when he sees his fathers ghost, 'he comes in so questionable a shape that I must speak to it'... the first Lord of the Treasury would be the best person to settle it.[7]

On 10 May, Allan held a conference with the Six Nations chiefs, who were refusing to believe that England could give away their country. They were confused by the Oneidas who had brought General Washington's letter for Allan. The Oneidas had visited the temporary encampment at Buffalo Creek, where they had relatives, and had told the refugee Indians that the Americans intended destroying all the Six Nations, and the white people who had served with them, especially Sir John Johnson and John Butler. Allan urged Haldimand not to evacuate the upper posts. He was convinced that the Iroquois would be "faithful & moderate" if the British garrisons remained, but if they were withdrawn "disagreeable scenes" would ensue.

Some Delawares had left to found a community along the Grand River, and many people, Indian and white, were enquiring where they might live if they could not return to their former homes. Butler was hoping to resettle his rangers along the west side of the Niagara River, and Allan, too, was wondering where the men of his 84th Regiment, who had come from the rebelling colonies, would find new homes. Butler thought Joseph Brant would be asking the same question of Haldimand while he was in "Canada." Glad that Brant was not on hand in this time of uncertainty, Allan wrote again, suggesting that Brant be detained until Haldimand could make plans for the refugee Indians and loyalists.

Allan feared Brant because he knew the implication of the boundary settlement. At the same time Allan admired the Mohawk war chief for his loyalty to his own people and for putting their best interests ahead of all else. "I do from my soul Pity these People, and should they Commit Outrages at giving up these Posts, it would by no means surprise me," he wrote to the governor.[8]

Early in June, Allan received a private letter from Haldimand. Much as he sympathized with him over his precarious financial situation, he could not give Allan leave at present. He would do so as soon as the confusion and discontent amongst the Indians was resolved. "Now that Lord North has returned to a share in the administration, I have not a doubt that you will experience his friendly offices." Here was welcome news, the first intimation Allan had of the Lord North-Charles James Fox coalition that had assumed power from Lord Shelburne on 1 April. Some of his pent-up tension eased and he knew he could be patient a while yet.

He squeezed time from his regular duties, directing the movement of provisions and soothing the Indians, to attend to his own 84th Regiment, which he had been neglecting of late. Haldimand had ignored his recommendation that Major Harris purchase the lieutenant-colonelcy, after which Allan would serve as colonel-commandant without pay. Now that the regiment would soon be reduced, there might not be many more promotions. Major Harris had arranged a few promotions some months before, and the captain-lieutenancy was vacant, for unfortunate reasons.

Archibald Maclean, who had purchased from Captain-Lieutenant Neil Maclean in 1781, had been court martialled at Carleton Island and dismissed. Allan's young kinsman was found 200 pounds in arrears to the regiment, and in arrears to his company and to several Montreal merchants for goods he had purchased. All told, Archibald owed 460 pounds, an appalling sum. Major Harris was willing to pay the 200 pounds owed the regiment unless Haldimand could meet this from public funds, which Allan knew the governor would never do.[9]

Harris had cleared the 2,222 pound debt to Cox, Mair and Cox by opening an account with Mr. Adair, of Chidley Court, London, and borrowing that sum from him. Yet a day of reckoning was approaching, and Allan desperately needed leave. In London he hoped to find a patron to settle the debt. In every letter he urged Haldimand to speed Sir John Johnson on his way. Once the Superintendent had visited the Indian allies, and defused the potentially explosive situation, Allan was certain that Haldimand would let him go back to England.

Chapter Nineteen

Uneasy Truce 1783

While Haldimand waited for specific instructions from London on what to do about the displaced Indians and loyalists (both provincial troops and civilians) the commanding officers in the upper country endeavoured to reassure those who had taken refuge at their posts that Britain would not abandon them. Allan borrowed 1,200 gallons of rum from the merchants Robert Hamilton and Richard Cartwright and ordered a like amount from Carleton Island to repay them. An alarmed John Butler crossed the Niagara River and told Allan that Sir John Johnson was supposedly at Cataraqui, looking for land on which the Mohawks could be resettled. Butler hoped the rumour was false. The land at Cataraqui belonged to the Mississauga Indians, and placing the Mohawks there could cause friction.

"A barrel of rum and a few trade goods will appease the Mississaugas," Allan told Butler. "But the Six Nations will be very distressed if they are not able to return to their homeland."

On 23 May, Haldimand wrote confirming that Sir John was at Cataraqui, and would soon come to Niagara with a good supply of clothing for the Indians. Haldimand was planning to resettle any of the Six Nations who did not want to return to their own country, and he was sending his surveyor-general, Major Samuel Holland (who had surveyed the Island of Saint John for Lauchlin Macleane in 1767) to Cataraqui to select suitable land. The governor had discussed his plan with Joseph Brant, who agreed and would accompany Holland. Allan was to say nothing to the Indians at Niagara. Sir John would tell them. Meanwhile, Major Harris was to furnish men and supplies to Major Ross, who would be constructing a new fort at Cataraqui. Carleton Island might have to be evacuated as the boundary was to run north of it.[1]

Allan wrote to Major DePeyster, for by now the Indians at Detroit must know about the boundary, to tell him that Sir John would be sending presents soon. DePeyster wanted to call a council of chiefs, but Allan advised against this. Chiefs brought "large suites" that had to be fed and given rum, which was expensive. Allan suggested that DePeyster send Indian Department officers to the various villages to distribute the presents, and to tell the natives that the only messages that were true were those coming from Niagara. All messages brought by agents of the American Congress should be ignored.

Allan complained to Haldimand that "designing Americans" kept sending emissaries to the Indians. Ten from Virginia had come to the Indian camp at Buffalo Creek with two strings of wampum. Allan dispatched John Butler with twelve men and a barrel each of rum, flour, and pork. The effrontery of the Americans knew no bounds, and they had no right to enter "this country" without Haldimand's permission. Allan was sending all white men who came among the Indians to Carleton Island, when he could catch them. DePeyster, too, was having agents of the Congress brought to Detroit when his officers found them.

Allan held a council at the Onondaga camp at Buffalo Creek on 2 July, to hear a report from two Oneidas who were friendly to Britain. The two had visited the Oneida castle of Kanowalohale, near Oneida Lake, and returned with an alarming story. In the spring, General Philip Schuyler, a rebel leader in Albany, had held a council which the Six Nations who were allies of Britain did not attend. Schuyler told the Indians that peace had come, and because the Six Nations had sided with the British, they were now in the same situation as the loyalists, their lands forfeited. The United States could dispose of their lands as they saw fit. These lands were United States territory by right of conquest, as were all the upper posts. The United States would look favourably on most of the Oneidas and some Cayugas, but the rest of the Six Nations ought to move north of the lakes into the King's territory. Should John Butler be captured, he would be hanged.

Now Butler addressed the council. He could not say whether the report of Schuyler's speech was false, for Haldimand had yet to hear from England, but he expected that Sir John Johnson would be apprised of more particulars when he arrived. "I ask you to remember the promise I made to you in 1775 when I moved to Niagara," Butler said. "I came to share the dangers and fatigues of war with my

Indian brothers. I was ready to leave my bones among you, and will still assist you if the enemy tries to to deprive you of your possessions.

"General Maclean promised his protection at the council last December. He stands ready to fulfil that promise when required. If any of your chiefs visit Kanowalohale, I want to know what messages they take and are sent."

The chiefs seemed mollified, and Allan fervently hoped that Sir John would come soon. He felt close to the breaking point. Nor did reports from Detroit reassure him. On 7 July, DePeyster wrote that Captain Matthew Elliott, of the Indian Department, found two agents of the Congress, Ephraim Douglass and a Captain McCully, near Detroit and brought them in. Douglass, whom DePeyster thought shrewd, said the Congress assumed that DePeyster had orders to evacuate Detroit. Douglass was to arrange the release of prisoners the Indians were holding. DePeyster recommended that the agents go to Niagara, where Sir John was expected daily, as he could give them more information. DePeyster was providing them with a guide to Fort Pitt, and he suggested Allan send them home by Lake Champlain or Oswego. DePeyster's honour would be sullied if a drunken Indian, or an irate loyalist, harmed the emissaries in the vast wilderness.

Allan was very suspicious of Douglass and McCully. Machiavelli, he told Haldimand, could learn from such designing knaves as the Americans. As long as Indians were receiving the King's provisions and clothing, they were British allies and "a part of our Family." He was also sceptical because Washington had not mentioned these agents in his letter of 14 April, and Allan wondered if Douglass might be an imposter.

Some Six Nations chiefs did visit the Oneida castle of Kanowalohale, and they reported that General Schuyler had not made a speech in which he said the Iroquois lands belonged to the United States. Some mischief-makers spread the story to provoke an Indian war. On 9 July, Joseph Brant arrived at Niagara, very pleased with the way Haldimand had received him. The governor had promised a tract of land along the Grand River for the Six Nations. Allan gave Joseph four gallons of rum and sent him to spread the good news among the chiefs at Buffalo Creek. Butler sent a belt of wampum to the Oneidas as a good will gesture, but Allan and Joseph were annoyed. Butler was playing into enemy hands, and Joseph sent out scouts who intercepted Butler's runners and brought the belt back.[2]

On the evening of 10 July, Ephraim Douglass and Captain McCully, the emissaries from the Congress, reached Niagara from Fort Pitt. Allan received them politely, but refused to allow them to talk with any of the Iroquois. Douglass, Allan decided, was shrewd, but he behaved correctly. Then, in a letter from Captain Elliott, Allan discovered that Douglass knew Indian dialects. He did not want Douglass to wait at Niagara until directions arrived from Haldimand, or the arrival of Sir John. Joseph Brant had sought out Douglass and had a long talk with him, to Allan's dismay, and he asked the two emissaries to leave on the 16th, in a bateau for Oswego. He provided them with an escort of a sergeant and seven men of the 8th and 34th Regiments. Douglass asked Allan for a letter, which he could show to the Congress, setting out the reasons why he had not spoken with the Indians. Allan complied, stating that he could not allow such conversations as long as Britain retained the upper posts. The 3,000 Indians being provisioned at Niagara were part of his garrison. Communicating Douglass' instructions from the Congress could have led to disorder, for which Allan would be blamed if he did not have authority from Haldimand.

From Detroit, DePeyster reported that "Kentuckers" had crossed the Ohio River and stolen horses from the Indians. He had met with 200 Southern Indians, seventy of them Cherokees, who had come seeking help. The war on the frontier of Georgia, their territory, was still raging. The major added that Douglass and McCully had hoped to tell the Indians that Pennsylvania had passed a law making it a felony for whites to cross the Ohio River, to show the Americans' good faith. Now DePeyster was trying to recover prisoners the Indians were holding, to co-operate with the Congress.

On 18 July, Sir John arrived with a vessel full of Indian presents, and he asked for plenty of rum before meeting his charges. Butler agreed, but Allan disapproved. While he sometimes resorted to rum himself, he wanted to wean the Indians away from expecting so much of the harmful liquor.

He had to borrow four barrels from the merchants, which Sir John said was not enough. Butler and Sir John went off to meet the chiefs, and Allan had presents for Detroit moved to Fort Schlosser. He was pleased with the results of Sir John's visit. When the baronet and John Butler met with Allan, all agreed that some Virginians wanted to start an Indian war as an excuse to help themselves to more Indian land.

"I'll write to General Schuyler," Sir John said. "I'll inform him that Virginians, not Indians, are the aggressors, and suggest that the Congress do more to restrain the frontiersmen."

"The Indians should band together, unite for protection," Allan said.

"I have advocated it," Sir John replied. "The Iroquois have agreed to send representatives to Sandusky to meet with some thirty other nations, their younger brethren, to form a confederacy so that they can resist the Virginians."

"I am pleased to hear it," Allan said. "Most of the Virginians at Kentuck are law breakers, who like living a long way from the United States government. Yet they will not hesitate to involve the Congress in their quarrels with the Indians if they can."

What Allan did not say to Sir John was that unless the Indians united, they would be divided and conquered as surely as the Highland clans had been divided and suppressed.

Instead, he said, "I'll write Colonel Willett to warn him of the dangers of an Indian War."

The following day, 1 August, half a dozen American merchants from Schenectady arrived with three bateaux full of rum, intending to trade at the upper posts. They had letters from General Schuyler, George Clinton the governor of New York State, and the mayor of Albany, giving them permission. Allan was bewildered that Captain Thomas Gumersall of Sir John Johnson's regiment, now in command at Oswego, had not turned back the merchants. He refused to allow them to proceed to Detroit, and ordered the rum locked up, as trade was improper before the final peace treaty had been signed. All the British merchants at the upper posts had permits from Haldimand, and those at Niagara protested vigorously when they learned of the arrival of the men from Schenectady. "Our Indian friends looked at those people, very crooked indeed," Allan informed Haldimand. When he finished his letter he went outside, where an incident occurred that made him glad Sir John was there. An Indian, the worse for rum, was swaying angrily in front of one of the merchants from Montreal, mistaking him for an American.

"You damn Yankee, what brought you here?" he demanded.

Sir John, who was watching, motioned to an Indian Department officer, who hastily placed himself between the merchant and the Indian before anyone was injured.

Sir John left for Cataraqui later in the day. At that time Major DePeyster was writing from Detroit that the Indian presents had arrived on the schooner *Faith* from Fort Erie. Once Sir John's orders reached him, DePeyster would conduct the solemn ceremony of burying the hatchet, and the presents would be distributed. The presents appeared to have been pillaged and they had come without an invoice. Once DePeyster knew the extent of the looting, he would inform Allan.[3]

A letter from home that arrived on 4 August brought distressing news. Allan's son, now nineteen, was without employment. His regiment, in which he had a lieutenant's commission, had been disbanded. Since fencibles were not regulars, he had no half-pay. He was back in London with Janet and wholly dependent on Allan. On the death of Lord Loudoun, who had commanded the 3rd Regiment of Guards, the Duke of Argyll had taken command of that regiment, but he had done nothing for Allan's son. Allan wrote Haldimand asking him to procure and ensigncy in an established regiment. "The young man wishes to follow the Army.... I have no other means of providing for him." In his reply, dated 14 September, Haldimand chided Allan for asking a favour at such a busy time, but "I shall endeavour to grant your Request in favor of the Young Gentleman—You forgot to mention his Name."[4]

The governor was busy with his plans to resettle the Indian allies and loyalists, and he had abandoned the British policy of reserving the interior of the continent for Indians. Land along the upper St. Lawrence and Lake Ontario would now be opened for white settlement. Hitherto the presence of some French-speaking farmers around Detroit had been tolerated because they were there before the reservation policy had been formulated. Sir John Johnson arranged for the purchase of the land from the Mississauga Indians. Haldimand agreed to allow white settlement because the refugee Indians wanted the loyalists near them as a protection against the Americans. John Butler left Niagara with sixty gallons of rum and presents for 500 Mississaugas, to visit their camps. Allan did not want them coming to Niagara for the negotiations, because they would have to be provisioned.

"I declare I have more plague with Rum than all the other businesses I have to do," Allan wrote Haldimand on 17 August. "It's a pity that such a Cursed Liquor has been found out." Seamen on the Lakes expected it as part of their wages and would desert if they did not get it. Allan was in a quandary because Haldimand gave the merchants Douglas and Symington an exclusive permit to retail rum to the garrison, for they charged a higher price. Officers complained, and so did competing merchants. Allan was sympathetic, especiialy to Hamilton and Cartwright, who had loaned him the rum when he needed it. As he tried to reduce the consumption of rum, he was convinced the Indian Department officers competed to see who could dispense the most liquor.

On 12 August, Allan received a letter from Captain Thomas Gumersall at Oswego, with an enclosure from Haldimand. Gumersall reported that General Washington was at Fort Stanwix, and he had troops in the Mohawk Valley, ready to occupy the upper posts. In his enclosure, Haldimand wrote that one of Washington's staff officers, the German Baron von Steuben, had come to Quebec City to demand the surrender of the upper posts. Haldimand resisted this kind of pressure. He ordered Allan to defend them at all costs, to hold an enquiry into the looting of the Indian presents that had been sent to Detroit, and to send home the merchants from Schenectady who had been at Niagara since the first of the month.

The Schenectady men claimed to be afraid that their three bateaux of rum would be captured. Allan agreed to let them store the rum with a Niagara merchant, Samuel Street, but he took the precaution of summoning Lieutenant-Colonel

Dundas, 8th Regiment, and Major Robert Hoyes, 34th Regiment, as witnesses. In their presence the merchants wrote certificates stating that no one at Niagara would be held responsible for the security of the rum. The merchants went aboard the *Mohawk* for Oswego on 15 September. On the 20th Allan opened his court of enquiry into the theft of the Indian presents. After hearing testimony for six days, Allan summed up his findings.

The goods had been stolen while they were being moved from Fort Schlosser to Fort Erie, by non-commissioned officers and privates of the 34th Regiment, men originally intended for Detroit who had not been sent because Haldimand decided DePeyster did not need them. Most of the culprits belonged to Captain Alexander Fraser's company, stationed at Schlosser, but a few were from Captain William Ancrum's at Fort Erie. Allan found that the value of missing goods amounted to some 5,000 pounds in New York currency, or nearly 3,000 pounds Sterling. He sent four corporals and eight privates, the most suspect, in irons to Montreal for trial. Sixteen other privates were locked up at Fort Niagara to await a court martial.

A grieving Captain Fraser wrote his own report, noting that his men were good soldiers. Fraser blamed the carelessness of the merchants at Montreal and Schlosser, who had put temptation in the men's way. Trunks from Montreal had been shipped without rope, keys tied to the handles. Of the goods which DePeyster reported missing, Fraser and his lieutenant found only five yards of calico and two prayer books. Everything else had vanished, most likely traded to local Indians. His men had opened the trunks, removed some goods, and substituted logs to give the right weight.[5]

John Butler returned to Niagara after helping reconcile the Mississaugas to parting with some of their land for the Indian allies and loyalists, and he reported he, too, had heard that General Schuyler had never made an inflammatory speech threatening the Six Nations with the loss of their lands. Nevertheless the Mohawks and some others wanted to remain in Canada, although the Senecas felt that their territory was sufficiently remote from white settlements to be safe. For months, men retired from Butler's Rangers who were farming on the west side of the Niagara River had been enquiring whether they could have titles to their farms, where they now wanted to live. Since all hope of having their properties returned was lost, most of the rangers wanted to settle close to the farmers. Allan told Haldimand, "they would rather go to Japan than go among the Americans where they could never live in peace."[6]

On 5 October, Allan wrote another request to Haldimand for leave, and he also wrote a covering letter to his nephew Captain Lauchlin Maclean, now serving as the commissary at Carleton Island. He asked Lauchlin to obtain leave from Major Harris to carry the letter to Quebec City. In his letter to Haldimand, he asked him to mention his name in letters to Lord North. He wrote other letters to friends in London "to refresh their Memory" and asked, if Haldimand could not spare him, to allow Lauchlin to go to England on his behalf. He was very worried that the present government might not last long, and Lord North would again be out of office.

On the 15th, a letter arrived from Haldimand. The governor replied that Allan's long, faithful service, zeal and present complicated command "forbids my refusing a Request so earnestly made." Allan was to come to Quebec City at once, and to bring all his records, returns, and accounts with him. Lieutenant-Colonel Dundas would also be going to England. He was retiring, and Major DePeyster would purchase his commission in the 8th Regiment. Allan was to order the detachments of the 84th Regiment at Niagara and Detroit to join Major Harris at Carleton Island, and Haldimand would replace the two companies at Michilimackinac with other regulars in the spring. Robert Hoyes, promoted to lieutenant-colonel of the 34th Regiment, would take over Allan's command at Niagara.

Allan sailed for Carleton Island on 17 October, where six companies of his battalion were on duty, while one remained at Oswegatchie. Disbanding the battalion would be Major Harris' responsibility. The unfinished business at Niagara would be handled by Lieutenant-Colonel Hoyes, who would preside over the court martial of the men who had stolen the Indian presents. Although Allan had not heard that a final peace treaty had been signed, the war was over, and he was thinking of retiring from the army. Before he left Carleton Island, his nephew Lauchlin returned after carrying his letters to Quebec City. Lauchlin gave him a powder horn, on which a map of northern New York was carved.

"Please send this to Torloisk, Uncle," he said. "I expect to stay in the new world, and I would like something of mine kept in our ancestral home."[7]

When he reached Quebec City, Allan had a final conference with Haldimand, who promised to use his influence to help Allan's never-named son obtain a permanent commission. The governor now had orders to disband all his provincial regiments, and the 84th. However, because the order had come late in the season, the 84th, Butler's Rangers, and Major Ross' second battalion King's Royal Regiment of New York would not be disbanded until the spring of 1784. The men of the 84th who had come from the rebelling colonies would receive grants of land in townships being surveyed for the disbanded provincials, while all the officers and men would be given generous allotments of land as a reward for their services. Haldimand had arranged a passage to Halifax, so that Allan could oversee the disbanding of his second battalion. The year before, Sir Guy Carleton had recalled Lieutenant-Colonel John Small and the five companies serving in Georgia to New York City, and now the entire second battalion was in Nova Scotia.

When he reached Halifax, Allan found that the peace treaty had been signed on 3 September. He met with the governor, John Parr, and arranged for the Township of Douglas to be awarded to his second battalion. Most of the rank and file who did not have homes in Nova Scotia would go there, but some of the officers wanted to return to Britain. These included Lieutenant-Colonel Small, the senior captain, Alexander Macdonald, as well as Captain Allan Macdonald, the husband of the legendary Flora, who had almost lost the use of his legs. Flora herself had returned home in the autumn of 1779 in poor health, after residing for a time in New York City and Nova Scotia.[8] Allan's nephew Lachlan Macquarrie, who had purchased a lieutenancy in the 71st Regiment, would return with that regiment when the time came.

Before he sailed for England, Allan visited the military cemetery near the little fort on the hill overlooking the harbour. He found the grave of his cousin Francis, and paid his last respects to the man who had become his comrade in arms in 1746, after the Battle of Culloden.

Monument to John Macdonald in Exeter Cathedral, Devonshire. John was left in Scotland to be educated when his parents emigrated to North Carolina in 1774. His mother, Flora, is famous for escorting Bonnie Prince Charlie from the Outer Hebrides to Skye after the '45.

Retirement 1784-1797

Allan Maclean left the army in 1784, soon after his return to London. There he lived quietly in Buckingham Street with Janet. Records reveal only glimpses of his life during his closing years.

Two pieces of news which he regarded as vital awaited him when he reached York Buildings some time in January 1784. His twenty-one-year-old brother-in-law was Sir Hector, the 23rd chief of clan Maclean. Sir Allan died on the Isle of Inch Kenneth on 10 December 1783. A week later, on the 17th, the North-Fox ministry resigned, news that confirmed Allan's fears over the past months. William Pitt the younger, son of Lord Chatham, was the new Prime Minister, and Lord North was a member of the opposition. Allan's only protector was Haldimand, who was himself under something of a cloud. Pierre du Clavet, the man Allan had had arrested too hastily in 1780, had come to London, and instituted a lawsuit against the governor for false imprisonment.[1]

With the coming of summer, Allan and Janet paid a visit to Torloisk, and with them went two precious mementos of his now-disbanded regiment—the colours, and his nephew Lauchlin's powder horn. He presented the colours to his niece Marianne, the most suitable person to whom he could entrust them since she was the heir to Torloisk. On 24 January 1839, Marianne wrote a short history of her uncle's life which concluded:

> Conscious that my uncle left me, by that deposit, the best possession he had, his military renoun, I should not deserve the trust, if I left his Banners without making the future possessor aware of the value of them.[2]

Another visitor to Torloisk in 1784 was the French naturalist Bartholemy Faujas de Saint-Fond, who, upon his arrival, found a "little musical concert" in progress. Of Marianne he wrote, "Miss Maclean, a girl of most charming figure, played on a harpsichord some excellent Italian music."[3]

In the autumn, on learning from a newspaper item that Governor Haldimand was to sail home on leave aboard the *Atalanta*, accompanied by his secretary, Allan wrote a letter to Major Robert Mathews and sent it to Plymouth, where a tender was known to deliver mail to incoming vessels. He warned Mathews that Monsieur du Calvet intended serving Haldimand with a writ upon his arrival. The governor would be in no danger at Plymouth, for the Captain of the *Atalanta* could prevent any bailiffs coming on board. It would be most unfortunate, Allan thought, if Haldimand's enemies could arrange to have him arrested, and then published the fact in newspapers to embarrass him. Allan suggested that Haldimand go from Portsmouth to Southampton by a fast row boat, and take a post chaise to London, rather than disembark at Southampton, where du Calvet's agents might be lying in wait.

Haldimand may have followed Allan's advice, for he did elude du Calvet's bailiffs, and reached London on 9 January 1785. He went to stay with his nephew, Antoine François Haldimand, who lived at St. Mary Axe, in Hampstead. There, Allan called on the governor on the 11th, a day before Haldimand was presented to the King, who made him a Knight of Bath.

What Haldimand did for Allan was obscure, but he helped him obtain a pension. Allan was able to live frugally in London, with sufficient funds to support his family and preserve his independence. Without a pension, Allan would have had to live at Torloisk, accepting help from his affluent elder brother, Lachlan the 7th laird. Allan remained in contact with Haldimand, who recorded on one occasion that Brigadier Maclean and some other officers had dined with him, "and we sat longer at table than I could have wished."[4]

Settling the regimental debt may have used up most of Allan's savings from the sale of commissions, including his own. The Army List shows that he sold his lieutenant-colonelcy to Robert Manners, the former major of the 80th

Regiment, on 14 February 1784, before the Royal Highland Emigrants were disbanded. The 1st battalion was disbanded at Carleton Island on 24 June 1784, and the 2nd battalion at Halifax on 10 April of that year. Allan's only wealth, apart from a pension, was a grant of 5,000 acres on the north shore of the Ottawa River which he received in 1788 for his service as commander of the first battalion 84th Regiment Royal Highland Emigrants. On 31 January of that year, Prince Charles Stuart died in Rome. As his only brother Henry was a Cardinal of the Roman Catholic Church, their sole heir was Charle's daughter Charlotte. The following year, at age thirty-six, Charlotte died without issue. The Hanoverians were then the closest descendants of the Stuart line, making them the legitimate rulers of Britain. The King was no longer o'er the water; the King was in London.[5]

Allan's son probably had a military career, for by 1793 Britain was again at war with France, a war that lasted, with truces, for twenty-two years, an era which spawned many army careers. Patrick Agnew, Lauchlin Macleane's unofficial stepson, was a major-general. Of Lauchlin's other children, John Macleane was a major in the 5th Madras Calvary in the service of the East India company. John's sister Harriet also went to Madras and married Colonel Mark Wilks, but she died at age thirty-three in London. Her two children, a son and a daughter, were brought up by, of all people, Jane Satterthwaite, their mother's old nurse and grandfather Lauchlin's mistress. Whether Lauchlin was really "Junius" will never be known, for the political journalist has never been satisfactorily identified.[6]

Allan's nephew, Lachlan Macquarrie of Ulva, his sister Alicia's son, remained in the British army, rising eventually to colonel of the 73rd Regiment and a major-general. In 1809 he was appointed Governor of New South Wales to succeed Governor William Bligh, of the *Bounty* mutiny fame. The New South Wales Corps, nicknamed the Rum Corps, had mutinied and deposed Bligh. Macquarrie succeeded in establishing the authority of the Crown where Bligh failed, mainly because he was allowed to take the 73rd Regiment with him, and had the troops to support him.[7]

Janet Maclean's brother Sir Hector lived what was termed a "retired life" and died in 1818, leaving no heirs. He was succeeded by their half-brother Sir Fitzroy Jeffreys

Grafton Maclean, the 24th chief. Sir Fitzroy, too, followed the army, receiving his first commission in 1787 and rising to general in 1837. The present chief, the 27th, the Right Honourable Lord Maclean of Duart and Morvern, former Lord Chamberlain to Her Majesty Queen Elizabeth II, is descended from Sir Fitzroy Jeffreys Grafton. Lord Maclean's grandfather, the 26th chief, purchased the ruins of Duart Castle in 1911 and undertook the work of restoration.

Duart Castle is more than a family home. All members of the clan are welcomed there by their chief. Belonging to the chief's collection is the miniature of Allan Maclean in the uniform of the lieutenant-colonel of the 84th regiment.

Allan was seventy-two years old when he died in London in March 1797, having lived to what was a good age for his time. In the restful atmosphere of his home, relieved of the rigours of soldiering, he suffered less from his bad leg than he had in the biting winters of Canada. Janet lived until May 1837, 111 years after Allan's birth.[8]

Three years after Allan's death, Torloisk again became the property of his family. His niece Marianne married in 1790, Douglas Clephane of Carslogie, Fifeshire, another military man who became a general in the army. She inherited the lease to Torloisk on the death of Lachlan the 7th laird in 1799. The following year, 1800, the Duke of Argyll put his hand on Mull up for sale, and the Clephanes purchased Torloisk, an event that would have warmed Allan's heart. Marianne and Douglas Clephane had three daughters. Margaret, the eldest and heir, married the 2nd Marquess of Northampton, and Torloisk passed to the Northampton family, which still owns the estate.

Torloisk House has been rebuilt since Allan saw it, but the colours of his regiment are there, displayed on the staircase leading from the front hall to the main reception rooms. In 1930, Major Edward Compton, father of the present owner, had the colours mounted in a glass case to preserve them, and in the case he placed the note which Marianne Maclean Clephane had written in 1839. William Bingham Compton, the 6th Marquess of Northampton, wrote a description of the flags:

The colours actually carried by the Royal Highland Emigrants. The regiment continued using these colours after it was placed on the British regular establishment and numbered the 84th Foot.

The Second, or Regimental, colour of the 84th Regiment. A group in Wisconsin re-created the colour party for the 84th Foot using the regulations of 1768 for numbered regiments. The 84th never carried the colours of a regular regiment.

There are two colours at Torloisk which were the colours of the 84th Regiment. One of them is a blue ensign [the regimental or second color] which has in its centre a thistle in a circle surmounted by a crown, with the motto 'Nemo me impune lacessit'; and below this is a riband bearing the words 'Royal Highland Emigrants'. The second flag is a Union Jack [the King's color] with similar devices in the centre.[9]

These are not the flags of a regular regiment of the era; they are the flags of the Royal Highland Emigrants 1775-1778. Two centuries would pass before the regulation colours of the 84th Regiment would come into existence. For the bicentennial celebrations, groups of volunteers in the United States created regiments of the revolutionary war period and formed the Brigade of the American Revolution. An enterprising group in Wisconsin formed a colour party of the 84th and had flags made in accordance with the regulations of 1768 for numbered regiments. In the centre of each flag is '84th Reg't'—true and yet not true. The volunteers knew the rules, but they did not know Allan, the poor but noble commander who could not afford to purchase new colours when his regiment was placed on the British establishment.

Allan Maclean's defence of Quebec is often cited as the highlight in his military career. His contribution then was short and showy. Much more significant was his less spectacular but sustained effort at holding together the garrison and Indians at Niagara.

He was not a leader of men, but a senior clansman, able to carry out the wishes of a chief. His talent, with few exceptions, lay not in taking initiatives but in doing what others wanted done. He was in every respect a true Highlander, which helped him have a rapport with the Iroquois Indians, whose clan system was very like his own. Allan's spirit is associated with many places, but if the Highlander roams anywhere it is among the hills of the Isle of Mull. His native isle is a haunted place where wraiths of many who have gone before may be sensed through the billowing mists after soft rain.

Notes

Prologue

1 G. F. G. Stanley, *Canada Invaded 1775-1776* (Toronto 1973) pp. 94-95.

Chapter One

1 John Patterson Maclean, *A History of Clan Maclean* (Cincinnati, Ohio 1889) pp. 312-315. The Macleans of Torloisk. All the genealogy is found in this section.

2 Dugald Mitchell, M.D., *History of the Highlands and Gaelic Scotland* (Paisley, Scotland 1900) p. 518; John Prebble, *Glencoe* (London 1966) pp. 180-181.

3 Bartholemy Faujas de Saint Fond, *A Journey Through England and Scotland to the Hebrides in 1784* (Glasgow 1907) pp. 63-64.

4 John Patterson Maclean, *History*, pp. 222, 225-227.

5 Divers have found the galleon, but raising it has been deemed too expensive. The story of the Maclean-Mackinnon feud is from Mull folklore.

6 *Isle of Mull and Iona.* Guide book produced by Adcom Limited (Edinburgh, no date) p, 14. "The Pirate of Torloisk."

7 *Dictionary of Canadian Biography* , vol. 4, p. 504. Biography of Francis McLean (Maclean) by Franklin B. Wickwire.

8 John Patterson Maclean, *History*, pp. 216-219, participation of the Macleans at Culloden.

Chapter Two

1 John Prebble, *Culloden* (London 1966 c 1961). Prebble's account is used as background for the chapter on this battle.

2 No account of how Allan made his escape has survived, but he must have known where, on the coast, to find a fishing boat. According to the *Dictionary of Canadian Biography* , vol. 4, p. 503. Biography of Allan Maclean by G. F. G. Stanley. Allan reached the Netherlands by May.

Chapter Three

[1] John Patterson Maclean, *History*, p. 225.

[2] *Harbottle's Dictionary of Battles*, third edition, revised by George Bruce (New York 1981) p. 41.

[3] *Dictionary of Canadian Biography*, vol. 4, p. 503.

[4] John Patterson Maclean, *History*, p. 314.

[5] Jean N. McIlwraith, *Sir Frederick Haldimand* (Toronto 1926) Makers of Canada Series, vol. 3, pp. 5-6.

Chapter Four

[1] John Patterson Maclean, *History*, p. 227.

[2] J. N. M. Maclean, *Reward is Secondary: the life of a political adventurer and an enquiry into the mystery of 'Junius'* (London 1963). This biography of Lauchlin Macleane, Allan's benefactor, was a main source for the interwar periods, 1750-1756, and 1763-1775. Lauchlin's arrival in Edinburgh starts on p. 39.

[3] Stanley M. Pargellis, *Lord Loudoun in America* (New Haven, Connecticut 1933). The discussion on promotions is on pp. 306-314.

[4] The Army List 1756. Allan's commission is dated 8 January 1756; War Office 12/7033 - S - BC2072. A muster roll of the fourth battalion 60th Regiment (formerly the 62nd), dated 24 October 1757, shows Allan as the senior lieutenant in the major's company. The major at the time was John Rutherford. Augustine Prevost had moved to the second battalion.

Chapter Five

[1] Pargellis, *Loudoun*, pp. 116-117.

[2] Lewis Butler, *The Annals of the King's Royal Rifle Corps* (London 1913), vol. 1, "The Royal Americans". The corps was founded as a rifle regiment.

[3] Pargellis, *Loudoun*, pp. 316-318.

[4] J. N. M. Maclean, *Reward is Secondary*, p. 48. The author assumed that Allan was in the first battalion, but the War Office records 12/7033 show him in the fourth in 1757.

5 British Museum, Add. Mss. 21666, p. 36.

6 Douglas Edward Leach, *Arms for Empire: A Military History of the British Colonies in North America 1607-1763* (New York 1975), p. 429.

7 A paper kept at Torloisk House states that Allan was "severely wounded" at Ticonderoga in 1758.

Chapter Six

1 Allan's condition was diagnosed by the late Dr. Allan Walters of Toronto, who was interested in the history of medical practice and had investigated the effects of bullet wounds in the 19th century.

2 The Army List 1759, Third New York Company.

3 Mary Beacock Fryer, *King's Men: the soldier founders of Ontario* (Toronto 1980), p. 131; Butlersbury, built in 1742 is now an historic building, the exterior of which cannot be altered.

4 Leach, *Arms for Empire*, pp. 455-456.

5 A paper kept at Torloisk House states that Allan was wounded at Niagara in 1759.

6 John Knox, *Historical Journal of the Campaigns in North America for the Years 1757,1758 and 1760*, edited Arthur G. Doughty (Toronto 1914) 3 volumes, vol. 1, p. 191.

7 *Dictionary of Canadian Biography*, vol. 4, p. 503. Stanley concluded that Allan was at Quebec with Wolfe in September, yet no documentation suggests that any of the independent companies were there. Allan was certainly at Niagara in August, and could not have moved his company in time to join Wolfe, but he was at Quebec in 1760.

Chapter Seven

1 J. N. M. Maclean, *Reward is Secondary*, pp. 67-68.

2 British Museum, Add Mss. 21789, p. 161, 12 September 1780. Allan told Haldimand that the only way to improve his leg was to be treated by Drs. John Hunter and Richard Huck in London. In 1760, Huck was serving in North America.

3 The Army List 1760, Third New York Company.

[4] The Army List 1760, Third New York Company.

[5] J. N. M. Maclean, *Reward is Secondary*, p. 96.

[6] The Army List 1763, 114th Regiment.

[7] John Patterson Maclean, *History*, p. 314.

[8] J. N. M. Maclean *Reward is Secondary*, p. 96.

Chapter Eight

[1] J. N. M. Maclean, *Reward is Secondary*. The substance of the chapter is from pp. 96, 104, 122, 125-126, 128, 135.

[2] British Museum, Add. Mss. 21763, p. 221. Maclean to Haldimand, 4 August 1783. Allan said his son was nineteen years old.

[3] The family genealogy does not give a date of death for Allan's mother.

[4] British Museum, Add. Mss. 21789, p. 68, 29 November 1779. Allan stated that Hector was seventeen, implying he was born in 1762.

[5] John Patterson Maclean, *History*, p. 229. Janet lived until 1836, which suggests she was much younger than Allan.

Chapter Nine

[1] J. N. M. Maclean, *Reward is Secondary*, pp. 155, 162-163, 166, 176, 182, 186-188, for the substance of the chapter.

[2] Prince Edward Island Land Records, list of original proprietors.

[3] John Prebble, *The Highland Clearances*. (Hamondsworth, Middlesex 1969) pp. 248-249.

Chapter Ten

[1] J. N. M. Maclean, *Reward is Secondary*, pp. 250, 253-266, 266-270, 279, 284, 286, 297.

Chapter Eleven

[1] J. N. M. Maclean, *Reward is Secondary*, pp. 302, 318-319, 354, 382-383, 386-387, 391-393, 395, 401, 410, 414, 431.

[2] The Maclean genealogy does not give a date of death for Janet's mother, but she died around this time. Janet's half-brother was born about 1773 to Donald Maclean's second wife.

[3] The Army List 1773, shows the date of Allan's commission.

[4] Robin May, *The British Army in North America 1775-1783*, Osprey Men-at-Arms Series (Reading, Berks., 1974) p. 28.

[5] The Army List 1779, 84th Regiment, until 1778 the Royal Highland Emigrants.

[6] *London Gazette*, War Office announcement 16 January 1779, 84th Regiment Royal Highland Emigrants; the Army List 1776, 21st Regiment.

[7] Public Archives of Canada, M G 23 B 1 #7583, Macdonald *Letterbook.*

[8] The Baron Porcelli, *The White Cockade* (London, no date) pp. 232-239, a short biography of Flora Macdonald.

[9] Canada Department of Militia and Defence, General Staff, Brigadier E. A. Cruikshank, ed., *A History of the Organization and Service of the Military and Naval Services in Canada from the Peace of Paris in 1763 to the Present Time* (Ottawa 1919-1920) vol. 2, p. 56. Memorial of Allan Maclean.

[10] McIlwraith, *Haldimand*, p. 103.

[11] John Patterson Maclean, *Renaissance of Clan Maclean* (Columbus, Ohio 1913) p. 129; Egerton Ryerson, *The Loyalists of America* (Toronto 1980) vol. 2, p. 262. Certificate of Allan Maclean for Munro.

Chapter Twelve

[1] Public Archives of Canada, War Office 28, vol. 4, p. 212. Commission of Allan Maclean.

[2] Ibid Macdonald, *Letterbook.* #7583

[3] Ryerson, *Loyalists*, vol. 2, p. 262.

[4] Cruikshank, *History and Organization*, vol. 2, p. 56.

5 Extract of a letter at Torloisk. The original is Family documents, Castle Ashby, Northampton, no. 1340.

6 E. A. Cruikshank, *The King's Royal Regiment of New York* (Ontario Historical Society 1931, Reprint 1984, with additions by Gavin K. Watt) p. 7.

7 Public Archives of Canada, *Quebec Gazette*, 20 July, 19 August, 14 September.

8 Stanley, *Canada Invaded*, pp. 31, 56, 60, 81, 84-86, 87, 95-101, 103.

9 Public Archives of Canada, Colonial Office, Ser. Q, vol. 12, pp. 195-196, Cramahé to Germain, 6 October 1775.

10 J. N. M. Maclean, *Reward is Secondary*, p. 383.

Chapter Thirteen

1 Stanley, *Canada Invaded*, pp. 105, 108, 125-127, 136, 145; 155, the officers of the 1st battalion Royal Highland Emigrants 1779.

2 Cruikshank, *History and Organization*, vol. 2, p. 56.

3 Cruikshank, *History and Organization*, vol. 2, p. 152.

4 Public Archives of Canada, Colonial Office, Ser. Q, vol. 12, p. 69.

5 Porcelli, *White Cockade* p. 236; Mark M. Boatner III, *Landmarks of the American Revolution* (New York 1975) pp. 358-362.

6 Cruikshank, *King's Royal Regiment*, pp. 10-11.

7 J. N. M. Maclean, *Reward is Secondary*, pp. 431-433.

8 John Patterson Maclean, *Renaissance*, pp. 131-132.

Chapter Fourteen

1 Lieutenant-General John Burgoyne, *A State of the Expedition from Canada* (London 1780), Appendix, iii.

2 Cruikshank, *King's Royal Regiment*, p. 14.

3 John Patterson Maclean, *Renaissance*, p. 135.

4 *Toronto Globe*, 16 July 1877, "Narrative of John Peters".

5 Public Archives of Canada, Colonial Office Ser. Q, vol. 41, p. 159, Beating Order 15 September 1777.

6 British Museum, Add. Mss. 21789, p. 95, 14 January 1780.

7 Public Archives of Canada, War Office 28, vol. 4, p. 266.

8 J. N. M. Maclean, *Reward is Secondary* p. 431.

9 Cruikshank, *History and Organization*, vol. 2, p. 255.

10 Ontario Archives, Haldimand Papers, incomplete set, old PAC numbering, B 54, pp. 84-86, 1 July 1778. Pain and wasting of the lower leg are characteristic of a bullet wound in the thigh.

11 John Patterson Maclean, *Renaissance*, pp. 135-136.

12 J. N. M. Maclean, *Reward is Secondary*, p. 431.

13 British Museum, Add. Mss. 21762, pp. 194-195. Allan referred to a family of nine, seven of them women. He said he had no children of his own, which he later contradicted.

14 The Army List 1779. This is the first list that includes the 84th Regiment.

15 British Museum Add. Mss. 21789, p. 60, 18 November 1779.

16 British Museum Add. Mss. 21789, p. 30, 2 June 1779.

Chapter Fifteen

1 Public Archives of Canada, Haldimand Papers, old reference numbers, B 128, p. 13.

2 Public Archives of Canada, Haldimand Papers, old reference numbers B 128, 30 August 1779, no page number.

3 British Museum, Add. Mss. 21789, p. 40.

4 British Museum, Add. Mss. 21789, pp. 54, 60.

5 British Museum Add. Mss. 21789, p. 46; 21791, p. 11

6 British Museum Add. Mss. 21789, p. 54; 21791, p. 13.

7 British Museum Add. Mss. 21789, p. 68; 21791, p. 43.

8 British Museum Add. Mss. 21789, p. 74, 8 December 1779.

9 Alexander Fletcher was not shown on the Army List as a captain-lieutenant, but he was shown as holding that rank in War Office 12/8741, 16 April 1781. Neil Maclean was the captain-lieutenant on the Army List from 1780-1782.

10 British Museum, Add. Mss. 21789, p. 110; 21791, p. 54. The Army List 1780, 1781, both show Ranald Macdonell and Duncan Murray in the 84th Regiment, therefore they were not dismissed.

11 British Museum Add. Mss. 21762, p. 221. Allan referred to his son's regiment as the Argyll Fencibles, which was part of the larger regiment.

12 British Museum, Add. Mss. 21791, p. 69, Haldimand to Maclean 17 April 1780.

Chapter Sixteen

1 British Museum, Add. Mss. 21817, p. 83

2 British Museum, Add Mss. 21789, p. 141; 21791 p. 83.

3 British Museum, Add. Mss. 21789, p. 147; 21791 p. 88.

4 British Museum, Add. Mss. 21791, p. 92; 21789, p. 157.

5 British Museum, Add. Mss. 21791, p. 92; 21789, p. 159.

6 British Museum, Add. Mss. 21791, p. 92; 21789, p. 161.

7 British Museum, Add. Mss. 21791, pp. 104, 106.

8 Cruikshank, *King's Royal Regiment*, pp. 56-57.

9 Public Archives of Canada, Haldimand Papers, old reference numbers, B 180, pp. 45-58, Sherwood's Journal.

10 British Museum, Add. Mss. 21791, pp. 118-119, 3 November, 1780.

11 British Museum, Add. Mss. 21789, p. 215; 21791, p. 142.

12 Cruikshank, *King's Royal Regiment*, p. 70.

13 British Museum, Add. Mss. 21791, p. 160.

14 British Museum, Add. Mss. 21789, pp. 158, 160.

[15] Public Archives of Canada, War Office 28, vol. 3, p. 185, 2 November 1781.

Chapter Seventeen

[1] British Museum, Add. Mss. 21762, pp. 190-191, 194-195, 196. On page 194 Allan claimed to have purchased three commissions, which was not true. His captaincy was a field promotion, and his other promotions were in new regiments where purchase was not required.

[2] British Museum, Add. Mss. 21762, p. 208.

[3] British Museum, Add. Mss. 21762, p. 213.

[4] British Museum, Add. Mss. 21762, pp. 213, 238.

[5] British Museum, Add. Mss. 21762, pp. 223.

Chapter Eighteen

[1] British Museum, Add. Mss. 21762, pp. 228-229, 230-231, 232-233. Allan spelled the name Tuguanda and Tioguando; 21714, p. 340, Haldimand spelled it Tuoni. This spelling is from Graymont's book. The text of Allan's speech is on pp. 228-229.

[2] British Museum, Add. Mss. 21762, p. 231.

[3] British Museum, Add. Mss. 21763, p. 52.

[4] British Museum, Add. Mss. 21763, p. 48.

[5] British Museum, Add. Mss. 21763, pp. 42, 70. Washington's letter is moved back to the date Allan received and replied, 4 May 1783, which is 21763, p. 86.

[6] British Museum, Add. Mss. 21714, pp. 358-359.

[7] British Museum, Add. Mss. 21714, pp. 114-115.

[8] British Museum, Add. Mss. 21714, pp. 118-119.

[9] British Museum, Add. Mss. 21714, pp. 148-149.

Chapter Nineteen

[1] British Museum, Add. Mss. 21763, p. 153; 21714, pp. 370-371.

2 British Museum, Add. Mss. 21763, pp. 175, 176, 177, 185.

3 British Museum, Add. Mss. 21763, p. 192, Maclean to Douglas 16 July 1783; 195, 199, 213, 214-215, 216-217.

4 British Museum, Add. Mss. 21763, p. 221, Maclean to Haldimand 4 August 1783; 21714, p. 304, Haldimand to Maclean, 14 September 1783.

5 British Museum, Add. Mss. 21763, pp. 228-229, 241-242, 252-264.

6 British Museum, Add. Mss. 21763, p. 77.

7 The powder horn with Lieutenant Lauchlin Maclean's name on it is a treasured artifact at Torloisk House.

8 Porcelli, *White Cockade*, p. 238.

Epilogue

1 McIlwraith, *Haldimand*, pp. 282-284.

2 From a paper at Torloisk House.

3 Faujas de Saint Fond, *Journey* p. 16.

4 McIlwraith, *Haldimand*, pp. 310-327.

5 Porcelli, *White Cockade*, p. 229.

6 J. N. M. Maclean, *Reward is Secondary*, pp. 437, 439.

7 Sir Leslie Stephen and Sir Sidney Smith, ed. *The Dictionary of National Biography* (London, 1921-1964). Biography of Lachlan Macquarrie.

8 John Patterson Maclean, *History*, p. 229.

9 William Bingham Compton, *History of the Comptons of Compton Wynants* (London 1930), p. 241. Courtesy of Alwyne Compton Farquharson.

Bibliographical Essay

The material for this book comes from four main sources. The first is information supplied by Mrs. Alwyne Compton Farquharson of Torloisk. In reply to my enquiries, she wrote me long, detailed letters, meticulously recording each source she consulted. From her I gained invaluable insight into Allan Maclean's early years, a gap I could not have bridged using only Canadian sources.

The second is the work of the late Dr. James N. M. Maclean of Glensanda. His book *Reward is Secondary*, a biography of Lauchlin Macleane, revealed an unexpected and intriguing relationship between Allan and the man who could have been "Junius", the author of vicious letters to the press in the 1760s.

Third is the contribution of two men, George F. G. Stanley, and the late Brigadier Ernest A. Cruikshank. The latter did so much to put into print any handwritten documents. Stanley's book *Canada Invaded 1775-1776*, for which he drew on some of Cruikshank's work, is an excellent account of Allan's role during the siege of Quebec.

Last and most extensive is the Haldimand Collection from the British Museum. By 1778, when Allan was governor of Montreal, his letters are frequent and detailed. Later, when he commanded at Fort Niagara, he wrote to Haldimand almost daily. However, some sifting was necessary. Many letters are clear and to the point, while others make little sense. He contradicts himself and makes statements that are not true.

When agitated, Allan may have thought in Gaelic. Also, because of war wounds, he needed pain-killers. His more baffling prose could have been written while he was less than sober, or taking laudanum. Some of his remarks are outrageous and others are hilarious. Yet his writings reveal a man who was somewhat arrogant, conscious of rank—including his own— and who took himself seriously.

Bibliography

Primary Sources

Colonial Office Records. Copies of these are in the Public Archives of Canada.

The Haldimand Papers, British Museum. Microfilm and transparencies are in the Public Archives of Canada, as Add. Mss. with various reference numbers, and as the old series B.

War Office Records. Copies of these are in the Public Archives of Canada.

Secondary Sources

Ainsley, Captain Thomas. *Journals* Sheldon S. Cohan, ed., published under the title *Canada Preserved*. Toronto,1968.

Army List, The. A list of general and field officers. London, various dates.

Beacock, M. E. "North Mull". M.A. Dissertation, Edinburgh University, 1954.

Boatner, Mark M. III. *Landmarks of the American Revolution*. New York, 1975.

Bond, C. J. J. "The British Base at Carleton Island". *Ontario History*. March 1960.

Bradley, A. J. *Lord Dorchester*. The Makers of Canada Series, vol. 3. Toronto, 1926.

Burgoyne, Lt.-Gen. John. *A State of the Expedition from Canada*. London, 1780.

Butler, Lewis. *The Annals of the King's Royal Rifle Corps*. London, 1813.

Canada Department of Militia and Defence, General Staff. *A History of the Organization and Services of the Military and Naval Forces of Canada from the Peace of Paris in 1763 to the Present Time*. Brigadier E. A. Cruikshank ed., Ottawa, 1919-1920.

Cappon, L. J. Ed. *Atlas of Early American History: The Revolutionary Era 1760-1790*. Princeton, New Jersey, 1976.

Compton, William Bingham, 6th Marquess of Northampton. *History of the Comptons of Compton Wynyates*. London, 1930.

Cruikshank, E. A. *Butler's Rangers*. Lundy's Lane Historical Society. Welland, 1893.

Cruikshank, E. A. *The King's Royal Regiment of New York*. Ontario Historical Society, 1931. Reprint 1984 with additions by Gavin K. Watt.

Debor, Herbert W. "German Regiments in Canada 1776-1783". *German Canadian Yearbook*, vol. 2. Toronto, 1975.

Dictionary of Canadian Biography, vol. 4. ed. Frances G. Halpenny. Toronto, 1979.

Faujas de Saint-Fond, Bartholemy. *A Journey Through England and Scotland to the Hebrides in 1784*. Glasgow, 1907.

Fryer, Mary Beacock. *King's Men: The Soldier Founders of Ontario*. Toronto, 1980.

Graham, Henry Grey. *The Social Life of Scotland in the Eighteenth Century*. London, 1900.

Graymont, Barbara. *The Iroquois in the American Revolution*. Syracuse, New York, 1976.

Harbottle's Dictionary of Battles, third edition. revised by George Bruce. New York, 1981.

Harper, J. R. *The Fraser Highlanders*. Montreal Military and Maritime Museum. Chapter 17. The Royal Highland Emigrant Regiment, 1775-1783. Montreal, 1979.

Knox, John. *Historical Journal of the Campaigns in North America for the Years 1757, 1758 and 1760*. Arthur G. Doughty, ed., Toronto, 1914.

Leach, Douglas Edward. *Arms for Empire: A Military History of the British Colonies in North America 1607-1763*. New York, 1975.

London Gazette, 16 January , 1779.

Macdonald, Alexander. *Letterbook*. Public Archives of Canada. MG23B1

Maclean, J. N. M. *Reward is Secondary: the life of a political adventurer and an enquiry into the mystery of 'Junius'* London, 1963.

Maclean, John Patterson. *A History of Clan Maclean*. Cincinnati, Ohio, 1889.

Maclean, John Patterson. *Renaissance of Clan Maclean.* Columbus, Ohio, 1913.

May, Robin. *The British Army in North America 1775-1783.* Osprey Men-at-Arms Series. Reading, Berks., 1974.

McIlwraith, Jean N. *Sir Frederick Haldimand.* The Makers of Canada Series, vol. 3. Toronto, 1926.

Mitchell, Dugald, M. D. *History of the Highlands and Gaelic Scotland.* Paisley, Scotland, 1900.

Mull, Isle of, and Iona. Guidebook. Edinburgh: Adcon Ltd., n.d.

Pargellis, Stanley M. *Lord Loudoun in America.* New Haven, Connecticut, 1933.

Porcelli, the Baron. *The White Cockade* . London, n.d.

Pound, Arthur, and Day, Richard E. *Johnson of the Mohawks.* New York, 1930.

Prebble, John, *Culloden.* London, 1966 c1961.

Prebble, John, *Glencoe.* London, 1966.

Prebble, John. *The Highland Clearances.* Hamondsworth, Middlesex, 1969.

Preston, Richard A. *Kingston Before the War of 1812.* Champlain Society. Toronto, 1959.

Quebec Gazette. Public Archives of Canada.

Ryerson, Egerton. *The Loyalists of America.* Toronto, 1880.

Seanachie. *Account of Clan Maclean.* London, 1838.

Stanley, George F. G. *Canada Invaded 1775-1776.* Toronto, 1973.

Toronto Globe. "A Narrative of John Peters". 16 July 1877.

Walker, J. Samuel. *The Perils of Patriotism, John Joseph Henry and the Attack on Quebec 1775.* Lancaster, Pennsylvania, 1975.

INDEX

Illustrations in bold face

Boyd, Capt. Hon. William. 82
Braddock, Gen. Edward. 49,52,56
Bradstreet, John. Captures Fort Frontenac 65,69
Brant, Joseph. 71,127,184,1947196; threats of 199;201,202,205-206
Brant's Volunteers. 187
Brass, Lt. David B.R. To erect mill 191-192
Bray, Jonathon. Murders Delaware Indian 197
Brick Court, house in. 103,105,106,107,113,115
Bridge Road, Lauchlin Macleane s house in. 105,106,107,109
Brigade of the American Revolution. **219**, 220
Brolass, Mull. 21
Buffalo Creek. 190,193,200,204,205
Bunker/Breeds Hill, Battle of. 122
Burgoyne, John. Accuses A.M. of being Jacobite and demands enquiry
    into affairs of East India Company 114;140,142; refuses to take
    R.H.E. on expedition 1777 148-149;150,152; at Saratoga 152;
    surrenders 153;155,157; provincials from army accepted into Northern
    Dept. 166;
Burke, Edmund. 96
Bute, Lord. 88
Butler, Catherine (Mrs. Walter Sr.). 69
Butler, John. A.M. meets for first time 70;71,**124**,125,127,139;
    commands Indians with St. Leger 148; asks for warrant to raise corps
    of rangers 152;157,162; ill 187;191.192,196,197,198,199-
    200,201,203;addresses Indians 204-205; threats against 204;205-
    206,207,209,210
Butler, Walter (son of John). 127; killed in action 1781 187;
Butler, Walter Jr. Killed in action 1755 70
Butler, Walter Sr. 66.67-70,71,72,73,76; death of 80;125
Butlersbury N.Y. **68**,67-69,125
Butlersbury (Butlersburg) at Niagara. 187-188
Butler's Rangers. 151,155; raids by 159;161; superfluous R.H.E. officers
    sent to 163;173-174,**178**; raid Mohawk Valley 1781 179; support
    western Indians 185;186,187; barracks at Niagara 191; barracks
    similar to Butler's **195**; too many know about boundary 199;201;
    wanting to settle along Niagara River 210-211; disbanded 212
Caldwell, Col. Henry. 133,135,137
Cameron, Alexander of Glen Nevis. 25
Cameron, DonaldT Young Lochiel. 24-25,27
Cameron, clan. 24,27,182
Campbelll clan. 15,16,19,20,22; attack on Mull 28;38,39
Campbelll Capt. Duncan R.H.E. Captured off Boston 140
Campbell, Sir James. Raising fencible regiment 168
Campbelll John 4th Earl of Loudoun. See Loudoun, Lord.
Campbell, Capt. Robert. 82
Cape Diamond battery. 133,135
Carillon. See Fort Carillon. Carleton, Maj. Christopher. 172-173
Carleton, Guy. 11,127,128,129,132,133,135,136; refuses to allow
    pursuit of rebels 137;138; lets rebels escape 139;140,142,143;

Macdonald clan. 24

Macdonald, Maj. Donald R.H.E. 118,120; to recruit in middle and southern colonies 121-122; captured at Moore's Creek Bridge 140; leaves R.H.E. 157;

Macdonald, Flora. 39,122,140,212

Macdonald, Lt. James (140,212 Bridge 140;141; freed, sent to Halifax 159; Macdonald, John (son of Flora). Monument to **213**

Macdonald of Keppoch. 24,27

Macdonell Lt. Archibald R.H.E. In drunken brawl 167

Macdonell, Lt. James K.R.R.N.Y. Injured by officers of R.H.E. 167

Macdonell, John. Ensign in 1st batt., offered lt's commission in 2nd batt. 147; Lt. Archibald Maclean to exchange with 151; captaincy in Butler's Rangers 157; accusations against A.M. 164; paymaster of Butleris Rangers 189;

Macdonell, Capt. John K.R.R.N.Y. Brings recruits for R.H.E. 150; son injured 167;

Macdonell, Ranald. Guides A.M. 128

Macdonell, Lt. Ranald R.H.E. In drunken brawl 167

MacDougall, Capt. John R.H.E. 129,135; death of 169

Macintosh, clan (Chatten). 29,31,38

Mackay, Francis. 43,51,53,54,91,98

Mackay, Samuel. 43,51,53,54,70,91,98; takes command of Pfister's men 152;

MacKinnon, clan. 15,19,20

Mackreth, Thomas. 113

MacLachlan, clan. 29

Maclaine, Archibald (merchant). 51,53,78,79,82,83,84,85,87,88,92, 101

Maclaine, Thomas (son of Archibald M.). 101-102

Maclean, ? A.M's natural son. Birth of 88; growing up in Paris 97;99; brought from Paris to live with A.M.and Janet 115-116;119,145,158,159,160; commission in fencible regiment for 168;181; hope of commission in lst Foot 182;190; no half-pay for 208; never named 212,216

Maclean, Alan of Drimnun 23,37

Maclean, Alexander (brother-in-law). 18

Maclean, Capt. Alexander (friend of A.M.). 109,110

Maclean, Allan of Torloisk, central character 8,**10**,11; Jacobite 12; background 15-19; birthplace 16; family 16-18; education 19; at Culloden 28-32; lieut. in Scots Brigade 35-43; takes oath of allegiance to George II 44-45; lionized by Edinburyh Jacobites 48; commission in 4th batt. Royal American (60th) Reg't 52; wounded at Ticonderoga 64-66; commissioned capt. Third New York Indep. Company 66; wounded at Fort Nigara 73; winters at Ticonderoga 77; leave of absence in London 78; resigns from Third New York Independent Company 81; commission to raise ll4th 82; major's half-pay 84; in Paris to evade creditors 85-89; birth of natural son 88; brother Hector's executor 90; resides in London 93-119; henchman for Lauchlin Macleane 95-115; receives grant on Island of Saint John

Maclean, clan. 15,29,118,163

Maclean of Coll. 47,49

Maclean, Donald, 5th laird of Torloisk (father). 8,15,18,19,20,22.38; death of 41;

Maclean, Donald of Brolass. 8,89; heir to Maclean of Maclean 22nd chief 90;93,105,108; second marriage 115;117; death of 158

Maclean, Donald, Cadet of Torloisk. 8,18,23

Maclean, Donald of Drimnin. 23,37

Maclean of Duart. 16

Maclean, Elizabeth (sister). 18,91

Maclean, Sir Fitzroy Jeffreys Grafton. Birth of 115,158; becomes 24th chief 216-217

Maclean, Francis of Blaich (cousin). 21,26,33; serves with A.M.35- 42; resigns from Scots Brigade 47; purchases comission in 42nd Reg't. 49;61,79; raises 97th Foot 81,84; in Portugese service 84, 86;91, receives part Lot 24, Island of Saint John 97; commands at Halifax 158;164; lt.-col. of 82nd Foot 158; leads expedition to Penobscot River 164-165;171; warns of French designs 174; death of 176

Maclean, Hector, 6th laird of Torloisk (brother). 8,18,22,23,26,28.29-30.31,33,34.39; lawyer in Edinburgh 41; orders A.M. to return to Scotland 43; Writer to the Signet 44- 45;47,48,49,51; moves to Glasgow 78;81,82;86; illness and death of 89-90

Maclean, Sir Hector, 21st chief. 8,15-16,21,22; death of 47

Maclean, Sir Hector, 23rd chief. 8;90,108,110,115; ensign in R.H.E. 117-118;121,122,141,146; lieutenancy for 159,163; invalided home 159-160;181; becomes 23rd chief 214; death of 216

Maclean Ensn. Hector R.H.E. (cousin). 156

Maclean, Janet of Brolass (wife of A.M.). 91,92,93,94,97,98,100,104,105; sisters 108; marriage to A.M. 108, 110-111;114; accepts A.M's son 115-116; pension for 119; remains in London while A.M. on active service 119;145,146,155,157,158,163,168; provision for 181;214; death of 217

Maclean, John, Lt. 1st batt. 8,122,123,125,128

Maclean, Lachlan, 7th laird of Torloisk (brother). 8,18,39,45,47,82,89; inherits from 6th laird 90;91,93; rebuilds Torloisk 97,100; in kelp industry 100,158; as poet 100;108,215; death of 217

Maclean, Lachlan of Drimnin. 8,23; death of 37

Maclean, Lachlan of Garmony. 8,18,91

Maclean, Lauchlin, merchant of Baltimore and capt. 1st batt. R.H.E. 9,91-92; sharea lot 23, Island of Saint John with A.M. 98; to serve in R.H.E. 121; misadvantures reaching Canada 147;150; capt. in grenadier company R.H.E. 183;185-185; at Oswego 186; commissary 211; sends powder horn to Torloisk 212,214

Maclean of Lochbuie. 47

Maclean, Rt. Hon. Lord, of Duart and Morvern. 217

Maclean, Margaret Wall (2nd wife of Donald of Brolass). 115,158

Maclean, Margaret Smith (wife of Lachlan 7th laird). 82,89,90,91.92; gives birth to daughter Marianne 97;

Maclean, Marianne, daughter of Lachlan 7th laird. Birth of 97;123; A.M. presents colours of R.H.E. to 214-215; marries Douglas Clephane 217; purchase of Torloisk 217

Maclean, Mary of Torloisk (sister). 9,16,18,45,89-90,91,108,110

Maclean, Mary Campbell (mother). 9, 15,23,43,45,50,85,90,182

Maclean, Mary Dickson (mother-in-law). 9,89-90

Maclean, Lt. Neil R.H.E. 122,123,125,128; ct.-lt.143;156; retires 166;

Maclean, Capt. William of Blaich. 21,26.38,39

Macleane, Elizabeth (Mrs. Lauchlin). 49,59,86,89,92,96,99,101,104

Macleane, Henry (brother of Lauchlin). Moves from Dublin 96-97; receives half Lot 55, Island of Saint John 98;99,101;104,105,107,110,112,113; hired by East India Co. 115; dies in India 145

Macleane, Harriet (daughter of Lauchlin Macleane). Birth of 114-115;145,158,216

Macleane,John (son of Lauchlin Macleane). 8; birth of 105.114,145,158,216

Macleane, Dr. Lauchlin (benefactor). 9; A.M. first meets 48;49,50; in Philadelphia 59; at Ft. Duquesne 66-67;77; in Agnew' Grenadiers 77;78,79,82; with A.M. in Paris 86-89, settles A.M's debt, invites A.M. to share house in Paris 88;89,91,92,93,94; manipulates East India Co. stock 95;96; replaces brother Hector as A.M s leader 97; appointed Under Secretary of State to Lord Shelburne 97-98; receives half of Lot 55, Island of Saint John 98;99,100,101-102,103; gives A.M. lot 21 104;105,106,107,108; Challenges Wilkes to duel 109-110,112;113; death of Penelope Agnew in childbirth 114; leaves London for Bengal 115;116; A.M. seeks L.M's Jacobite friends in Philadelphia as agents 123;145,148,155- 156; death of 157-158;216

Maclean's Highlanders. See 114th Regiment.

Macleod, clan. 29

Macleod, Capt. Donald R.H.E. 121; to recruit in southern colonies 123; killed at Moore's Creek Bridge 140;141

Manners, Robert. Purchases A.M's lt.-cols commission 215

Macquarrie of Ulva. 47

Macquarrie, Lachlan (brother-in-law). 18

Maquarrie, Lachlan (nephew). Commission in R.H.E. 117,212; governor of New South Wales 216 Martin, Gov. Josiah of North Carolina. 141;

Mathews, Maj. Robert (Haldimand's secretary). 163,166-167;169,170,172,173,183,215

McAlpin, Daniel. 148; inspector of Loyalists 167; ill 168; death of 171

McArthur, John. 83

McCabe, Pte. Michael. Rapes landlady 163-164

McCauley, Lt. Archibald. 66,67,77

McCully, Capt. Agent of Congress 205,206

McDonald, John R.H.E. Asks for back pay 171

McGill, James (magistrate). 167

McKee, Alexander. 192

Mexico. 112

Michhilimackinac. See Fort Michilimackinac.

Militia, British. 133
Militia, Canadian. 129,133,140,142,152-3,160,175
Mirabelle, M. 27
Mississauga Indians. 203; Sir John Johnson buys land from 209,210;
Mohawk Indians. 67,128,170,189,203; decide to settle in Canada 210;
Mohawk Valley. 67,120; A.M. recruits in 125-127;169,172,209
Monkwell Presbyterian Meeting House. 110
Moore's Creek Bridge, Battle of (North Carolina). 140
Montagne, Rue de la. 133,135
Montcalm, Marquis de. 11,56 captures Ft. Wm. Henry 59;67
Montgomery, Gen. Richard (rebel). 11,12,132,133,135,136; death at
    137;
Montour, John. A.M. angry with for taking scalps 191
Montreal. 75,76,77.78,79; captured by Amherst 80;127,128; captured by
    rebels 132; rebels reinforce 138; liberated 142; A.M. governor of
    150;153,155,
Moravian missionaries. 185
Morning Chronicle. 109
Morvern Peninsula. 28.83
Mull, Isle of. 15,16; map 17;19,21,28,38,45-46,81,82,83,90
Munro, John. Warns A.M. of danger in New York City; to be ct.-lt. in
    R.H.E. 120;123,125; prisoner of rebels 143; capt. in K.R.R.N.Y. 166;
    raids Ballstown 172-175; escape of prisoners from Coteau du Lac 175-
    176;
Murray, Quartermaster Duncan R.H.E. In drunken brawl 167
Murray, Lord George. 24,29,31
Murray, Brig. James. 77,79,81
Musgrove, Dr. Samuel. Claims France ended Seven Years' War with a
    bribe 88,89,92
Muswell Hill, Lauchlin Macleane's house on. 105
Nairne, Maj. John R.H.E. 129,135,136;138; commands R.H.E. in A.M's
    absence 143;150,153; major for R.H.E. 157,161; commandant of Fort
    Haldimand 162; commandant of Ile aux Noix 179; in 53rd Regiment
    179
Nesbitt, Lt.-Col. William. 140,141,142
Newfoundland. Recruits for R.H.E. from 130,166,168
New Jersey. 55,56
New York City. 52,53,54,55,57,59; A.M. convalesces at
    66;67,77,81,118,120,121,122,125; captured by the British 146
Niagara Falls. A.M. visits 75
North Carolina. Battle of Moore's Greek 140; prisoners in 157
North Carolina Highlanders. R.H.E. officers purloined for 141
North, Lord. 103,104,105,109,112,113,116,118; promises pension for
    Janet 119;143,146,158,168,176; government falls 181; in coalition
    201; resigns 214
Northern Dept. (Quebec City). 155; Burgoyne's provincials accepted into
    166; Nova Scotia. Batt. of R.H.E. to be recruited there 121;
Old Pretender, The. See James the Old Pretender. Oneida Indians. 189;
    carry Washington's letter to A.M. 197,200,206

Onondaga Indians. 189; council fire 193;204
Orange, House of. 12
Orange, William IV Prince of. 36-37,39,44
Orme, Robert. 94,95,115,116,157-158
Oswego. French capture of 56,59;67,70,72,73,75,77,122,127,128; St.
  Leger's expedition to gather at 148; St. Leger withdraws to 152; 179;
  2nd batt. K.R.R.N.Y. occupies 183;184; A.M. inspects
  186;190,196,197,205,206,207,210
Panchaud, Isaac, banker. 94,95,96
Paris. A.M. in 85-89; stock exchange 94;95; peace talks in 193;
Parr, John, Governor of Nova Scotia. 212
Pay, rates of. 52
Paymaster's Dept. 84,118
Perth, Duke of. 24
Peters, Ann (wife of John). 151
Peters, John. 148,151,153
Pfister, Francis. 148; killed at Bennington 152
Philadelphia. 53,57,59,60,67,77,123,127; prisoners held in 140;
  captured by British 157; evacuated by British 159;
Pillon, Dr. Arrested 173 pitt, William the Elder (1st Lord Chatham).
  87,96
Pitt, William the Younger. 214
Pointe au Fer. 173
Pointe aux Trembles. 132
Portneuf, Chevalier. 75
Pouchot, Capt. Pierre. 70; surrenders Fort Niagara 73
Powelll Capt. John. 200
Powell; Brig.-Gen. Watson. 142,150; commands garrison at Ticonderoga
  152; evacuates Ticonderoga 153;155,167,174; resigns command of
  upper posts 185;
Prenties, Widow. 129
Pres de Ville. 132,133,135,136,138
Presbyterians. 19
Prescott, Col. Richard. 132,139,141;150
Presqu'ile (Erie Pa.). 75
Prestonpans, Battle of. 31
Prevost, Maj. Augustine. 52,53;54,55,57,58,59
Prevost, Col.James. 52,53; harshness and incompetence of 56- 58;59;
  removed from command 60;69
Prideaux, Col. John. 70; death of 72
Prince Edward Island. See Saint John, Island of. Prisoners. Taken at
  Quebec 136; allowed to enlist in R.H.E. 137- 138; shortage for
  exchanges 139; taken at Saratoga and lack of rebel prisoners to
  exchange 153-154; R.H.E. officers held prisoner 156; loyalist
  prisoners 157; rebels held in Montreal 161; to be exchanged 172; need
  for new prison for 176;
Privateers. 171
Protestants. 50,53,98
Provincial Marine. 169; rum for seamen in 209

St. Leger, Brig.-Gen. Barry. Leads expedition into Mohawk Valley
  148,151,152;174,184
St. Roch. 132,133,135
Saratoga. 152; Burgoyne surrenders at 153
Satterthwaite, Jane (mistress of Lauchlin Macleane),
  106,115,145,155,158,216
Satterthwaite, Margaret (sister of Jane). 106,107
Sault au Matelot, Rue. 133,135,136,138
Savannah, Ga. British capture of 160
Schenectady N.Y. 66,67,69,125; merchants from at Niagara 207-208;
Schuyler, Gen. Philip. 204,205,207,210
Scots Brigade (Dutch service). 21;26,33;34; A.M. serves in 37-43;118
Scott, Capt. Caroline. 24,27
Secord, James. 189
Seneca Indians. 189,196; decide to return to tribal lands 210
Shawnee Indians. 187;189; village of Standing Stone attacked 192;193
Shelburne, Lord. 97,99,100,101,105; in Whig ministry 181-182; 184;
  out of power 201;
Sheriffmuir, Battle of. 15
Ships.
  Angelica. 191
  Asia. 123,146
  Atalanta. 215
  Caldwell. 191
  Faith. 208
  Fell. 132
  Lizzard. 130,133 Mary (Lachlan 7th Laird's) 45;90; sold 97;
  Mohawk. 210
  Nottingham 53;
  Ontario. Sunk in storm 174
  Seneca. 190,191
  Surprise. 139
  Wyandot. 191,192
Sinclair, Capt. Patrick R.H.E. 169,183
Six Nations. See Iroquois Confederacy
Skye, Isle of. 39
Small Lt.-Col. John (Commander 2nd Batt. R.H.E.). In Scots Brigade
  43,118;121,123,125,130,140,141,147,157,159,160,179,212
Smith, Adam. 87
Sorel, rebel outpost at 138,142; fortified 161;170
Spain. At war with Britain 181
Stamp Act. 116
Standing Stone. Shawnee village 192,193
Stapleton, Brig.-Gen. Walter. 27
Stewart, Capt. James. 82
Stewart, John (Jack the wine merchant).
  100,101,108,110,113,114;115,145
Stewart, John (Little John). 100, 101,106,107,113,145
Stirling Castle. 168,181

Stock Exchanges. Amsterdam 94; London 94, Paris 94;
Stratton, Lt. Alexander R.H.E. 156
Street, Samuel, merchant. 209
Stuart, Andrew, lawyer. 86,l01,110,112
Stuart, Prince Charles Edward the Young Pretender. 21,22-
  23,24,28,30.31; army of 31-32;33,36;38; reaches France 39;50,92
  118,119;death of 216
Stuart, Charlotte (daughter of Charles Edward) 216
Stuart, Gardinal Henry (brother of Charles Edward) 216
Stuart, Dr. John. 48; in Phildelphia 59; in Faris 86-
  89;92,94,95,110,115
Stuart, House of. 11,15,89,101
Sullivan, Maj.-Gen. John. 142
Sutherland, Capt. George. 82
Symes, Lt. James R.H.E. Captured off Boston 140
Thomas, Maj -Gen. John. 139
Thompson, Brig.-Gen. William. 141
Tice, Capt. Gilbert. 200
Tiree, Isle of. 83
Tobermory, Mull. 19
Toconando. Seneca chief, addresses council 193
Tonge, Capt. Messenger from Carleton 197
Torloisk. Descr. of 16; 28,29,33,34,38,39,41; A.M. visits 1750-51 45 -
  47;50,83,85,90,91,93,100;103,108; Lauchlin Maclean's powder horn
  sent to 212; A.M. visits 1784 214,215; colours of R.H.E. on display
  at 217-220; colours do not conform to regulations of 1768 220
Townshend Acts. 116
Townshend, Brig. Geo. 78,79
Treaty of Aix-la-Chapelle 1748. Ends War of Austrian Succession 41
Treaty of Paris 1763. Ends Seven Years' War 84.
Trois Rivieres. 140; rebel defeat at 141;142
Tuscarora Indians. 189
Ulva, Isle of. 18,46
Uniforms. K.R.R.N.Y. 144; R.H.E.11,,119,131,134,135; Butler's
  Rangers 178
Van Ingen, Lt. Peter. 52,53,56,58
Voltaire. 87
Von Barner, Col. Lt. Archibald Maclean rude to 175
Von Creutzburg, Lt.-Col. Orders Bouteillet's horse taken 165;166
Von Riedesel, Baron Eriedrich (German commander). Arrival of
  140;142,151,157
Von Speth, Brig. Ernst. 164; replaces A.M. as governor of Montreal
  177,184
Von Steuben, Baron. Demands Haldimand surrender upper posts 209
Voyer, Lt. Col. Noel. 133
Walker, Lady Mary (mistress of Lauchlin Macleane). 156
War Office. 51,58,79,81,82,83,84,116,117,118,158,177,182
Washington, Gen. George. 146,174,179-181,183; writes to A.M. 197-
  198;200,205; ready to occupy British posts 209;

Webb, Maj.-Gen. Daniel. 53
Western sector. Map of 180
Westminster Bridge. 106
West Point N.Y. 125
Western Regiment of Fencible Men in North Britain. 168
Wheeling Va. Raid on 187 White cockade (Jacobite). 22; A.M. sports at
    Quebec and Montreal 130,133,151
Whitehall, 51,79,116,118
Wilkes, John. Published Essay on Women 87; exile in Paris
    87;89,91,96,99,104; A.M. carries challenge to 109-110; Bill of
    Rights Society to assist 109;110,112,113
Willett, Col. Marinius. 197,198,207
Wolfe, Gen. Jameg. 11,76,78,79
Woodfall, Henry. 78,79,99; prints "Letter to the King" 103; trial of 104-
    105;108,109
Woodfall, William, 109
Wooster, Brig.-Gen. David. 138
Wyandot Indians. 187;189
Yamaska River. Blockhouses on 175
York Buildings, A.M. lives in
    100,108,110,113,115,119,158,159,181,214
Yorktown, Va. 179,181
Young, Lt.-Col. John. Takes command of 4th batt. Royal American
    Regiment 60.
Young Pretender, the. See Stuart, Prince Charles Edward.

Printed in Canada